M000215195

T H E   H U M A N

Embrace

THE HUMAN

Embrace

The Love of Philosophy
and the Philosophy of Love

Kierkegaard, Cavell, Nussbaum

RONALD L. HALL

THE PENNSYLVANIA STATE UNIVERSITY PRESS
UNIVERSITY PARK, PENNSYLVANIA

Library of Congress Cataloging-in-Publication Data

Hall, Ronald L., 1945–
    The human embrace : the love of philosophy and the philosophy of love :
Kierkegaard, Cavell, Nussbaum / Ronald L. Hall.

        p.   cm.
    Includes bibliographical references and index.
    ISBN 0-271-01952-2 (alk. paper)
    ISBN 0-271-01593-0 (pbk. : alk. paper)
    1. Kierkegaard, Søren, 1813–1855—Contributions in philosophy of love.
    2. Cavell, Stanley, 1926–   —Contributions in philosophy of love.
    3. Nussbaum, Martha Craven, 1947–   —Contributions in philosophy of love.
    4. Love—History—19th century.   5. Love—History—20th century.   I. Title.
    B4378.L6H35   2000
    128'.46—dc21   98-54929
                                                                                          CIP

Copyright © 2000 The Pennsylvania State University
All rights reserved
Printed in the United States of America
Published by The Pennsylvania State University Press,
University Park, PA 16802-1003

It is the policy of The Pennsylvania State University Press to use acid-free paper for
the first printing of all clothbound books. Publications on uncoated stock satisfy the
minimum requirements of American National Standard for Information Sciences—
Permanence of Paper for Printed Library Materials, ANSI Z39.48–1992.

For Taylor,
Whose Friendship Sustains My Love for Philosophy

And for Maggi (Again),
Whose Love Sustains My Life

Yet Abraham believed, and believed for this life. Yea, if his faith had been only for a future life, he surely would have cast everything away in order to hasten out of this world to which he did not belong. But Abraham's faith was not of this sort. . . . Abraham believed precisely for this life, that he was to grow old in the land, honored by the people, blessed in his generation, remembered forever in Isaac, his dearest thing in life, whom he embraced with . . . love.

—SØREN KIERKEGAARD

I am here, the relation is mine, what I make of it is now part of what I make of my life, I embrace it.

—STANLEY CAVELL

When the spring brings round its sequence of beauties and pains and fears, she will . . . embrace the pain and the fear along with the delight; for she will see how they are connected.

—MARTHA NUSSBAUM

CONTENTS

ACKNOWLEDGMENTS

Greetings!

This book had its beginnings in an invitation by Professor Jeffery Geller asking me to present a couple of lectures at the neighboring university where he teaches (the University of North Carolina at Pembroke) relating to my work on, well, roughly, Kierkegaard. At the time, I was reading Stanley Cavell's new book on film, *Pursuits of Happiness,* and Martha Nussbaum's major work, *The Fragility of Goodness.* Taking this opportunity to combine these various interests, I presented two talks: one a Kierkegaardian interpretation of Cavell, the other a Kierkegaardian interpretation of Nussbaum. Later, and after considerable revision, these two lectures found their way into journals, as I cite below, and form the germ, if that is the right word, for this present work.

As this germination proceeded, I came to see the writing of this book as an opportunity to expand my treatment of my favorite of Kierkegaard's works, *Either/Or.* In my first book, *Word and Spirit,* I concentrated on Volume I of *Either/Or,* and on the aesthetic modality of existence (Don Juan and Faust). Out of a sense of wanting completion of some sort, I began to see this project as an opportunity to present my interpretation of Volume II, and, accordingly, the ethical modality. And so, while at this, it also seemed appropriate to take up the religious modality, in its variations, as the alternative to both the aesthetic and the ethical modalities of existence. These efforts turned out to be published papers of their own, one on Judge William and two others on Kierkegaard's conception of faith, all of which form the basis of Part 1 of this book, just as the essays on Cavell and Nussbaum form the bases of Parts 2 and 3 respectively. (See citations below.)

It was not until after I had completed this book, that I came across Stanley Cavell's companion to *Pursuits of Happiness,* I mean, *Contesting Tears.* For me, this was unfortunate, since I found in this new book on film more support for my thesis that Cavell and Kierkegaard employ a similar kind of thinking. I have included an extended footnote in Chapter 4, recounting some of the relevant themes in Cavell's treatment of the Hollywood melodramas of the unknown woman. (See footnote 2, Chapter 4)

It has been my good fortune to have a colleague throughout this writing process. Unlike many an isolated scholar, I have been lucky to have had someone to talk these ideas through with. My friend and colleague, Taylor Scott, has patiently listened to me read portions of the text, has read the entire manuscript, has made helpful suggestions, and has constantly encouraged me in this project. I am quite sure that I could not have completed the book without the lively colloquy we have shared on its subject. Thank you, Taylor.

As Taylor has provided me with the friendship and collegiality necessary to inspire and sustain a love for philosophy—and I have come to think that philosophy can be loved only when it is humanized, or at least brought back from its esoteric, or metaphysical, extravagances or abstractions, to the everyday—so my wife, Maggi, has given me a human, existential, basis for developing a philosophy of love, call this love itself. I assume that it is just a fact that human beings naturally seek such a genuine love; perhaps it is the only daily bread that can sustain our deepest human hunger. But what some only seek, I have been lucky enough to find—dare I call this happiness? Thank you, Maggi.

As promised above, let me cite the previously published materials included in this book. With the exception of Chapter 2 (on Judge William), the inclusion of this material is not obvious, since the text, and some of the ideas, have undergone extensive revisions since they were originally published.

"A Critical Note on Edward F. Mooney's Reading of *Fear and Trembling*" *Søren Kierkegaard Newsletter* 29 (April 1994): 5–8.

"Pursuits of Knowledge and Happiness: A Kierkegaardian Reading of Stanley Cavell," *Soundings* 77, 1–2 (SpringSummer 1994): 145–61.

"Transcending the Human: A Kierkegaardian Reading of Martha Nussbaum," *International Philosophical Quarterly* 34, 135 (September 1994): 361–73.

"Kierkegaard and the Paradoxical Logic of Worldly Faith," *Faith and Philosophy* 12,1 (January 1995): 40–53.

"Judge William's Marriage to What's Her Name: An Exploration of Aesthetics, Ethics and Faith," in *The Ethical Aesthetic: Perspectives on Kierkegaard's* Either/Or, ed. David Humbert (Forthcoming AAR/Scholar's Press).

ABBREVIATIONS

AR Rudd, Anthony.*Kierkegaard and the Limits of the Ethical.* New York: Clarendon Press, 1993.

CA Kierkegaard, Søren. *The Concept of Anxiety.* Translated by Reidar Thomte and Albert B. Anderson. Princeton: Princeton University Press, 1980.

CE Thompson, Josiah, ed. *Kierkegaard: A Collection of Critical Essays.* Garden City, N.Y.: Anchor Books, 1972.

CH Cavell, Stanley. *Conditions Handsome and Unhandsome: The Constitution of Emersonian Perfectionism.* Chicago: University of Chicago Press, 1990.

CR Cavell, Stanley. *The Claim of Reason: Wittgenstein, Skepticism, Morality, and Tragedy.* New York: Oxford University Press, 1979.

CUP Kierkegaard, Søren. *Concluding Unscientific Postscript.* Translated by David F. Swenson and Walter Lowrie. Princeton: Princeton University Press, 1968.

EM Mooney, Edward F. *Knights of Faith and Resignation: Reading Kierkegaard's* "Fear and Trembling." Albany: State University of New York Press, 1991.

EO Kierkegaard, Søren. *Either/Or.* 2 vols. Edited and translated by Howard V. Hong and Edna H. Hong. Princeton: Princeton University Press, 1987.

FG Nussbaum, Martha. *The Fragility of Goodness: Luck and Ethics in Greek Tragedy and Philosophy.* New York: Cambridge University Press, 1986.

FT Kierkegaard, Søren. *Fear and Trembling, Repetition.* Edited and translated by Howard V. Hong and Edna H. Hong. Princeton: Princeton University Press, 1983.

HC Arendt, Hannah. *The Human Condition.* Chicago: University of Chicago Press, 1958.

JOU Urmson, J. O. *Aristotle's Ethics.* New York: Basil Blackwell Inc., 1988.

KDI   Dunning, Stephen. *Kierkegaard's Dialectic of Inwardness: A Structural Analysis of the Theory of Stages.* Princeton: Princeton University Press, 1985.

KK   Green, Ronald M. *Kierkegaard and Kant: The Hidden Debt* Albany: State University of New York Press, 1992.

LK   Nussbaum, Martha. *Love's Knowledge: Essays on Philosophy and Literature.* New York: Oxford University Press, 1990.

LP   Walsh, Sylvia. *Living Poetically: Kierkegaard's Existential Aesthetics.* University Park: Pennsylvania State University Press, 1994.

PH   Cavell, Stanley. *Pursuits of Happiness: The Hollywood Comedy of Remarriage.* Cambridge: Harvard University Press, 1981.

PK   Polanyi, Michael. *Personal Knowledge: Towards a Post-Critical Philosophy.* New York: Harper Torchbooks, 1964.

QO   Cavell, Stanley. *In Quest of the Ordinary: Lines of Skepticism and Romanticism.* Chicago: University of Chicago Press, 1988.

SUD   Kierkegaard, Søren. *The Sickness unto Death: A Christian Psychological Exposition for Upbuilding and Awakening.* Edited and translated by Howard V. Hong and Edna H. Hong. Princeton: Princeton University Press, 1983.

TD   Nussbaum, Martha. *The Therapy of Desire: Theory and Practice in Hellenistic Ethics.* Princeton: Princeton University Press, 1994.

UA   Cavell, Stanley. *This New Yet Unapproachable America: Lectures After Emerson After Wittgenstein.* Albuquerque: Living Batch Press, 1989.

WS   Hall, Ronald L. *Word and Spirit: A Kierkegaardian Critique of the Modern Age.* Bloomington: University of Indiana Press, 1993.

INTRODUCTION
THE LOGIC OF PARADOX

In this book, I undertake to bring to light some common themes running through three important philosophers, each of whom, on the surface at least, has a different philosophical interest and agenda. I refer to the nineteenth-century, Danish, Christian, existentialist philosopher, Søren Kierkegaard, and two contemporary American philosophers, Stanley Cavell, whose interest is in ordinary language philosophy and recently in philosophy and film, and Martha Nussbaum, whose interest is in ancient philosophy and the intersection of philosophy and literature. One of these common themes is found in the fact that all three are interested in, and develop a philosophy of, love. Another related theme is found in the fact that they all articulate in their own distinctive way, deeply held convictions about what it means to be human, about the value of being human, about our human challenge to embrace our own humanness.

Also, there is something beyond these common thematic convictions that brings these apparently divergent thinkers together. As I would put it, all three of these figures seem to be guided by a similar logic. I began to see this when I noticed that all three claim, in one way or another, that for human beings, the (or at least, a) defining element of being human is our freedom not to be. All three of these lovers of philosophy and philosophers of love seem to agree that a unique feature of human being is that we humans must decide to be human, to embrace our humanness, a decision that presupposes alternative possibilities, possibilities that range all the way from fantasies of being gods, to flirtations with the inhuman, the monstrous. But whether these alternatives to being human take the form of rising above the human or sinking below it, they are all forms of refusal, denial, and avoidance. Convinced of this, Kierkegaard, Cavell, and Nussbaum spend a great deal of their time indirectly considering the value and meaning of the human quest to understand what it means to be human, or fully human, or more existentially, the human quest to be fully human, by directly exploring the myriad techniques human beings have developed for finding and living in modes of existence that are alternatives to being (fully) human. Their common assumption seems to be that it is peculiar to the human condition not only that we are called to embrace our humanness, and have the power to do otherwise, but that this embrace is possible only on the other side of an existential confrontation with these alternatives, call these our human temptations to flee from, avoid, or otherwise deny, our own humanness. In this sense, these failures to be human play a decisive, important, and in a paradoxical sense, even a positive role in the views these thinkers develop concerning the human call to be human.

Another way to put this is to say that all three of these philosophers employ a dialectical logic of paradox. Since *paradox* is so often associated with Kierkegaard, I will take my cue from him in order to offer a preliminary brief that I hope will serve to introduce this logic and to begin an explanation of what such a dialectical logic finally comes to.

We may say that a paradox, or more precisely, a paradoxical relation, for Kierkegaard, is a peculiar kind of dialectical relation in which a positive reality is taken to include within itself what it, by its very nature, excludes. This dialectic of paradox is different from a Hegelian dialectic as follows: in Hegel, the tension of the negation of thesis and antithesis is relieved in a synthesis; in the dialectic of paradox, opposites form a structural unity in which the tension of negation is accentuated not resolved. It is Stephen Dunning, despite what he most likely intended in his marvelous book *Kierkegaard's Dialectic of Inwardness,* that has helped me to see this difference between Kierkegaard and Hegel.[1]

Relying on Kierkegaard's discussion of these matters in *The Concept of Irony,* Dunning defines a dialectical structure as follows: "Such structures involve a series of opposed poles, and the way in which those oppositions are related to one another determines the character of the dialectic" (KDI, 8). There are four such structures: (1) the dialectic of contradiction; here, two opposites simply negate one another and that's it; the relation has no further

---

1. Stephen Dunning, *Kierkegaard's Dialectic of Inwardness: A Structural Analysis of the Theory of Stages* (Princeton: Princeton University Press, 1985), 8–9 (hereafter KDI). When I say "despite what he intended," I mean to point out that Dunning is out to show that Kierkegaard took over, more than he explicitly acknowledged, the very dialectic of Hegel that he so vehemently excoriated.

possibility for unity; (2) the dialectic of reciprocity; here two opposites are regarded as equally legitimate, and mutually supportive, but the most one can do is to go back and forth between them; no moment of further unity is possible; (3) the dialectic of paradox; here, for the first time, a new unity between opposites is possible; but in this new unity, the oppositions are accentuated, not resolved; and (4) the distinctively Hegelian dialectic of mediation; here the opposites are taken up into a unity in which their negation is negated and thus the tension between them is relieved, at least for a moment—that is, until a new tension is created with some other opposite; and so on it goes (KDI, 8–9).

I will not get into a dispute with Dunning here as to which of these dialectical structures is most characteristic of Kierkegaard or into the matter of Kierkegaard's consistency in using only one sense of dialectic throughout his work. I will simply say that the kind of dialectic that I am concerned with here is what Dunning calls the dialectic of paradox.

Even though Kierkegaard employed the dialectic of paradox throughout his work, he did not invent it. Rather, he would no doubt maintain that he was simply being true in his own thinking to the dialectic of the Christian faith. In embracing Christianity, Kierkegaard embraced its dialectic. But he did so with a novel and unprecedented awareness. Let me illustrate.

As Kierkegaard has Author A put the matter in *Either/Or I,* Christianity brought sensuality into the world.[2] His elaboration of this startling claim shows that the logic of Christianity is the logic of paradox. In this elaboration, Kierkegaard shows us as well just how complicated, and how seemingly convoluted this logic can be. As Kierkegaard has it, Christianity introduced sensuality into the world insofar at it introduced spirit into the world, and spirit dialectically excludes sensuality. He says, "But if the thesis that Christianity brought sensuality into the world is to be understood properly, it must be comprehended as identical to its opposite, that it is Christianity that has driven sensuality out of the world, has excluded sensuality from the world. . . . This is quite natural, for Christianity is spirit, and spirit is the positive principle it has brought into the world" (EO I, 61). So sensuality was posited in the world in a paradoxical relation to spirit: spirit included sensuality but as an excluded possibility. What can this mean?

To see how spirit excludes sensuality, and yet dialectically includes it as

2. Søren Kierkegaard, *Either/Or,* 2 vols., ed. and trans. Howard V. Hong and Edna H. Hong (Princeton: Princeton University Press, 1987) (hereafter EO I and EO II). See especially "The Immediate Erotic Stages" of vol. 1. See also my *Word and Spirit: A Kierkegaardian Critique of the Modern Age* (Bloomington: Indiana University Press, 1993) (hereafter WS).

a possibility, an excluded possibility, we must first see that Christianity was the first to introduce into human consciousness a model of the relation between spirit and the sensuous that is essentially dialectical (we must be careful to distinguish between the *sensuous* and *sensuality,* just as we must distinguish between *spirit* and *spirituality*). On this Kierkegaardian (Christian) model, spirit is thought of as excluding, or as constantly negating, or as emancipating itself from, the sensuous, and at the same time as essentially requiring the sensuous as the medium of its expression. To illustrate this dialectical relation, Kierkegaard uses examples of the following sort: "If a person spoke in such a way that we heard the flapping of his tongue etc., he would be speaking poorly; if he heard in such a way that he heard the vibrations of the air instead of words, he would be hearing poorly. . . . Language is the perfect medium [to express spirit] precisely when everything sensuous is negated" (EO I, 67–68).

It is quite obvious that if we listen to someone speaking in such a way as to concentrate our attention on the sounds of his or her words, then we will lose the meaning of what the person is saying. Yet without the sounds that convey the meaning in this oral/aural phenomenon, no meaning would be conveyed. Meaning is constantly emancipating itself, constantly disengaging itself, from the sensuous, but at the same time, and by this very exclusion, the sensuous sounds of speech are included as essential within it as a phenomenon. Again, however, the sensuous is dialectically included as excluded, as annulled, as constantly negated.[3]

When the dialectic of inclusion/exclusion between spirit and the sensuous is broken, when the two are no longer seen as bonded together, as mutually requiring one another, that is, when they are seen only in terms of their mutual exclusion, then a new form of existence becomes actual, something Kierkegaard calls the demonic. Held together, as only language can do, spirit requires and excludes the sensuous. If broken apart, as in fact the two have become in the modern age, that is, in the wake of the demise of language— that is, in the wake of the modern rise of mathematics (science), and music (romanticism)—the dialectical relation between spirit and the sensuous gets transformed into a relation of pure exclusion. In this state of brokenness, the sensuous becomes sensuality, and spirit becomes spirituality, two forms of what Kierkegaard calls the demonic. The figures Kierkegaard uses to express

---

3. See my *Word and Spirit,* where I discuss in detail Kierkegaard's conception of the impact of Christianity on pagan (Greek) sensibility. In paganism, neither spirit (as psyche) nor the sensuous were conceived as dialectically excluding (negating) one another, but as in harmony and accord. Christianity disrupted this harmony by positing spirit as standing to the sensuous in a dialectical sundered/bonded relation.

these demonic possibilities are, respectively, Don Juan and Faust: the first represents the pursuit of a life within a sensuous world completely emptied of spirit; it represents the pursuit of a life of pure sensuality; the second represents the pursuit of a life of spirit as it would be when completely uprooted from the sensuous; it represents the pursuit of a life of pure disembodied spirituality.

The point here is that when Christianity introduced spirit into the world, it also introduced, it could not help also introducing, the opposite of spirit, that is, the demonic. Spirit is a possibility, on this dialectic of paradox, only if the demonic is also a possibility. And yet, spirit excludes the demonic (sensuality and spirituality) just as surely as it posits it, that is, includes it, as a possibility. In a spiritually determined world (that is, in the post-Christian world), spirit can exist only if the possibility of the demonic also and simultaneously exists; in the psychically determined world of antiquity (in pre-Christian paganism), spirit did not exist *as spirit* (it existed as psyche), hence in antiquity, there was no room for the demonic either.

Fortunately, not all of the illustrations of the dialectic of paradox are this complicated. Consider, for example, what is perhaps the most famous such relation of inclusion/exclusion that Kierkegaard discusses, that is, the relation between despair and faith. Faith is the condition of having rooted out every trace of despair.[4] And yet despair is also included within faith as its "first element" (SUD, 78), as its absolutely essential condition. To use one of Kierkegaard's little noticed turns of phrase, we might say that despair is both excluded from and included within faith insofar as it is always "an annulled possibility."[5] This idea will be very important in my interpretation of him and of Cavell and Nussbaum. I take his concept of an annulled possibility to capture what I mean by saying that, in the dialectic of paradox, a positive relational reality can *include* within itself what it also *excludes*.

While this dialectic of paradox—wherein one phenomenon is necessar-

---

4. Søren Kierkegaard, *The Sickness unto Death: A Christian Psychological Exposition for Upbuilding and Awakening,* ed. and trans. Howard V. Hong and Edna H. Hong (Princeton: Princeton University Press, 1983), 14 (hereafter SUD).

5. Kierkegaard introduces this notion in a footnote. Since this note plays so large a part in my interpretation of Kierkegaard, I will quote the full text: "Note that here despair over sin is dialectically understood as pointing toward faith. The existence of this dialectic must never be forgotten (even though this book deals only with despair as sickness); in fact, it is implied in despair's also being the first element in faith. But when the direction is away from faith, away from the God-relationship, then despair over sin is the new sin. In the life of the spirit, everything is dialectical. Indeed, offense as *annulled possibility* is an element in faith, but offense directed away from faith is sin. That a person never once is capable of being offended by Christianity can be held against him. To speak that way implies that being offended is something good. But it must be said that to be offended is sin" (SUD, 116n, italics added).

ily present within some other one, but *present as absent*—may sound at first a bit strange and even though it can be very complicated, I also want to claim that it is in fact an essential element in our ordinary experience. This dialectic of presence-in-absence is as ordinary as, as familiar as, the common experience of discovering the presence of what was right before us only when it has been taken away. This common, ordinary experience finds its voice in the popular expression "You don't know what you've got 'til its gone." The dialectic of paradox is no less familiar than this.

Although I say this paradoxical logic is part of our ordinary common sense, some have found it altogether bewildering. Some have thought that Kierkegaard's rhetoric simply defies reason. This has led to the most famous criticism of Kierkegaard, the charge that he is an irrationalist.[6] In the following chapters, I will show that the embrace of the logic of paradox is not only not a retreat into irrationalism, but to the contrary, an embrace of the familiar. But like so much that is right before our eyes—too close for us to see, we might say—it may be hard to recognize. For me, recognizing it has opened new paths in our common human quest to understand our existence, and our existential call to embrace it.

6. See, for example, Alasdair MacIntyre's *After Virtue: A Study in Moral Theory,* 2d ed. (Notre Dame, Ind.: University of Notre Dame Press, 1984). He says, e.g., that "the doctrine of *Enten-Eller* is plainly to the effect that the principles which depict the ethical way of life are to be adopted *for no reason,* but for a choice that lies beyond reasons, just because it is the choice of what is to count as a reason" (42).

One

KIERKEGAARD

To Be or Not to Be Human

RELIGION AND PHILOSOPHY
AS REFUSALS OF FAITH

It is perhaps a startling claim, but Kierkegaard argues, and I think correctly, that religion in general, and Christianity in particular, can be, and often are, at odds with faith. He identifies such faithless religions with a modality of existence he sometimes calls religiousness A, and sometimes, infinite resignation. I read his notion of resignation as a form of refusing the human, the human world, a kind of turning of one's back on it, spiritual or literal, for the sake of a world elsewhere, a world perceived to be higher or better than this human world. These faithless religions I call religions of resignation and refusal. Again, these religions are marked definitively by the efforts they devise and promote to provide human beings with ways of salvation, all of which turn out to be ways of resigning from, or denying, or avoiding, or otherwise refusing the existential embrace of our own humanness.[1]

---

1. Kierkegaard treats religiousness A in his *Concluding Unscientific Postscript,* trans. David F. Swenson and Walter Lowrie (Princeton: Princeton University Press, 1968) (hereafter CUP). And in agreement with my opening point about the possibility that religion, in particular popular Christianity, can be at odds with faith, he says, "Religiousness A can exist in paganism, and in Christianity it can be the religiousness of everyone who is not decisively Christian [that is, who does not live in faith], whether he is baptized or not" (495). He also treats it, although not explicitly in *Fear and Trembling, Repetition,* ed. and trans. Howard V. Hong and Edna H. Hong (Princeton: Princeton University Press, 1983) (hereafter FT). In this work, I take Kierkegaard's discussion of the movement of resignation that the knight of resignation makes to be essentially identical to the movement made in religiousness A. While Stephen Dunning takes resignation to be but the first movement of Religiousness A, along with suffering and guilt, I will take resignation to be its central and defining element (KDI, 190). For my purposes in this book, I will take the discussion of infinite resignation in FT, and the discussion of religiousness A in CUP to be variations on the type of religion that I call the religion or philosophy of resignation.

I construe Kierkegaard to be saying that the mode of existence in such religions of resignation and refusal (religiousness A), along with the other modalities of existence he is famous for naming and exploring—I mean, the aesthetic and the ethical modes of existence—stand in contrast to existential faith. Kierkegaard identifies existential faith with authentic Christianity, and sometimes calls it religiousness B. For Kierkegaard, such a Christian faith is the only authentically existential modality of existence; it is defined for him paradigmatically in the biblical figure of Abraham, the father of faith. In Abraham, existential faith is represented (especially in the story of the sacrifice of Isaac) as a double movement of giving up and getting back. I understand this double movement of existential faith in terms of human *freedom*. In existential faith, freedom embraces the human, but only on the other side of having faced, in fear and trembling, its power to give it up, something that makes the free embrace of the human a matter of both giving up and getting back.

On my view, Kierkegaard's religions of resignation and refusal are matched by corresponding philosophies. That is, the refusal of faith is not confined exclusively to religion; it can also find expression in philosophy. Indeed, for Kierkegaard, the greatest spokesman for religiousness A is a philosopher, Socrates. This is so because Socrates (well, Plato) is the one who articulates most clearly the metaphysical rationale for resignation and refusal. As such, authentic Christian faith, that is, existential faith, will always find itself at odds with the metaphysics of Platonism, and this despite the oft-made claim that Christianity is Platonism for the masses.

To see this, we need look no further than to the history of the early Christian church. In its beginnings, Christianity's most formidable enemy was a religious form of Platonism known as Gnosticism. As Jonas defines it, Gnosticism was, and is, a religion of spiritual transcendence born and bred of a deep-seated alienation from the world. He puts this religious urge to escape from the world as follows: "[T]he material universe . . . is like a vast prison whose innermost dungeon is the earth, the scene of man's life. . . . The goal of Gnostic striving is the *release* of the inner man from the bonds of the world and his return to his native realm of light."[2]

The historical gloss on the struggle between early Christianity and Gnosticism has it that Christianity was the victor. Arguably, however, this second-century heresy was not put to rest. Indeed, it may just be the case that

---

2. Hans Jonas, "Gnosticism," in *The Encyclopedia of Philosophy,* ed. Paul Edwards, vol. 3 (New York: Macmillan, 1967), 339–40 (italics added).

what won the day in official Christian doctrine actually lost within popular Christian belief and practice. In this light, it may make perfectly good sense to say that Christianity is Platonism for the masses.

And the situation has not changed within modern popular Christianity. In fact, it is Harold Bloom's thesis that modern American religion is essentially Gnostic. He says, "We [America] are, alas, the most religious of countries, and only varieties of the American Religion finally will flourish among us, whether its devotees call it Mormonism, Protestantism, Catholicism, Islam, Judaism, or what-ever-you-will. And the American Religion, for its two centuries of existence, seems to me irretrievably Gnostic. It is a knowing, by and of an uncreated self, or self-within-the-self, and the knowledge leads to freedom, a dangerous and doom-eager freedom: from nature, time, history, community, other selves."[3] Whether we call it Gnosticism or not, philosophy or religion, popular Christianity, American or otherwise, seems shot through with elements of world-alienation and with the wish to transcend the human.

In a recent treatment of *Fear and Trembling,* Edward Mooney makes much ado of the connection between the religion of resignation, as Kierkegaard himself does, and the philosophy of Socrates. I quite agree. I find no human figure a better model of religiousness A than this philosopher. Mooney characterizes Socrates as follows: "To escape a painful vulnerability, Socrates devotes himself to resignation. His is not a mere denial of the value of worldly attachment, a kind of nihilism, but a resignation powered by an embrace of eternal value, an absolute good that gives him leverage against the weight of the worldly. . . . Letting go, resigning the world, they grasp the virtues of honesty, courage, freedom, and integrity—virtues that secure an eternal consciousness because they are not conditioned by threat, temptation, or corruption from worldly influence."[4]

On my reading, the contrast between religiousness A and the existential faith of authentic Christianity is most illuminated in the contrast between the human figures of Socrates and Abraham. Clearly, it is our human existence in the world—its temporality, its contingencies, its concrete particularity, its risks, its vulnerabilities to loss, and so forth—that Socrates refuses and seeks to escape or deny; and it is just these concrete actualities that Abraham embraces, every inch.

Socratic religiousness A has its aesthetic and ethical counterparts.

---

3. Harold Bloom, *The American Religion: The Emergence of the Post-Christian Nation* (New York: Simon and Schuster, 1992), 49.

4. Edward F. Mooney, *Knights of Faith and Resignation: Reading Kierkegaard's* "Fear and Trembling" (Albany: State University of New York Press, 1991), 141 (hereafter EM).

Seeing these analogies (along with disanalogies) goes a long way toward establishing that, for Kierkegaard, existential faith is not just a next higher rung on a ladder leading from the aesthetic to the ethical to the religious. As I read Kierkegaard, existential faith stands on the other side of an abyss and can be reached only by a leap. There are no bridges, no way to inch closer. On one side of the abyss is existential faith, on the other, all of the other modalities of existence. My claim is that the feature that unites all of these modalities of existence that fall short of faith is their common refusal of the human embrace.

Such an existential embrace of the human, in requiring a leap across an abyss, interestingly enough, makes sense only if the leap is *from* a position of nonfaith, that is, *from* one variation or another of the modalities of religious and/or philosophical resignation and refusal—aesthetic flight, ethical abstraction, and so forth—that is, *from* positions Kierkegaard often characterizes in terms of despair. Such a leap is called for only if the failures of the modalities of existence other than faith are existentially confronted and refused. This makes my reading of Kierkegaard all the more obviously paradoxical: since I read the modalities of existence that are outside of existential faith as basically modalities of refusal, the leap of faith can only be characterized as something like a dialectical refusal of refusal.

In the next chapter, I will focus on the ethical modality (a life-possibility that is seemingly very close to the existential embrace of the human) as itself a subtle form of refusal and avoidance. As I will put it, the ethical mode of existence represents a form of resignation similar to, but also different from, religious or philosophical resignation; or more precisely, I will say that the ethical mode represents a way of resignation *to,* rather than a religious or philosophical resignation *from,* the finite world and our human existence in it.

To anticipate this discussion, let me admit at the outset that this interpretation of Kierkegaard's stages is highly unorthodox. Consider, for example, a recently published, typically orthodox, interpretation of Kierkegaard's ethical modality, Anthony Rudd's *Kierkegaard and the Limits of the Ethical.*[5] In this book, Rudd reads the ethical stage as a decisive advance over the aesthetic stage. (And I might add here, that he reads the aesthetic stage in the same way that I do, and most others, namely, as the self's flight from itself, from others, and from the world.) As Rudd sees it, again in agreement with most others, the ethical stage represents a step in the right direction, a step

5. Anthony Rudd, *Kierkegaard and the Limits of the Ethical* (New York: Clarendon Press, 1993) (hereafter AR).

into existence, a step that brings the self closer to, indeed, to the very edge of, existential faith. If nothing else, the ethical stage is taken to represent a step away from despair. Here I differ. I suggest that the ethical stage is itself simply another form of, a different mode of, despair, at least as it is embodied in Kierkegaard's most notable representative of this stage, Judge William of *Either/Or II.* As such, the ethical represents a different way of refusing existential faith, not a step toward it. Basic to my reasons for saying this, as most agree, Rudd included, is that the ethical individual falls short of, or lies outside of, existential faith.

My argument for reading the ethical as a form of despair is simple: the minor premise is, as I just indicated, that the ethical falls short of existential faith; the major premise is Kierkegaard's famous definition of faith, namely, that it is the state of the self in which despair is completely rooted out (SUD, 14). From these premises, it follows that the ethical modality of existence has not completely rooted out despair, or what is the same thing, is itself still a modality of despair, and hence not faith. Again, I will try to show this is true with Kierkegaard's central human representative of the ethical, Judge William.

On the reading that I am proposing, the most basic either/or for Kierkegaard is that between faith and despair. It is an absolute disjunction: in faith there are no traces of despair and so in despair there are no traces of faith. At the same time, this radical, absolute, disjunction is understood, in the logic of paradox, as a dialectical either/or. As absolutely mutually exclusive, faith and despair are, at the dialectical same time, never far from one another. Indeed, they are inconceivable apart from one another: they are included within each other, but included as excluded. The more conscious one is of despair, the more conscious one is of the possibility of faith, and vice versa. (Animals cannot exist in faith, and so neither can they despair!) But not only does the actuality of despair presuppose the possibility of faith, so the actuality of faith presupposes the possibility of despair. And not only must we have the possibility of one to have the actuality of the other, the abyss that separates the two, and keeps them together, is an abyss that can be crossed in *both* directions. Moreover, this crossing, this leaping, is not done once and for all; rather, the embrace of existential faith is an embrace that must be reaffirmed continually, perhaps daily.

But let us return to Rudd for a moment. On his analysis, the aesthetic modality is best described and understood in terms of *disengagement,* or *rootlessness.* Rudd's claim is that these are the terms that best describe human existence within modernity. As he sees it, and as I agree, it is this rootless disengagement from the world that is the source of our uniquely modern forms of both individual and cultural despair.

For Rudd, a key element in the etiology of modern aesthetic disengagement and rootlessness is the human discovery of individual freedom, or what is the same thing, the discovery of the individual. This discovery issued in the rejection of traditional social roles, roles that engaged human beings in the world among others and defined the (telos of the) good life for them. In a traditional culture, the individual was identical to whatever social roles he or she was born into—a king, a warrior, a craftsman, a citizen—all of which were clearly defined. In this society, Rudd says, "to be good is to perform one's social role successfully, and there are criteria to establish definitely how well one has performed" (AR, 2).

The modern age, Rudd argues, was born when human beings realized that they were not locked into a particular social role, that they possessed the power to step back from such roles, the power even to reject them—call this the power of (another sort of?) disengagement, or it you will, freedom. Enthralled by this power to choose one's place, the modern person became intoxicated with this newfound liberation from caste, clan, tradition. Fearing a return to the bondage of traditional society, the modern person chose to hover in aesthetic, disengaged, rootless, freedom from the world—as if this were the only way that freedom could be maintained.

But Rudd's and Kierkegaard's point is that a life lived in perpetual disengagement is but an illusion of freedom and ultimately renders concrete existence in the world unbearably problematic and leads finally to despair. For both, however, this despair has a remedy: an existential reengagement in the world through the exercise of positive freedom in concrete worldly projects. This is not a return to traditional society, for social roles are no longer simply given by birth, fate, or circumstance, but are taken up as ethical (teleological) projects: one's social role is now a matter of freedom, of existential responsibility.

As Rudd puts this, the remedy for despair is found in coming to a proper understanding of how freedom (disengagement) and rootedness can both be embraced. He says:

> Kierkegaard describes the self as a self-conscious synthesis of "the infinite and the finite, and the temporal and the eternal, of freedom and necessity." In each of these three sets of contrasting qualities, there is one that stands for our limitations, our 'rootedness', as I have called it, and one that stands for our power to transcend those limits, our capac-

ity for 'disengagement'. . . . [Yet] the human being is not simply a combination of factors . . . the synthesis of the different factors in a human being is the task of that human being, which he must actively strive for. The possibility therefore exists that the synthesis will not be properly developed and maintained, and that the elements in human nature will become misrelated. This misrelation Kierkegaard calls 'despair'. (AR, 24–25)

I certainly agree with Rudd that a completely disengaged self, a self completely untethered from its rootedness in the world, the general state of the self in modernity, is a self in despair. And moreover I agree with Rudd that the remedy that Kierkegaard proposes for the modern despair of disengagement lies in some form of existential reappropriation of our rootedness within the world among others. Surely Rudd is correct in thinking that it is just this rootless disengagement that is at the heart of Kierkegaard's critique of the many forms of aestheticism. I would quarrel with this only by suggesting that it might be that, for Kierkegaard, this disengagement is an element in *all* of the modalities of existence short of existential faith, even in the modality of existence, namely, the ethical, that Rudd thinks is at least the partial cure for the aesthetic despair of disengagement.

Rudd thinks of the ethical as a decisive alternative to aesthetic disengagement (and, of course, it is different) and as a step toward faith. Indeed, for Rudd, Kierkegaard's ethical sphere of existence is the opposite of aesthetic disengagement, or as we might say, a sphere in which all traces of this disengagement have been rooted out. This makes the movement from the aesthetic to the ethical, for Rudd, the major leap toward an existentially authentic human life. Nevertheless, Rudd also interprets the ethical as limited: even though the leap from the aesthetic to the ethical takes us closer to faith, still the ethical falls short of it. The problem with the ethical, Rudd claims, is that it is incomplete; it needs faith to be complete. For him, oddly enough, this completion comes by way of an infusion of a new religious transcendence (a new form of disengagement?).

In disagreement with Rudd, I argue that Kierkegaard's ethical existence may not be the embrace of the world that he thinks it is. It may not even be as close to faith as he thinks it is. Indeed, my argument is that Kierkegaard's ethical mode of existence is still on the other side of the abyss—on the side other than faith, we might say, as much so as any of the other alternatives to faith. As I will suggest, the ethical may turn out to be just another subtle form of resignation, another subtle form of rootless disengagement, not its (even partial) remedy. Since I interpret Kierkegaard as saying that the only real remedy for the despair of disengagement, of world-resignation, is religiousness B, I cannot agree with Rudd that religiousness B is simply a completion of the ethical, that it is simply something added on to the ethical in order to overcome its inherent limits, thus making it a complete and proper remedy for disengagement. Although I agree that religiousness B has an essential ethical component, I read religiousness B not as a completion of the ethical modality, but as a decisive alternative to it.[6]

But let me turn from this criticism of Rudd's position and return to the discussion of religious and philosophical forms of resignation and refusal. In the following section, I will set out in more detail my interpretation of Kierkegaard's modalities of existence. I will then turn to the task of continuing to highlight what I take to be the basic contrasts between religions and philosophies of resignation and refusal and religiousness B, what I am calling existential faith. I will show how these two perspectives differ in their interpretations of immortality and eternity. And in the concluding section of this chapter, I hope to make it clear what I mean by saying that religions and philosophies of resignation and refusal have an essential role to play *within* existential faith.

Faith and the Other Modalities of Existence

In the logic of the Kierkegaardian framework, faith is the opposite of a religion and philosophy of resignation and refusal: existential faith for Kierkegaard is always essentially worldly; a religion and philosophy of resignation and refusal are always essentially, however subtly, other-worldly. To live in faith, to live as a knight of faith, for Kierkegaard, is synonymous with existing as spirit, as self. To live in resignation and refusal, to live as a knight of infinite resignation, is to forfeit self, to forfeit spirit, to forfeit our humanness, even in the face of the usual judgment that such a world-denial is the defining mark of a spiritual existence.

True to the incarnational character of biblical religion, the Kierkegaardian vision of the life of faith sees it as an existence deeply connected to the historical actuality of finite particularity. Or to put this differently, spirit, for

---

6. For further criticism of Rudd's position, see my review of his book, *International Journal for Philosophy of Religion* 37 (1995): 57–59.

Kierkegaard, is always incarnate; the self, for him, is always a particular, embodied, individual self among others within the world. Existential faith, for Kierkegaard, entails a love for, and a wholehearted embrace of, the world in all of its historical particularity.

To be sure, to live as a knight of faith is to take up a covenantal relation with God. But what is most often left out of the popular conception of faith is that the knight is also and at the same time called to establish an affirmative bond to the historical world. The Kierkegaardian knight of faith is called to establish such a dual relation: a relation of the self to God and a relation of the self to the world; existential faith requires *both* components.

In the typical gloss on the self's relation to God and to the world that existential faith requires, its paradoxical character quickly becomes evident: the knight of faith is called on existentially to confront at once both transcendence and immanence. She is called to exist in such a way that every moment of her life includes within itself—is a paradoxical synthesis of—seemingly mutually exclusive components: the finite and the infinite, the temporal and the eternal, freedom and necessity (SUD, 13).[7] If, however, such characterizations are not to be dismissed as nonsense, if they are to have intelligible substance, we must specify more precisely the logic of such a paradoxical embrace of opposites.

I take it that the key paradoxical aspect of existential faith is found in the fact that it both includes and excludes within itself the possibility of taking up alternative postures toward the world. Grasping the paradoxical role that these alternatives play within faith is essential for understanding the nature of the self-world relation that the knight of faith is called upon to enter—essential, that is, for grasping that Kierkegaardian faith is fundamentally, albeit paradoxically, a worldly faith.

To do this, we must first adumbrate the class of relations that a human being can take up vis-à-vis the world that constitute the alternatives to the world-relation established in existential faith. Again, a religion and a philosophy of resignation and refusal are not the only such alternatives to faith; there are also the paths of the aesthetic per se and the ethical. But common to all of these life-possibilities is the refusal of the human embrace.

My interpretation of the alternatives to faith converges and diverges from the standard tripartite analysis of the Kierkegaardian stages of the aesthetic, the ethical, and the religious in the following ways. As I have sug-

---

7. In *Word and Spirit,* I have called this paradoxical relation of the self to the world a sundered/bonded relation.

gested above, I propose that common to all of these alternatives to faith is the structural element of *resignation and refusal.* This interpretation differs from the usual insofar as the single self-world movement of resignation is associated almost exclusively by Kierkegaard himself with the religious alternative to faith, namely, religiousness A. As I see it, resignation, though of a different sort, is also an essential feature—but more subtly—of Kierkegaard's ethical modality of existence. I also take it for granted that aesthetic existence, or rather the aesthetic flight from existence, is also a form of resignation from worldly existence, different to be sure from its counterparts, but nevertheless a refusal of the human, a mode of transcending it.

My way of reading Kierkegaard is similar in one respect to the twofold analysis that I learned from Stephen Crites.[8] Crites proposes that there are only two basic modes of existence for Kierkegaard, namely, the aesthetic and the existential. What I accept from Crites is the idea of the dichotomy—call this the bedrock Kierkegaardian either/or. Unlike Crites, and other variations on his position,[9] I will not take the ethical, or religiousness A, to fall *within* the existential modality. Rather, I will say that the aesthetic, the ethical, and religiousness A, are simply variations of modalities of existence that lie across the abyss from faith. On my reading then, there is a twofold either/or analysis of the stages: there is existential faith and then everything else (that is, despair). This does not mean that I want to deny all of the differences among the alternatives to faith. This would be unfaithful to Kierkegaard himself who goes to so much trouble to work out these differences. Yet, it would also be a mistake, I think, not to see the abyss that separates all of these life-possibilities from faith. Perhaps Kierkegaard goes to so much trouble to work out the differences among the alternatives to faith so as to make sure that we understand what faith is by telling us the myriad things that it is not. I reiterate: on my reading, Kierkegaard thinks that the only properly authentic modality of existence is the modality of existential faith (religiousness B).

8. See Stephen Crites, "Pseudonymous Authorship as Art and as Act," in *Kierkegaard: A Collection of Critical Essays,* ed. Josiah Thompson (Garden City, N.Y.: Doubleday Anchor Books, 1972) (hereafter CE) where he says, "[I]n certain respects one best grasps the intent behind the notion of the stages in reducing the scheme to the distinction between the aesthetic and the existential, regarding the ethical and religious as existential discriminations" (202).

9. See Edward Mooney, for example, who seems to be in basic agreement with Crites's aesthetic/existential dichotomy, affirmingly quotes Alastair McKinnon, who is also in "rough agreement" with Crites in thinking that all of the stages boil down to a single "either/or." Yet in citing McKinnon, Mooney emphasizes, tellingly, what is important for him in this interpretation: "*either* the aesthetic on its own terms, *or* religiousness B [the existential], *including within it,* as dethroned or subsumed stages, religiousness A, the ethical, and the aesthetic" (EM, 146, n11). My reading of Crites's dichotomy is different. For me, *the either/or* is as follows: *either* the aesthetic, the ethical, the religious (the religion of resignation, religiousness A), *or* the existential (religiousness B).

In some ways, my interpretation of the alternatives to faith is fairly standard. I read Kierkegaard as proposing at least three basic alternatives, with variations within each, to existential faith: (1) the aesthetic life-possibility in which the self adopts the strategy of flight from historical particularity achieved via a refusal of responsible ethical choice/action and the attachments to the world that such a responsible existence entails (Author A, Don Juan, Faust, Johannes the Seducer); (2) the ethical life-possibility in which the self appears to exist within an existential attachment to the world, an attachment based on a willingness to engage in responsible action, a willingness to embrace the concrete historical actuality as one's own, but which turns out to be a relation that is simply another, albeit veiled, form of refusing the human, that is, an illusion of faith in which attachments to historical particularity are made only insofar as they serve as the concrete occasions for manifesting a higher, deeper, more absolute attachment—an attachment to abstract, timeless, eternal, universal, ethical ideals (Judge William); (3) the life of religious resignation from historical particularity—a detachment which may be based on a recognition of the failure of the ethical to realize the universal within the muck and mire of concrete historical actuality (religiousness A). It is just the failure of the ethical project of making the abstract, universal principle absolute—of making the relative, the temporal, the concrete particular, and so forth, conform to timeless, abstract generalizations (the failed attempt at absolutizing the relative)—that leads the knight of infinite resignation to seek a more perfect world elsewhere (Socrates).[10]

All of these self-world relations stand in contrast to the self-world relation proposed by existential faith insofar as only in the latter do we find a true, full, albeit paradoxical, affirmation and embrace of our human existence within the finite historical world.

---

10. Kierkegaard's Judge William discusses two examples of such religions of resignation within Christendom, namely, mysticism and monasticism. About the mystic, the Judge remarks as follows: "The mystic chooses himself in his perfect isolation; for him the whole world is dead and exterminated, and the wearied soul chooses God or himself. . . . For the mystic the whole world is dead; he has fallen in love with God. . . . The mystic chooses himself abstractly; one can therefore say that he is continually choosing himself out of the world" (EO II, 241, 242, 249). And about monasticism, he says, "If those who withdrew from life had been honest and frank with themselves and others, if they had loved being a human being above all else, if they had felt with some enthusiasm all the beauty there is in being human, if their hearts had not been unacquainted with genuine, deep human feelings, they perhaps would have also withdrawn into the solitude of the monastery, but they would have foolishly deluded themselves into thinking that they had become extraordinary persons, except in the sense that they were more imperfect than others; they would not have looked down pityingly on the ordinary people but would have looked at them sympathetically, with a sad kind of joy that they succeeded in accomplishing the beautiful and the great that they themselves were unable to accomplish" (EO II, 328).

When I say that resignation and refusal are the common elements of all of the stages of existence, save one (faith), I mean that all of these alternatives to faith represent, in one way or another, the persistent human desire to retreat from, to transcend, our human existence, our embodiment in time and place. As well, I mean to set this desire in its proper paradoxical context. I claim that this desire for transcendence of the human is both definitive of human existence—only human beings can desire not to be human!—and, at the same time, born of a deep-seated human resentment of, and alienation from, the human condition.

Where does this paradoxical resentment come from? There are no doubt many sources, but surely high among these are the disappointments of finitude: its sufferings, losses, vulnerabilities, broken promises, or more generally, the realization that human existence in the world is intrinsically and inextricably fragile to the core.

Before I take up a more detailed discussion of the paradoxical place of the alternatives to existential faith within the very structure of faith itself, let me turn to a more specific contrast between the interests of a religion or philosophy of resignation and refusal and the interests of existential faith.

Immortality and Eternity

The contrast between a worldly existential faith and an other-worldly religion or philosophy of resignation and refusal, between Christianity and Platonism say, or between religiousness B and A, is clarified when we see how each brings a different conception to common religious and philosophical preoccupations. Let me illustrate this with two examples: the concept of immortality and the concept of eternity.

The term *immortality* means, of course, not mortal, that is, not subject to death. Since all life on earth seems to be subject to death, the question arises as to whom or to what the term can apply?

One early and quite surprising answer is, immortality applies to everything in the cosmos but human beings. Whatever else we may doubt, one thing is certain: "All men are mortal." It was this conviction that all but human beings are immortal that dominated pre-Platonic Greek culture. The primary metaphor that these early Greeks used in picturing the cosmos was nature, that ever-recurring cyclical order of life (and death). While plants, animals, etc. die, the natural order itself is immortal, deathless; human beings alone die. As Hannah Arendt has pointed out, "[I]ndividual [human] life is distinguished from all other things by the rectilinear course of movement, which, so to speak, cuts through the circular movement of biological life. This is mortality: to move along a rectilinear line in a universe where everything, if it moves at all, moves in a cyclical order." [11]

The anthropomorphic figures that symbolize this cosmic immortality are, for the Greeks, the Olympian gods, those deathless, ageless beings who stand as such over against mortal human beings. Yet, paradoxically, even though human beings alone are mortal in an immortal cosmos, amongst immortal gods, it is thought possible that mortal beings can attain to immortality, to divinity, we might say. Once again, to quote from Arendt, "The task and potential greatness of mortals lie in their ability to produce things— works and deeds and words—which would deserve to be and, at least to a degree, are at home in everlastingness, so that through them mortals could find their place in a cosmos where everything is immortal except themselves" (HC, 19).

For the Greeks, then, at least for the Greeks prior to Socrates/Plato, immortality was intimately connected to life on earth, to human worldly existence. Immortality was thought to be achieved in the great works (of art, architecture, sculpture, poetry, etc.) or the great deeds (political deeds, in Arendt's sense of the term) of human beings, works that would last in the memory of future generations. Here, immortality is a worldly achievement of greatness *within* human existence. [12]

Later, an alternative conception of immortality developed within Greek culture. It was Plato who gave this other conception of immortality its decisive formulation. Plato's most famous expression of this doctrine of immortality is in the *Phaedo*. [13] Here Plato extends his metaphysical doctrine of

---

11. Hannah Arendt, *The Human Condition* (Chicago: University of Chicago Press, 1958), 19 (hereafter HC).

12. Related to the pre-Platonic Greek idea of a this-world immortality—immortality as remembered human greatness—is the notion that we achieve immortality through our children. Our physical identities do survive, as a matter of genetic fact, through our children in family resemblances; but we also pass on to them our names, our beliefs, our values, our occupations, and so forth. The attempt at achieving this kind of immortality, however, may entail the loss of individuality; it may be an attempt to absorb human life back into the immortality of animal existence, an existence in which the immortality of the species is guaranteed through procreation.

13. On the day of his death, Socrates says in calm cheerfulness that he is looking forward to what he has been preparing himself for all of his life—through the practice of philosophy—namely, the release of his soul from his bodily imprisonment in the world. At death, he goes on to say, the soul "departs to that place which is, like itself, invisible, divine, immortal and wise; where, on its arrival, happiness awaits it, and release from uncertainty and folly, from fears and uncontrolled desires, and all other human evils" (*Phaedo,* in *The Last Days of Socrates,* trans. Hugh Tredennick [New York: Penguin Books, 1969], 133).

forms—a doctrine according to which forms are separate from worldly, temporal, concrete, sensuous existence—and develops a conception of the soul as the form of the human being, a form that is not only essentially separable from, but indeed hostile to, worldly, embodied, temporal existence. For Plato, a person's body, and the whole world of its senses and pleasures, are not real. This sensuous world comes into being and dies along with one's body—it is essentially temporal, transient, temporary. The soul, however, is independent of time, of its ravages of change and decay; as such, the soul alone is real in a person—it alone is lasting and immortal. For Plato, a human being simply *is* a soul, a soul temporarily trapped in time (and space). Insofar as the soul is essentially independent of time and embodiment, the soul, like all forms, is immortal.

In a momentous shift, Plato managed to define immortality as an impossibility *within* human, worldly, temporal, embodied existence—the shadowy realm of appearances. Immortality now was understood as an other-worldly, disembodied, atemporal, contemplative state of being. It is only in this state of rest and repose outside the temporal, historical world that human beings come to their final perfection; it is only by being released from human existence in the world, from the cave of ignorance and shadows, that the good life can reach its telos. On this view, death in both its biological and philosophical senses, is the goal of life, the doorway to the good life: biological death brings the final escape from the human, the release that accounted for the cheerfulness of Socrates in the face of his imminent execution, and the death-in-life of the philosopher about which he talks to his disciples just prior to his drinking the hemlock—the philosopher who puts all of his energies, as much as possible, into the contemplation of the other world of eternal forms and so dies to the pleasures and ignorance of a life focused on *this world.*

It is this other-worldly focus that has dominated doctrines of immortality subsequent to Plato. And in an ironic twist, it is just this Platonic notion of immortality, or more precisely, a spiritually qualified version of it— Gnosticism—that has dominated Christendom.[14] The Gnostic doctrine of immortality—a doctrine that is essentially excarnational and ultimately misanthropic—is essentially alien to the incarnational faith of Christianity (religiousness B).

---

14. Here I am assuming the Kierkegaardian distinction between Christendom and Christianity: the former being the actual beliefs and practices of those in the Church and the latter being the faith revealed in the Christ event. For Kierkegaard, Christendom most often does not reflect the faith of Christianity; indeed, most often it reflects some form of the religion of resignation, that is, some form of spiritlessness, or faithlessness.

While Gnosticism grew up with Christianity, and even though it is not always clearly distinguishable from it, and even though some of the documents of the New Testament seem more Gnostic than not, Gnosticism—its docetic denial of the incarnation, its denial of the hope for the redemption of the created order, its denial of the goodness of the creation and human existence within it, its longing for another spirit-world, and so forth—was declared heretical by the Church and supposedly rejected. But as I pointed out earlier, the fact is that in popular Christianity the dominant belief system is essentially Gnostic, essentially Platonic. Again, popular Christianity has rightly been called (Gnostic) Platonism for the masses. It has become religion without existential faith.

The irony of this is that the Gnostic doctrine of the immortality of the soul is foreign to biblical faith. It is certainly foreign to the passion narratives where the resurrection of the body, not the immortality of the soul, is central. And this is not surprising since Christianity (like its older sister Judaism) is governed from beginning to end by the notion of incarnation. In the biblical tradition, spirit is always incarnate—indeed, so much so, that even in its doctrine of the afterlife, (for the Pharisee and for the Christian) it is the body/soul, the whole person, that really dies and that is redeemed in the resurrection of the body.

The New Testament scholar Oscar Cullmann comments as follows on popular Christianity's widespread embrace of a doctrine (the immortality of the soul) that is essentially alien to the Bible:

If we were to ask an ordinary Christian today (whether a well-read Protestant or Catholic or not) what he conceived to be the New Testament teaching concerning the fate of man after death, with few exceptions we should get the answer: "The immortality of the soul." Yet this widely accepted idea is one of the greatest misunderstandings of Christianity. There is no point in attempting to hide this fact or to veil it by reinterpreting the Christian faith. . . . The concept of death and resurrection is anchored in the Christ-event, and hence is incompatible with the Greek belief in immortality.[15]

For Plato and Gnosticism, it is our human embodiment in the world that is the enemy of the soul. In this cave of ignorance, the soul is hindered from

15. Oscar Cullmann, *Immortality of the Soul or Resurrection of the Dead* (New York: Macmillan, 1958), 15.

its lofty desire to return to its disembodied home, from its desire to overcome the limitations of human existence. And so life is preparation for death, for it is death that is the great liberator of the human from its humanness.

For Christianity, it is death that is the enemy of the human, for it destroys the whole human being, body and soul. For Christianity, it is this enemy of the human—death itself—that is taken seriously in the passion and crucifixion of the man Jesus. And in the resurrection of Christ, it is not the body or the world that is conquered, but death itself. Yet even this conquest is not a denial of the reality of death; rather, it curiously betokens its acceptance as the fate of all human life: resurrection takes death seriously for it is a myth of life *after* death, not a myth of continued deathless existence. But the Christian acceptance of death is no fatalism, for it is tempered by the hope of resurrection: the hope that God will not allow death the last word.

Whenever we find in a religion or philosophy an intense drive for the immortality of the soul, for a disembodied other-worldly immortality, we can expect to find in that position a contempt for human existence—the decisive mark of a religion or philosophy of resignation and refusal. And the extent to which popular Christianity is so driven, is the measure of the extent to which it has become a religion of spiritual resignation and refusal. And again, the irony of this is nowhere more sharply evident than in the defensiveness of the biblical fundamentalist, who disavows the biblical doctrine of the resurrection of the body and openly embraces the Greek/Platonic/Gnostic doctrine of the immortality of the soul.

Popular Christianity has also tended to embrace an other-worldly conception of eternity—a conception that implies a denigration of, and an ultimate rejection of, worldly human existence. Eternity is commonly defined within popular Christianity in terms of its exclusive relation to historical time. According to this definition, the eternal is an atemporal, static, ahistorical realm; a realm outside of ordinary human affairs; a divine realm outside of human existence.

This conception of eternity as timeless, as ahistorical, etc., found its earliest philosophical formulation among the pre-Socratic philosophers in ancient Greece (especially Parmenides) and again culminated in the philosophy of Plato who gave the concept what has become, for the Western philosophic tradition, its most decisive definition.

For Plato, the Real (Being) is defined as that which, above all else, so to speak, *is*. In Plato's ontology, existence is the realm of time and change. Consequently, Being (what is) cannot find its home in existence. For Plato, Being does not come into nor does it go out of existence; Being does not change; it is not historical; in an important sense, it does not exist. Plato assumed that changelessness implies timelessness. As a consequence, Being (Reality) became virtually synonymous with atemporal, ahistorical eternity.

Human existence, on Plato's view, is the realm of becoming. Even though he does not think that this realm of becoming is completely without reality, completely disconnected from Being—as it was for Parmenides—he does think that Being is prior (ontologically) to, and the goal of, becoming. The realm of becoming has whatever meager, shadowy, reality it has only insofar as it imitates Being, insofar as it strives to let itself as movement and change be undermined and supplanted by the stasis and rest of Being. Being in its pure essence lacks every trace of movement and change, every trace of time, every trace of existence. Religions or philosophies based on views of this sort, wherein Being is thought to lie outside of existence, far from embracing the human, aim at an extrication from it.

But we need not define eternity in this other-worldly fashion; the term can also be given an existential, worldly meaning. Just as the other-worldly definition of eternity has its cultural roots in Greek culture, we can locate the roots of the existential meaning of eternity in the cultural matrix of the biblical narratives. There could be no greater contrast than that between the Platonic and the biblical definitions of eternity.

The locus classicus of the biblical definition of eternity is from Isaiah: "The grass withers, the flower fades; but the word of our God will stand forever" (40:8). As for Plato, the issue here is the relation of eternity to historical time; here, however, that relation is not exclusive, but inclusive. God's word, promises, covenants with God's creatures, are not phenomena outside of the world, outside of time, outside of human existence. Rather, God's word is given in history, in historical time, and it endures throughout all time. This is a conception of eternity that is not ahistorical but *transhistorical.* Here eternity is not the enemy of historical time, but the principle of its continuity. God's faithful promises constitute the stabilizing thread that weaves the mere flux of a succession of moments into a story, a plot, and transforms it into a purposeful, meaningful historical narrative—a narrative of creation, fall, and redemption. Such an incarnational picture of eternity has its perfect culmination in the idea that the Eternal has come into historical time—an idea that Saint Paul recognized to be foolishness to the Greeks.

To the extent that the Hebrews, and subsequently the Christians, lived within this existential faith, within its covenantal bonds to God and to the world, they neither yearned for an eternity outside the world, nor did they simply embrace the temporal flux as the ultimate reality. In place of these alternatives, existential faith conceives of eternity in terms of personal transhistorical faithfulness. The ultimate model of such a worldly faithfulness is the personal word *(dabhar)* of God. It and it alone stands forever—not outside of time, outside of the world, but *within the world,* and *for all time.*

If there is such a stark contrast and exclusion between existential faith and a religion or philosophy of resignation and refusal, how can we make sense of Kierkegaard's paradoxical claim that faith must *include* its alternatives within itself? We will be in a better position to address this question, I believe, if we first say more about what existential faith is. To do this, we will turn to what I take to be Kierkegaard's favorite model for faith, I mean, the biblical character of Abraham, and to the story of his willingness to sacrifice his only son.[16]

Abraham as the Knight of Faith

I take my reading of existential faith primarily from Kierkegaard's reading of the biblical story of Abraham's sacrifice of Isaac. In terms of Kierkegaard's writings, this means that my primary source for my interpretation of existential faith comes from his book *Fear and Trembling.*

In this book, I hear the (indirect) voice of Kierkegaard, writing under the pseudonym Johannes De Silentio, as he recounts and analyzes this puzzling biblical story, a story at once of sacrifice, of temptation to murder, of obedience, of embrace. I read Kierkegaard to be saying that Abraham is the very embodiment of a knight of faith, a perfect embodiment of existential faith. As I read Kierkegaard on this, Abraham's faith is found not so much by focusing on his courageous response to God's command to sacrifice his son Isaac as it is by focusing on his fear and trembling. Let me explain.

Kierkegaard wants us to see something in this courageous knight that we may not be inclined to associate with faith. This something, I think, he believes to be essential to faith. What is this? I would call it faith's essential dreadful and wrenching confrontation, via temptation, with the alternatives to faith. It is as if Kierkegaard were trying to tell us that every would-be knight of faith must, as Abraham did, confront the abyss, face the choice and ask, "On which side will I take my stand?" As I might put this, I do not think that

---

16. Of course, Isaac was not Abraham's *only* son, but, from the Jewish perspective, he was his only *legitimate* son.

in the story of the sacrifice, Abraham makes a leap of faith. He had already made the leap of faith when God first called him out of Ur and promised him the world, in the form of a son. Abraham's agony, the temptation he is faced with in fear and trembling, is the temptation *to renounce his faith*. What he found is that faith is no safe haven free from the threatening possibilities its alternatives pose.

My imagination pictures the abyss as separating two sides of the bedrock human either/or, and the two sides as being on different planes. I picture the side of the abyss, where the alternatives to faith are, as flat and inviting, maybe even comfortable; the side where faith is, as slanted upwards. In this picture, it takes considerable attention and balance for one to keep his or her footing on the side of faith. It is, I think, easy to fall, that is, to fall back into an alternative to faith, into despair.

At the same time, I don't mean to suggest that the life of faith is too hard for anyone to achieve, beyond our reach as it were. No. Faith, I assert, is a real human possibility and as such can and often is actualized in a human life.

In any case, it is clear from his analysis of this story that, for Kierkegaard, the alternatives to faith, that is, forms of resignation from, or refusal of, the human are essential elements *within* faith. Resignation and refusal are, however, not faith, but faith is not faith apart from them. Kierkegaard's way of putting this is to say that resignation is but the first movement in the *double movement* of faith. To make this double movement, to answer the call of God to live in faith, one must first realize the possibility of resigning from the finite world, of turning away from, of going beyond, all that is finite.

This first movement of faith is not faith. In the double movement where faith is chosen, the whole of the finite world, every inch, is embraced at the very dialectical moment when the possibility of giving it up is existentially (in fear and trembling) realized. In faith a new relation to finitude is thus established. This new relation lies on the other side of resignation and refusal, but it does not leave them completely behind. The movement of resignation—if it is not too easy, if it is a real existential struggle—brings with it the fully concrete awareness of my power (my freedom) to turn away from the world, to relativize the finite.

Such an awareness of my power to renounce the world prepares the way for faith insofar as faith is realized in the existential movement (moment) in which I receive back—from the hands of the Eternal—every inch of the finite that I have been willing to give up. Faith receives and embraces the world just as Abraham was enabled by faith to receive and embrace Isaac when his willing hand was stayed. I can only be said to be able to receive the world, to be able to embrace it, to be able to choose it, and hence to be able to make it my own in a deeply personal way, if I have the power to turn away, the power of renunciation, the will to resignation and refusal. For this reason, the elements of resignation and refusal are permanent structural elements within faith.

While we cannot forget that Isaac is Abraham's son, his only (legitimate) son, we must remember that in the biblical story, and in Kierkegaard's interpretation of it, he is also a symbol of worldly attachments in general. Does the story aim to tell us that Abraham's attachment to Isaac was wrong? that worldly attachments in general are wrong? Did Abraham care too much for Isaac? the world? It has seemed to some that Abraham's love for his son was wrong, that Abraham was guilty of possessiveness, of absolutizing the relative; or perhaps guilty of a kind of will-to-power, a desire to control his son. On this view, God is not only out to humble Abraham, to knock him down a peg or two, he also wants to teach him the lesson of how fathers must learn to let their children go, to liberate them from parental proprietary claims, to undo possessiveness.

To see an example of such an interpretation of Kierkegaard's interpretation of this biblical story, let us return to Edward Mooney's book, *Knights of Faith and Resignation.*[17] A general aim of Mooney's argument is to show that the key existential difference between resignation and faith is that in the former there is only a *single* movement, whereas, in the latter there is a *double* movement. The knight of resignation seeks to transcend the human; the knight of faith seeks to embrace it. I could not agree more. We differ, however, on how to characterize this embrace. According to Mooney, the exact quality and nature of the knight of faith's embrace of the human, his embrace of the world, of finitude, and so forth, is captured in the concept of *"selfless care."* What Mooney means by this term is found in the following paradigm: "[N]ot all cases of love or care are tied up with proprietary claim. I may *enjoy* and warmly anticipate the appearance of a sparrow at my feeder. Yet I would claim no rights over this object of my *enjoyment.* The matter of its life and death is something over which I have no claim. Of course, I would *feel* indignant were someone maliciously to injure it. But in the course of things, the sparrow will go its way. Meanwhile, I will adjust myself to its goings and comings" (EM, 53, italics added).

---

17. Much of the following appeared as "A Critical Note on Edward F. Mooney's reading of *Fear and Trembling* in *The Kierkegaard Newsletter"* (Spring 1994.) In that same issue, Mooney gives his reply to my criticisms.

Mooney begins his discussion of selfless care by commenting on the commonplace fact that care for something is linked to proprietary claims, to attachment, to possession, and hence to the vulnerability to loss, disappointment, grief, suffering, and so forth. As well, he rightly notes that human beings have long sought for, and found in many a religious tradition, including, of course, most forms of Christianity, a *techne* for coping with this vulnerability to loss. The formula of such a *techne* is simply this: renounce ones proprietary claims, disown and detach oneself from anything that is vulnerable to loss, that is, everything that is finite and temporal. If we don't care for something, then its loss cannot hurt us. And the corollary to this is that we ought only to care for what cannot be taken away, that is, the eternal, the changeless, the divine, etc. (EM, 53).

It has been my persistent claim here that it is just this technique of transcendence that we find in all of the alternatives to existential faith. In all of these alternatives, this world—because it is seen (and rightly so) as the center of uncertainty, change, anxiety, suffering, pain, loss, and death—and our existence in this world, are found to be unbearable. As such, especially given that we must, short of suicide, continue to live "down here," some technique to cope with the fragility of human existence must be found. It is these techniques of transcendence that the alternatives to faith explore. Their common assumption is that the only way that we can secure ourselves from being buffeted by the effects of time and finitude is to turn our interests, our concerns, our loves, elsewhere. And there is no end to the cleverness human beings are capable of when it comes to finding a way of refusing their own humanness. All of these alternatives agree, the real human disease, the real sickness unto death, is the condition of being human itself; all agree that the remedy for this, or as it is more often put, that our salvation from this vile human condition, is a transcendence of it.

Mooney seems to agree that existential faith contrasts with its alternatives insofar as it is a real embrace of the world, an existential embrace of our humanness. But as he develops his notion of selfless care as the model of existential faith, we can't help but wonder if the embrace he envisions is robust enough. Is the embrace of selfless care an existential embrace of the world and of our human existence in it?

For Mooney, faith as selfless care, makes no proprietary claims on the world, but nevertheless continues to embrace it, to care for it. Recall that a paradigm of such a selfless care is the claimless enjoyment Mooney feels for the sparrow that comes to his feeder. This paradigm would have us think that the knight of faith is called to keep his joyful eye on the sparrow (the world) without interfering with its comings and goings, without making any proprietary claims upon it. So here is the crux of the knight of faith's relation to finitude: care for it—love it, be concerned for it, keep a joyful eye on it, etc.—affirm it, but make no proprietary claims in relation to it; avoid, at all costs, the making of finitude one's own. Or, as we might expect to hear from the wisdom of pop self-help psychology, learn to love and to let go![18]

Again I ask, "Does Mooney's selfless care really amount to an embrace of the world?" I think that it does not. And accordingly, I think that his interpretation of Kierkegaardian faith as selfless care does not really move it to the other side of the abyss. Mooney's mistake, I submit, is in his claim that only in forswearing proprietary claims is the knight of faith able to take up a proper affirmation of the world.

Why does Mooney think it a good thing to forswear proprietary claims? I speculate that it is because he conceives of all forms of ownership, and perhaps all forms of possession, as ultimately forms of possessiveness. If this were true, and if faith therefore required a divestment of all of my ownership relations to the world, in what sense can I be said to receive it as my *own* from the hands of the Eternal? Gift-givers certainly expect us not only to receive the gifts they give, but to watch over them, to care for them, to protect them, to possess them, to claim them as our own.

Clearly it is worthwhile to point out that existential faith's affirmation of the world is not a form of possessiveness, that it is not a form of absolutizing the relative. Such relations fail to acknowledge the otherness of persons and things that we love, that we are concerned about and that we are attached to. But why must we believe that proprietary claims of care inevitably lead to possessiveness? Can there be a nonpossessive sense of ownership? Can we embrace the relative without absolutizing it? It seems to me so, and importantly so.

To see this, we must see that possessiveness is a perversion of possession, indeed an ironic transposition of it into a form of dispossession. That is, possessiveness betokens either an inability or ultimately an unwillingness to possess, to accept, and to claim as one's own what one cares for, in any usual or ordinary sense of the term. In our ordinary use of the term *possess,* we assume that we can possess something only if it is both possible for us to let it go, and in fact we do not let it go. If it were not possible to let it go then we

---

18. As I will point out presently, there is a very big difference not only between not being able to let go, and being able to, there is also a tremendous difference between being able to let go and not actually doing so.

could not posses it, just as we would not possess it if we did in fact let it go. When I possess something, when I have made it my own, in this nonpossessive sense, I have chosen it, accepted it, consented to it; *I can let it go, but I do not!* In possessiveness, I am not free in relation to what is possessed; in fact, I am possessed (perhaps obsessed or consumed) by it: *I can't let it go!* In this light, it is not surprising that the passive notion of *being possessed* is a metaphor for being in a state of unfreedom, and ultimately a state of madness; at the same time, the active notion of being *in possession,* as in *self-possession,* betokens both freedom and health.

While Mooney is right to caution against possessiveness, he has made the mistake of throwing the baby out with the bathwater. He assumes that what we can let go we must actually let go. This would be like saying that the only way we would know that Abraham was willing to sacrifice his son, to let him go, is if he had actually plunged the knife. There is certainly a difference between willing to let the knife fall and actually letting it. Abraham learns that he can sacrifice his son, but that faith does not require that he actually do it; indeed the opposite.

Consider the difference between a marriage as a covenant of existential faith and the example that Mooney gives of selfless care, viz., the experience of enjoyment he feels for the sparrow that comes to his feeder. What kind of marriage would it be for one spouse to say to the other that he or she does not make any claims on the other, but will simply adjust to the other's comings and goings? And what would we think if both mutually acknowledged that in the course of things the other will go his or her own way? What does such a disavowing of all proprietary claims on the other have to do with the covenant of marriage? Isn't it just the point of the wedding vows publicly to enter into the mutual proprietary claims of each on the other? Don't we in fact say in the vows something to the following effect: "I *take* you to be *my* lawfully wedded wife/husband . . . "? And if it is not a shotgun wedding, or otherwise arranged, this mutual giving and taking will be a matter of free consent; I can say "no" when the priest asks, "Do you take. . . ?"

I suppose that Mooney would think that such proprietary claims of one spouse on the other implied in the mutual giving and taking of one another before others and before God would be a compromise of the autonomy and independence of one or the other or both. It is as though Mooney might think that the worst possible sin in a marriage is jealousy. After all, jealousy, which is all too often confused with a genuinely destructive emotion, envy, implies a proprietary claim, a desire to protect what is one's own. (I remind you that, from the biblical point of view, jealousy is a virtue since it characterizes

God's care for his creatures, his own desire to be acknowledged by them: "for I the Lord your God am a jealous God . . . "). What indeed would a marriage be without an appropriate sense of jealously on the part of both spouses? To be without any hint of jealousy is possible only on condition that no proprietary claim whatsoever is made. Moreover, this is possible only when one no longer cares about the comings and goings of the other. This is no marriage! This is no human relationship!

And such proprietary claims certainly are involved with our children. They are, after all, *our* children, and we are *their* parents; we belong to each other in bonds of blood and/or choice. No less for Abraham and Isaac, indeed, perhaps more so. All of his hopes for the future are in his only son, the fulfillment of God's promises are found in him, he is everything to Abraham. He could not care more for Isaac, nor could he dread more the prospect of his son's having to suffer, much less of his having to die.

Is Abraham's attachment to Isaac a form of possessiveness? Has he absolutized the relative? Does he care too much for him? Mooney seems to think so (EM, 59). In the story of the sacrifice, as Mooney interprets it, God wants to teach Abraham the lesson of how fathers must learn to let their children go, to liberate them from parental proprietary claims, to undo possessiveness. After Moriah, according to Mooney, Abraham relates to Isaac in this new healthier way: he no longer makes any proprietary claims on him; he has let him go; but he still cares, in a selfless care, for him. He now *enjoys* his son, now he recognizes that in the course of things Isaac will eventually go his own way, and he now knows that he must find a way to adjust himself to his son's free comings and goings.

But on Mooney's interpretation, does Abraham really get Isaac back every inch? Is he able to embrace him and care for him ever as much as he did before he gave him up? Maybe more? It seems to me that on Mooney's reckoning Abraham gets Isaac back only tentatively, with a kind of distance now imposed between them that did not exist before, a distance that will not allow a full and complete embrace. That is, on Mooney's interpretation, Abraham gave up something that is not completely given back, at least not every inch of it.

Contra Mooney, I do not think that Kierkegaard thinks that Abraham is guilty of loving his son too possessively—of making inappropriate proprietary claims on him—or that he is in some way guilty of idolatry, or guilty of absolutizing "the relative." Indeed, Abraham never hesitated one moment in obeying God's command to sacrifice Isaac; and never did he flinch one moment in believing that God would fulfill his promise to him that he would be the father of a great nation. As I see it, Abraham does not need to be humbled, or knocked down, as Mooney suggests, for he has already made the leap of faith; he is already the Father of faith, he has been from the moment he was first called and offered a promise.

What then is the point of the story of the sacrifice? I suggest that the purpose of the story is to show us something about Abraham's faith, that is, something about existential faith. I do not think the story is out to show us that Abraham was able to put an inward distance between himself and his son, as though he was in danger of interfering with Abraham's reliance on God. The story is not trying to warn us of the dangers of getting too attached to finitude. Rather, and to the contrary, I claim that it is precisely the point of the story that God is attempting to show us just how deep Abraham's attachment is to finitude, to his son, to historical particularity, to this world. As Silentio puts it, "Yet Abraham had faith, and had faith for *this life*. In fact, if his faith had been only for a life to come, he certainly would have more readily discarded everything in order to rush out of a world to which he did not belong. But Abraham's faith was not of this sort" (FT, 20, italics added). Along these lines, I will say that the story of Abraham has three related lessons to teach us about existential faith.

The first lesson is that faith not only does not demand that Abraham withdraw his claim on his son (and finitude in general); it demands that he *deepen* it! This deepening of his claim on his son is a matter of particularizing and personalizing it: "Faith is the paradox that the single individual is higher than the universal" (FT, 55). This particularizing is an element within Abraham's deepening awareness of his own (and Isaac's) personal presence. He realizes that God is calling him (in the first person) to make his claim on Isaac in the first person; he realizes that God is calling him to make his son all the more *his own*.

The biblical text and context make it perfectly clear that the particularity of first-person presence is a central element of the story. As the account has it, Abraham is repeatedly addressed in his own name (by God, by Isaac, by the angel) and he repeatedly responds in the first-person present: "Here am I." Context suggests that the biblical story intends to present God's address as directed to this single individual, who is faced with (the threat of the loss of) another single individual, his own, his only, son.

As Silentio says it:

You to whom these words ["Abraham . . . N. . . . where are you?"] are addressed, was this the case with you? When in the far distance you saw overwhelming vicissitudes approaching, did you not say to the mountains, "Hide me," and to the hills, "Fall on me"? Or, if you were stronger, did your feet nevertheless not drag along the way, did they not long, so to speak, for the old trails? And when your name was called, did you answer, perhaps answer softly, in a whisper? Not so with Abraham. Cheerfully, freely, confidently, loudly he answered: Here am I. (FT, 21)

Expressed more negatively, we can say that the lesson the story would teach us about faith is that it is not a technique for transcending the contingencies and vulnerabilities of personal historical particularity. To live in existential faith is not to live above the threat of loss, of suffering, of death; it is not to live inured to change, unaffected by chance events that lie beyond our control, beyond our choice. Yet, to live in faith is to become conscious of such negative possibilities: to become conscious of the fact that such a transcendence, such refusal of our own personal presence in the world is possible.

Hence faith always involves an existential struggle, it always carries the necessity of working it out for ourselves in fear and trembling. To live in faith, I must choose—in full recognition of its fragilities and vulnerabilities—my own humanity among others; I must really invest myself fully and without reservation in the concrete, finite, historical actuality. To live in faith requires that I recognize and welcome my worldly condition among others as my own, that I do not resign myself to it or from it as an inevitable limitation of my human being or to my being truly human; to live in faith requires that in the midst of the possibility of doing otherwise I say, "Here am I!"

But there is a second lesson that Kierkegaard would have us learn. In addition to calling Abraham to take up his own particular, unique, personal vocation, to deepen his claim on his son, God is also teaching us, with Abraham as the example, that such a first-person claiming is ongoing, indeed, that it is a continual claiming; or what amounts to the same thing, the second lesson is that faith is *repetition*! This wholehearted embrace of the world that the knight of faith engages in is something that she must continually choose; faith is an intrinsically temporal modality of existence.

Thirdly, the faithful reception of the world from the hands of the Eternal presupposes an ongoing possibility of doing otherwise—an ever-present temptation not to receive it. Moreover, this temptation to turn away from the world in resignation—perhaps just because we know we can—never goes away. But this is necessarily so, since faith is a choice and choice presupposes a context of temporally unfolding possibilities.

It would have been easy for Abraham to have come to rest with the birth of Isaac in the belief that now everything was safe, that the fulfillment of God's promise had effectively ended anxiety, indeed, even ended the need for further faith. This would have made faith into nothing essentially different than infinite resignation insofar as in the latter "there is peace and rest" (FT, 45). But faith is not like this, God instructs; it is not a momentary, once-for-all choice, an emergency measure to get us through some crisis of uncertainty, some passing anxiety. The fact is, human existence is intrinsically subject to possibility, and hence to anxiety, to vulnerability, to loss. The faithful self does not put these elements to rest, she plunges forward through them. The faithful self is continually called to embrace the world in all of its fragility, for she recognizes that it is, at any moment, in her power to refuse. The knight knows that such a refusal would bring with it a form of existence that would be other than human; to this possibility she must continually say "no!".

Refusing Refusal

If existential faith is not a completion of resignation but must be radically distinguished from it, if faith is not simply a matter of adding a second step to the first step of world-denial, if the knight of infinite resignation fails not because he does not go far enough but because he goes in the wrong direction completely, then how can we make sense of the claim that resignation and refusal are necessary elements *within faith?* Well, my reading of this paradox has it that resignation and refusal are structural elements within faith insofar as existential faith would be impossible if resignation and refusal were not real, albeit excluded, existential possibilities. Or, as I like to put it, following Kierkegaard's suggestion, faith includes resignation and refusal within itself as annulled possibilities.

In the logic of paradox, in the logic of annulled possibilities, inclusion comes by way of dialectical exclusion. Spirit, for example, includes within itself the possibility of demonic spiritlessness precisely by annulling it as such. As well, the human includes within itself the possibility of sinking into the monstrous and the possibility of desiring to rise to the divine. Faith includes these possibilities, however, precisely by saying "no" to them, for this "no" ipso facto acknowledges their reality as ever-present, peculiarly human possibilities—as ever-present human threats.

As I have said, this is the same paradox at work in the logic of the relation between faith and despair. I come back again to *Sickness Unto Death,* to Anti-Climacus's famous definition of faith as a paradigm of this paradox. Kierkegaard certainly seems to presuppose such a relation of mutual inclusion/exclusion between despair and faith. But this is no relation in which two things are combined by putting a little of one and a little of the other together, as though faith were not faith if it did not contain a little despair. Rather the relation is one of absolute exclusion and absolute inclusion. On the one hand, Kierkegaard says that despair has no place at all within faith. His prefatory remark that introduces his definition of faith is as follows: "The formula that describes the state of the self [the self in faith] when *despair is completely rooted out* is . . ." (SUD, 4 italics added). Faith, then, is a state—we might call it a state of spiritual health—in which it seems there is no trace of despair; for despair is, after all, a sickness, the sickness unto death!

On the other hand, in his usual maddening dialectic, Kierkegaard says that despair is an essential element within faith. He says, "Note that here despair over sin is dialectically understood as pointing towards faith. The existence of this dialectic must never be forgotten (even though this book deals only with despair as sickness); in fact, it is implied in despair's also being the first element in faith" (SUD, 116).

So it seems that even though despair is the very opposite of existential faith, as resignation and refusal are its opposites, it is also an element within faith—indeed, an indispensable element. How can Kierkegaard have it both ways?

My suggestion is that we make sense out of this, that we save what may seem like a blatant contradiction, by turning to the notion of *annulled possibilities.* Kierkegaard remarks, "Not to be in despair must signify the destroyed possibility of being able to be in despair; if a person is truly not to be in despair, *he must at every moment destroy the possibility*" (SUD, 15 italics added).

If a person cannot be in despair, if he or she does not have this capacity to be able to be, then the person cannot exist in existential faith. It is in this way that despair figures essentially in the structure of faith, for it is what faith, at every moment, destroys, negates, annuls, as a possibility. As such, to the extent that despair is not possible, neither is faith. Despair, then, like resignation and refusal, is an essential dialectical moment in faith: despair, like resignation and refusal, is present within faith, but dialectically present as absent; despair, like resignation and refusal, is present within faith as an annulled possibility; in fact, resignation and refusal *are* despair.

To grasp this logic, I suggest, helps us not only to understand the sense in which Kierkegaardian faith includes within itself the movement of resignation and refusal, but also the sense in which, more generally, existential faith (religiousness B) both includes and excludes within itself every form of existential refusal, whether it be aesthetic, in the form of the sensual (Don Juan) or intellectual (Faust),[19] or ethical, in any of its many forms.

And so we arrive at what I might call the truth of resignation and refusal. This truth is what the story of Abraham would teach us about existential faith. It comes to something like this: we can own or truly possess something only if we have chosen it in the first person; such a choice always implies a context of historical possibility and hence repetition; and finally, we can own or truly possess only what it is possible for us to disown, to dispossess, to refuse. Again, refusal is not faith, but faith must include this negation within itself as an ever-present possibility. Indeed, it is just this refusal of the human that the knight of faith must be prepared continually to encounter in fear and trembling and continually to annul in faith.

This is the paradoxical thing about human beings: we do not have to accept our humanness. We can turn away from, resign from, our humanness, seek to live in eternity as gods or angels, rising above the vulnerabilities of historical time and finitude, or otherwise block out historical consciousness by sinking into the brute immediacy of a series of discrete moments. But this fact, this possibility of refusing the human embrace, the human possibility of not being human, the temptation to a kind of spiritual other-worldliness, profoundly qualifies the prospect of the embrace of the human and of the human world.

My claim is that the existential import of Abraham's embrace of Isaac, or more generally the full import of the faithful embrace of the world, comes in the concrete, existential recognition of the fact that we have the power to do otherwise; it is this power to do otherwise that is a permanent possibility *within* faith, a possibility faith must continually annul. Faith requires that the faithful knight continually say "no" to what is within his power to say "yes" to; yet the awareness of this requirement to say "no" to resignation and refusal is dependent on the awareness of the possibility of a "yes." The knight of infinite resignation embraces the "no" to human existence, says "yes" to the temptation to refuse it, to turn away from its hurts, its fragility; he says "yes" to the temptation to disown it, to give it up. Yet recognizing, or say, coming to terms with, this real existential possibility of resignation and refusal is absolutely necessary for faith to be vested with it full personal, existential significance.

19. For a discussion of these aesthetic figures see my *Word and Spirit,* chapters 3 and 4.

Abraham realized via an existential confrontation, that is, a confrontation in fear and trembling, that it was possible for him to give up all that was dear to him. He found out, with God's help, that he could do it, that he could raise the knife, that he had the resources, the freedom, the power, to resign, to give up his son. And this he realized even though he never stopped believing that God would be good to his promises. And further he realized that the possibility of loss is a permanent element within human life—that the gift of Isaac would have to be continually received.

Resignation and refusal are not moments that one passes through to get to faith, leaving resignation and refusal behind for good. Rather these are elements *within* faith, permanently a threat to it, possibilities that must continually be annulled. The existential awareness of the fact that I can, that I have the power to, run away from my fragile human existence occasions the paradox of human existence: as a human being I must choose either to embrace or to reject my own humanness. The constant temptation to search for a way of transcending the world has the paradoxical effect of occasioning my decision to live in it and to embrace it, every inch.

Faith must continually say "no" to the temptations of religious and philosophical resignation and refusal; faith must continually say "no" to the temptation to seek or to follow a spiritual technique of world-resignation; it must continually say "no" to the temptation to find a way of mastering time. Existential faith is a real attachment to history, to finitude, to the world, to others—an attachment always conscious of the possibility of loss. Yet within this existential consciousness, within the full awareness of the vulnerabilities, risks, threats, mortality, fortune, and uncertainties of worldly existence, faith courageously makes its full and unequivocal worldly claims. The knight of faith does not rise above, even inwardly, finitude or historical temporality; the knight of faith lives in commitment to the historical actuality; indeed, she is fully aware that the context of historical particularity does not limit her as a person, but provides the conditions that enable her to come to her self, to exist as a human being.

The devotee of a religion or philosophy of resignation and refusal ultimately says "no" to the finite historical world, to concrete particularity, to his own humanness within the world among others. He lives exclusively within the single movement of resignation, within the single-minded drive to refuse the human embrace; he lives in despair. The knight of faith differs from the knight of infinite resignation however, not simply by virtue of saying "yes" to the world, to his own humanness among others within it; rather, he realizes that in order freely and of his own choice to say this "yes," he must first concretely face the possibility of resignation, the possibility of saying "no" to the historical actuality. The condition of the possibility of his making the world and his own humanness within it his own is the realization that he has the power to do otherwise. The knight of faith says "no" to this possibility of saying "no"; and therefore his "no" dialectically annuls the concretely realized possibility of refusal. In the paradoxical logic of Kierkegaardian worldly faith, the "yes-to-the-world" is a refusal of refusal; it is an affirmation via a dialectical double negation.

Two

MARRIAGE AND THE
ETHICAL ILLUSION OF FAITH

In my (peculiar) reading of Kierkegaard, it is the human figures, historical or literary, that carry the most weight when it comes to giving us a picture of the life-possibilities that the stages represent. I trust these figures more than I trust Kierkegaard's more abstract conceptual analyses, which I find can be inconsistent.[1] In particular, the three figures who best exemplify for me the three stages are A, the aesthete *(Either/Or I),* Judge William, the ethical *(Either/Or II),* and Abraham, the religious (religiousness B), the knight of existential faith *(Fear and Trembling).*

My approach to the stages also recognizes variations within the three basic stages, but again in terms of human figures. For example, within the aesthetic stage there are Don Juan, Faust, Johannes the Seducer, and others; within the religious, Socrates is the primary exemplar of religiousness A, but we could also include the monk and the mystic; and of course, within reli-

---

1. It is certainly possible to take a reading of Kierkegaard from his more conceptual work, rather than my approach that focuses on the human exemplars of the stages. For example, if one were to begin with *Concluding Unscientific Postscript,* we might come to very different conclusions about the stages, especially the ethical modality. In that work, Kierkegaard's pseudonym, Johannes Climacus, interprets the ethical as though it were the embrace of ethics within the faithful embrace of human existence. Here the ethical (and religiousness A) is (are) part of what Climacus calls the "existential pathos." With regard to the ethical, Climacus says, for example, "Ethically, the individual subject is infinitely important" (CUP, 132). Nevertheless, even in this work, Kierkegaard holds consistently to the idea that the ethical individual falls short of existential faith. That is, he continues to hold to the idea of the ethical that was expressed by the pseudonym Frater Taciturnus in *Stages on Life's Way* who says, "[T]he ethical [is] the sphere of requirement (and this requirement is so infinite that the individual always goes bankrupt)" (trans. Howard V. Hong and Edna H. Hong [Princeton: Princeton University Press, 1988], 476).

giousness B, there are, along with Abraham, Christ, and perhaps, the Priest from Jutland.

I do not intend my focus on these human figures to exclude, or discount, Kierkegaard's more philosophical or theological treatments of the stages. Rather, I try to read these more abstract accounts of the stages in terms of their human exemplars. I do this especially with *Sickness Unto Death,* where Kierkegaard gives his conceptual analysis of despair (and by implication, faith), two of the most basic dialectical categories in his thought.

My guiding question always is, How do these figures, these life-possibilities, differ from Abrahamic existential faith? My conviction is that my approach is consistent with Kierkegaard's indirect method: what existential faith is, as a life-possibility, can be shown only in relation to life-possibilities that fall short of, that are different from, Abrahamic existential faith. For Kierkegaard, to know what this faith is, and to embrace it, requires that we know what it is not, something that requires us to confront its various alternatives existentially.

We can draw differences between the ethical modality of existence (Judge William) and faith (Abraham) that are parallel to the lines of difference I have drawn in the last chapter between faith (Abraham) and certain forms of the religious modality (Socrates). Like the knight of infinite resignation, someone who lives within the ethical modality—call him or her the ethical knight—also does not fully embrace, that is, existentially embrace, the historical actuality, his or her own and others' first-person connections within it, his or her own and others' unique particularity. Like the knight of resignation, the ethical counterpart refuses to embrace the human in any existential sense.

I read the ethical knight's refusal of the human in the terms Kierkegaard uses (via his pseudonym Johannes de Silentio) in *Fear and Trembling* to describe and define the ethical modality of existence. Here, the persistent claim is that "The Ethical is the universal, and as the universal it applies to everyone, which from another angle means that it applies at all times" (FT, 104). *Fear and Trembling* is as central in my reading of the ethical modality as it has been in my reading of existential faith, that is, in my reading of Abraham as its knight. Further, I read the judge's unbridled and absolute embrace of the universal as a modality of refusing the human, of refusing to embrace existentially our concrete human particularity, of refusing faith. It is in this sense that I see the ethical as just one more of the many alternatives to faith, rather than as a step closer to it, as if we could inch closer to it, as if faith did not require a leap across an abyss.[2]

It is not easy to see that Judge William represents a version of the human refusal of the human. Yet I hope that it was Kierkegaard's intention to present the judge's pretensions of an ethical embrace of the human as very near existential faith in order to show us just how it is possible to appear so very close to existential faith and yet actually to be so far from it. The judge's ethical pretension to have embraced the human in all of its historical particularity, his rhetoric of world-affirmation, his claim to value the historical particular, worldly engagement, and so forth, are, as I read him, deceptive illusions.[3]

The judge is similar to his religious counterpart insofar as both employ techniques of *disengagement* from historical particularity via absolute *commitments* to something else. The religious knight of resignation forswears the historical actuality for the sake of a god outside of time, or perhaps, for the sake of a god-wish to be outside of time; the ethical knight, professing his embrace of the human, in the final analysis, abandons his commitments to historical particularity in favor of an absolute commitment to universal ethical abstractions, abstractions that are embodied and mediated in and through the social order, its laws, its institutions, religious and secular, its customs, its traditions.[4] Of particular interest to him, and to me, is his treatment of the institution of marriage.

2. To put this point in the context of contemporary debate, I might say that the judge, the ethical, represents a typical conservative reaction to liberalism, or perhaps, libertinism—a retreat into the absolute as a defense against a relativism gone mad. But, as I see this, such a retreat into the absolute harbors its own despair, its own evil perhaps. Absolutism easily becomes, indeed, invites, authoritarianism, something that always threatens freedom. If the either/or of *Either/Or I and II* is between aesthetic negative freedom from the world, or absolute duty, then surely the ethical (the judge) cannot be seen as an advance toward existential faith. Perhaps Kierkegaard was wise beyond his time, seeing these options as merely flip sides of despair. To see this matter thusly is to see the judge's debate with A as a precursor to the contemporary debate between certain versions of what might be called "the left"—I mean things like relativism, post-modernism, permissivism, and so forth—and the right, especially its emphasis on family values, and law and order (things so important for the judge), and its alarming drift toward fascism.

3. A decisive reason that the ethical fails is that it always ends by absolutizing the relative, that is, the laws, institutions, customs, of some particular people. Judge William, I will claim, does this with regard to the institution of marriage. The judge, we might say, lacks humor. As Climacus points out, humor is the transition between the ethical and the religious; if the judge had humor, or the distance of humor, he would be poised to make the leap of, or into, faith. It does not seem that he and his wife have any laughs together; marriage is much too serious for this; he has no distance at all on his own marriage; it is too absolute for this, its requirements, its duties, too formidable. Clearly, the judge could not possibly conceive of divorce, much less feel the existential threat of this possibility.

4. Perhaps this abstract orientation makes the judge sound a bit like a Platonist. And indeed he does speak of the universal as having an eternal validity (like Platonic forms) and as being ab-

Here I must make a distinction that is critical to my interpretation of Kierkegaard. I read Kierkegaard to be implying a distinction between the *ethical,* as a modality of existence, and ethics, as the values one lives concretely. Every modality of existence, ethical, aesthetic, and religious, implies an ethics, since each way of life is guided by a set of values, by a conception of what is worthwhile and important. This distinction between ethics and *the ethical* is similar to a distinction I also draw between aesthetics and *the aesthetic.* Certainly, existential faith, as an embrace of the human, necessarily embraces ethics and art, but, as I argue, it also necessarily excludes the aesthetic and the ethical modalities of existence.

Furthermore, as I understand it, existential faith (religiousness B), for Kierkegaard, is, of all the stages, the only truly existential one, the only one that fully embraces historical particularity, the only one that is truly worldly, that is truly human—perhaps, the only one that is truly Christian. All of the

---

solute. But as Merold Westphal has pointed out, the judge is no Platonist, at least in this respect: for the judge the universal is not "an abstract, formal principal" apprehended by "an intellect that has somehow become pure reason." And he goes on to say, "The right and good are to be found [for the judge], not abstractly in a rational principle but concretely within one's social order, which is, for each individual, the essential mediator of the absolute and eternal." Westphal seems to have a point. Yet it seems mistaken to think that the universal for the judge is not abstract, or that it is concrete, at least if it is true for Kierkegaard, as I think it is, that the center of the concrete lies within historical, contingent particularity. But what happens to the concrete historical particular when it is simply the mediator of the eternal? Perhaps this is more Platonic than Westphal is willing to acknowledge, or perhaps it makes Kant more Platonic than is usually thought. See *Becoming A Self: A Reading of Kierkegaard's* "Concluding Unscientific Postscript" (West Lafayette, Ind.: Purdue University Press, 1996), 24. And Westphal also says, in this same passage, that Judge William is not a Kantian, and for the same reason that he is not a Platonist. This claim, of course, depends on one's reading of Kant. Westphal apparently thinks, as I do, that Kant, like Plato, does not acknowledge in any sufficient way the reality and value of the concrete historical particular. Kant is often criticized for ignoring the historical. For Westphal, this is reason enough to think that Judge William is not a Kantian, and for me, reason enough to think that he is. This is further complicated by the position of Ronald M. Green. He thinks that Judge William is a Kantian of sorts, precisely because in his treatment of the universal he, like Kant, does give due consideration to the particular. Green interprets Kant's ethics to be "considerably more content filled than it is ordinarily taken to be" (88), and Kierkegaard to be more Kantian than he is usually taken to be: "If we assume, as is true in Judge William and Kierkegaard's expression of this theme [self-choice and personal individuation] is always a 'universal choice' in the sense of being a willingness to conform one's particularity to shared human limitations and needs, then Kant's ethic is not opposed to this Kierkegaardian idea" (94). Ronald M. Green's *Kierkegaard and Kant: The Hidden Debt* (Albany: State University of New York Press, 1992), (hereafter KK). If what Green says is true, he might agree with Westphal who says that Judge William is really an Aristotelian, something I cannot see. My reading of Aristotle—something we will come back to in Part 3, when we discuss Martha Nussbaum's interpretation of Aristotle, an interpretation I tend to agree with—places Aristotle closer to existential faith than to the judge, at least in this respect: Aristotle does attempt to give what Nussbaum calls a due ethical "priority to the particular" that I find missing, or rather disguised, in Judge William.

other stages, I claim, are simply variations among the alternatives to existential faith's embrace of the human.

To put this slightly differently, I take it that existential faith is the only modality of existence in which a full-fledged, thoroughgoing *ethical engagement* in the world among others is fully actualized. Correlatively, I take everything short of existential faith—*ethical, aesthetic,* or *religious*—as variations on the human temptation to refuse the human. Only when ethics (and I would say, aesthetics, and even religion) is (are) placed within the existential dynamics of faith, does it get vested with its existential reality and power; only then does it become the telos of human existence, the measure of the human quest to become fully human.

What happens to ethics when it is placed within the dynamics of existential faith? To understand this, we must first remember that for Kierkegaard existence is defined in terms of human historical particularity: the concrete here and now of an individual human life among other human beings. To grasp the difference then between ethics within the *ethical* modality and ethics within existential faith is to grasp the place of, the value of, the love of, human historical particularity within each.

In both the religious and ethical forms of resignation and refusal, historical finite particularity suffers, but in two different ways. In the spiritual turning away from historical actuality in religiousness A—in Socrates/Plato, Gnosticism, mysticism, monasticism, etc.—the particular is simply and straightforwardly renounced, left behind with good riddance, as it were, in favor of a divine eternity outside of historical time and place; in the ethical refusal of the human, the matter is less straightforward.

While Judge William embraces the universal as absolute, he also strongly praises—unlike his religious counterpart—the historical particular, the individual, the world, finitude, time, choice, responsibility, and all the rest. The ethical knight seems to think highly of these worldly matters; he rails and rages against aesthetic disengagement and flight, religious or otherwise. In fact he concludes that a fully human existence, a fully human happiness, he might say, is actualized only when the universal and the particular are *harmonized.*

Yet, despite his slippery rhetoric, the judge has much in common with the religious knight of resignation. The fact is, in the final analysis, the ethical knight's proposal of harmonizing the universal and the particular comes at the expense of the particular, that is, at the expense of the historical concrete actuality of the individual who exists here and now before, and in relation to, some other existing individual. In the end, because the ethical knight thinks of the universal as being what is absolutely important, absolutely valuable, the concrete historical particular suffers. But again, not straightforwardly. Insofar as the judge absolutizes the relative, that is, the concrete historical institutions, laws, customs, traditions of his day, he subtly transforms them. By this slight of hand, the judge manages to turn the particular into the universal, a metamorphosis of the particular that finally amounts to an abandonment of it. As I see it, this abandonment is itself a kind of flight, or at least disengagement, from the radical contingency of an existing individual's concrete historical time and place before others.

We do not see just how the judge is guilty of this abandonment of the particular, especially in the face of his high praise of it until the issue of conflict arises. (This is, of course, also where Kant runs into trouble.) Indeed, if there were a conflict between the universal and the concrete particular, a prospect the judge must at all costs seek to avoid, the particular must be sacrificed to the universal. The judge's proposal for harmonizing the particular and the universal is thus a harmony achieved via subsumption. The ethical knight's ultimate preference for the universal over the particular, when push comes to shove, shows it to be another technique for sneaking out of the muck and mire of historical existence.

The ethical knight hopes that a conflict between the particular and the universal will not arise; he waits till the last minute professing his allegiance to the particular, all the while standing ready in his inward resolution to withdraw from the particular into the safety of the universal. How ever long the knight plays along with the idea that the particular is important and indispensable, it is clear in the end that his choice has already been made: he has already chosen the universal. It's the only clean way to resolve conflict, he thinks, to secure himself from the fear and trembling of uncertainly, anxiety, and concrete personal responsibility.

When ethics is radically transfigured by faith, the particular finally comes into its own, into its existential significance. Now the particular is higher than the universal! But this does not mean that there is no place for the universal within existential faith; rather, it means that the universal in faith is radically historicized and itself transfigured into what we might call the concrete universal.[5] The universal can have its place, indeed must, in ethics,

---

5. See Martha Nussbaum's "Introduction: Form and Content, Philosophy and Literature," in *Love's Knowledge: Essays on Philosophy and Literature* (New York: Cambridge University Press, 1986) (hereafter LK) where she distinguishes between the universal and the general. Her claim here is that Aristotle's argument against generality, his argument "against general rules as *sufficient* for correct choice," establishes "the need for fine-tuned *concreteness* in ethical attention and judgment" (38). But Aristotle's preference for the concrete, for perception, does not entail that he was not also deeply

but not as an absolute. Existential faith dethrones every pretension to absolutize the relative. But it does not do this to destroy the relative, but to bring the relative into its own. In the ethics of existential faith, the particular comes into its place in all of its existential power, value, and importance.

It is my central concern in this chapter to elaborate and substantiate these broad claims: (1) that the ethical modality of existence in Kierkegaard's thinking is simply another version of a resignation and refusal of the human; (2) that this is seen in the fact that the ethical modality of existence refuses historical particularity in favor of an abstracted universal—something seen in the fact that the ethical modality places duty higher than love; and (3) that existential faith transfigures ethics by embracing the concrete historical particular as higher than universal ethical ideals.

But I will also continue my previous concern. That is, I will continue to try to show how the ethical transfiguration of ethics into abstractions figures dialectically in existential faith, in its transfiguration of ethics into a concern and a love for the historical particular. Paradoxically enough, the ethical praise of the universal opens into an existential recognition of the value of the concrete historical particular.

Judge William: In Praise of Marriage

What Judge William of *Either/Or II* praises, the knight of Abrahamic faith would also praise, namely, *the human*! The judge praises the human by praising the ordinary, time, finitude, historical continuity, choice, responsibility, faithfulness, work, and so forth, but most especially marriage. All of these, the knight of faith would also praise; yet, the judge is no knight of faith. In fact, in the end, the judge's praise of the human turns out to be faint and damning—indeed, so much so that his advice for finding happiness reduces finally to one more faithless technique for transcending the human; one more technique for subduing the anxieties of a contingent historical actuality.

The pretext of the judge's praise of the human, of the ordinary, and especially of marriage, is his critique of aestheticism in general, and his critique in particular of the aesthetic misanthropy of a close friend of his, Author A of

interested in "the universal and in the universalizability of ethical judgments" (LK, 38). For Aristotle, and for Nussbaum, the universal is deeply concrete. And for Nussbaum, even the most concrete universal has its limitations: "[T]he universalizable does not, it would seem, determine every dimension of choice; and there are silences of the heart within which its demands cannot, and should not, be heard" (LK, 39–40). I will return to these issues later in this chapter, and in Part 3.

the first volume of *Either/Or*. He writes two very lengthy letters to A, the first entitled "The Aesthetic Validity of Marriage," and the second "The Balance Between the Aesthetic and the Ethical in the Development of the Personality." The volume ends with an "Ultimatum"—a last word from a priest from Jutland.

I read the judge to be claiming that the aesthete, the paradigmatic romantic seducer, has himself been seduced by a false sense of freedom: a negative *freedom from,* rather than a positive *freedom to.* Because A thinks of freedom negatively, he thinks that he can be free only if he hovers above worldly human existence and only if he refuses at all costs *to act.*[6]

The aesthete might agree with the judge that responsible action is definitive of human existence; he might agree that the embrace of positive freedom is absolutely necessary if we are to embrace our humanness. And both know that to embrace positive freedom requires the embrace of the historical, the here and now of concrete temporal possibilities.

The judge is clearly aware of this last point. He knows that positive freedom, ethical action "is essentially future tense" (EO II, 170). But to know this, to know that action is essentially connected to a future orientation, is to know full well that action is tied up essentially with historical existence. No doubt both A and the judge are quite aware that ethical engagement in free and responsible action situates the agent squarely within historical time and place.

Yet the aesthete acknowledges something that the judge seems not to (be able to), or more accurately, *will not,* acknowledge, namely, the essential fragility, the radical contingency, of historical actuality. A knows how dangerous the historical actuality is; he seems to know just how deep the anxiety of worldly existence invariably is, just how much worldly existence is always threatened with loss, pain, suffering, just how vulnerable, how dangerous, actually existing as a concrete individual in the world before others is. It is this anxiety that he hasn't the faith for; it is this anxiety that is the basic motive of A's ridicule of historical actuality as confining and as boring, the ultimate reason he constantly denigrates the human (especially marriage) and seeks perpetually to emancipate himself from it.

As we might put this, A acknowledges that if he acts, if he chooses to choose, if he exercises positive freedom, he must existentially embrace the constant possibility of *suffering*—what he thinks of (and rightly) as an in-

---

6. Although I shall not argue the point here, I am convinced that the distinctive feature of human action is that it is conducted in, through, and by means of speech. Human action is either directly or indirectly a speech-action. See my *Word and Spirit,* especially chapter 2.

escapable consequent liability of positive freedom; he knows that positive freedom carries within itself an essential anxiety, a perpetual fear and trembling; he knows that to be positively free he must be prepared actually to suffer. A simply hasn't the resources for all of this; indeed, he is terrified by its prospect. Rather than face his terror of freedom, of being human, A turns to a denigration of the historical actuality as the realm of daily drudgery, habit, routine, unfreedom.[7]

This darkness that the aesthete sees in the historical actuality of worldly existence, the terror that lies behind his ridicule of it, is something the judge does not fully acknowledge, or existentially face. His criticism of A reflects more the judge's own superficiality than that of the aesthete. He says to A, "Your mistake is that you do not think historically" (EO II, 128). What the judge does not fully grasp is that A's failure to think historically is not a mistake but a considered strategy, a technique for coping with his terror of the historical actuality. Granted the aesthete does not think historically, but he does seem to have his reasons, reasons that the judge seems strangely (willfully?) oblivious to. And, ironically, it may just be that it is the judge who makes the mistake of not thinking historically.

Who is right here, the judge or the aesthete? Does a life of action lead to happiness or does it inevitably entail only suffering? Is the realm of temporality the realm of darkness or light? the realm of unbearable anxiety or restful peace and security?

Before I try to answer these questions, I want to explore further the lines of agreement and disagreement between the judge and the aesthete. As I have just been claiming, both agree that a person cannot be free outside of a context of historical possibility—a future. They disagree, however, about what it means to be free: A defines freedom negatively, the judge purports to define it positively. This difference entails two very different interpretations of, two very different responses to, historical possibility.

Both the judge and the aesthete would agree that to act, to exercise pos-

---

7. The judge objects to A's use of habit to characterize all that recurs in life, including marital love. For the judge, the term *habit* should be reserved only for what is evil, as in the condemning expression we might expect to hear from an ethically upright judge, "You would do better to abandon your bad habits!" As William puts it himself, " 'Habit' is properly used only of evil, in such a way that by it one designates either a continuance in something that in itself is evil or such a stubborn repetition of something in itself innocent that it becomes somewhat evil because of this repetition. Thus habit always designates something unfree. But just as one cannot do the good except in freedom, so also one cannot remain in it except in freedom, and therefore we can never speak of habit in relation to the good" (EO II, 127). And to A he says, "[W]hat you abhor under the name of habit as inescapable in marriage is simply its historical quality, which to your perverse eyes takes on such a terrifying look" (EO II, 140).

itive freedom, closes off future possibilities, and necessarily so, since a specific act (in the present moment) by some person in some concrete historical time and place before some other effects a transposition of what was, the moment before, a future possibility (among other such possibilities not chosen) into a concrete actuality (and once chosen, this actuality is now established as part of the past). Actualizing a possibility among alternative possibilities, that is, acting, entails that the possibilities not chosen must perish, some, perhaps only for the time being, but others permanently. If I choose to marry Margaret, and marry her, I close off the possibility, at least for now, of marrying Kathy, and permanently close off the possibility of having Kathy as my first wife.

Beyond these agreements, that to act is to enter essentially into the historical, that to act is to enter into the realm in which reality comes into actuality from possibility, that to act is to actualize some possibilities and necessarily to annihilate or postpone others, the judge parts company with A. As far as A is concerned, it is just this closing off of possibilities in the act that will limit him and rob him of his freedom. As the judge sees it, A loves possibility and hates actuality; he rightly thinks that positive freedom is the enemy of negative freedom, but wrongly, that actuality is the enemy of possibility. Indeed, A thinks that the more one acts, that is, the more one exercises positive freedom, the more possibilities are closed off and hence the more one is caught in the snares of worldly responsibility. He closes the circle: the more responsibility one accrues, the less the freedom. The only way to be really free—in the aesthetic negative sense—is to remain aloof from action, to remain within the realm of pure possibility, to float in a hovering pattern above the historical actuality.

The judge does not disagree that action has, in some sense, the effect of closing off possibilities. He knows that to act is to transpose a possibility into an actuality and that in so doing one closes off the possibility of having done otherwise—a possibility which that act presupposes. In disagreement with the aesthete, however, the judge thinks of action as always opening onto a future limitless horizon of yet further possibilities: positive freedom does not ultimately limit possibilities, rather, and to the contrary, it produces an inexhaustible expansion. Actuality, for the judge, is the unequivocal friend of freedom, not its enemy, for actuality continually opens to further opportunities for action, for positive freedom.

Whereas the judge sees the realm of possibility, the future, as a door of opportunity forever opening onto the joys and the blessings of life that make human existence truly happy and worthwhile, the aesthete flees from temporality into the security of the eternal, but fleeting, moment. Or as I might put this, for the aesthete *the particular* is higher than the universal, but this *particular* that he values and relentlessly pursues is not the historical concrete particular, but the particular that exists in the vanishing moment, the particular as the accidental, the particular stripped of historical continuity. As the judge puts it, what the aesthete prefers is the particular when it is placed outside of the universal, when it becomes the bare momentary particular (EO II, 90).

Because the aesthete does not have the resources to face an open future that is bound up with uncertainty, vulnerability, the possibility of loss, and so forth, he ridicules human existence precisely because it is bounded by temporality; and he seeks his escape from the human. The difference between the aesthete and the judge comes down then to a fundamental difference in the attitude and response they respectively adopt to temporal possibilities, or more precisely, to the future: for the aesthete, the future is unequivocally the enemy, it is the realm of darkness and suffering; for the judge, the future is our unequivocal friend, it is the realm of light and joy. But neither A nor the judge embrace the future as the equivocal realm it essentially is.

The judge seems to understand perfectly the logic of the aesthete's escape from his own humanness, his flight from his own human existence, his ridicule of the temporal world of human affairs. Moreover, his characterization of the rationale of A's escape is no straw man that he sets up simply to insure that his critique of aestheticism will be successful. He is right in characterizing the aesthete as overwhelmed by the darkness of temporality, by the confinement of actuality. He is right that the aesthete's ridicule of the temporal world of human affairs as boring, as unfree, as routine, as deadening, and so forth, is a function of his deep-seated anxiety about its uncertainty, its vulnerability to loss, its unreliability, its unpredictability. The judge sees through the aesthete's pretense to arrogance; he sees that behind this is the aesthete's fear of loosing control.

The judge knows that A is painfully aware that to enter this world he will be accountable before others, before moral and civic laws, before divine laws. He knows that he will be implicated in responsibility for the choices he makes, that he will be obliged to suffer the consequences of his actions, consequences that are unpredictable and unforeseen, consequences that may not have been intended. The judge knows that A thinks of such a responsibility and accountability as a trap—a trap that will rob him of his autonomy.

The judge perfectly describes A's technique of escape. He points out to A that his mode of existence is hovering. As the judge puts it, "You continually hover over yourself. . . . You scorn everything that is established by divine or human laws, and in order to be free of it you snatch at the accidental. . . . you do not want to act at all; you want to experiment, and you regard everything from this point of view, with utmost effrontery. Action is always the object of your ridicule" (EO II, 11, 14, 15).

But what the judge is *not* willing to understand is why the aesthete insists on seeing temporality and human existence within it in such exclusively dark terms; that is, he can't seem to grasp why the aesthete insists on ridiculing time and the human, rather than appreciating them as the positive realities he concretely knows them to be. And herein lies the heart of his disagreement with, his critique of, A.

The disagreement focuses on the issue of marriage: A sees marriage as a confining trap that will inevitably lead to the pain and suffering of everydayness; the judge welcomes the commitment of marriage as an essential stepping stone in the human quest for happiness. For the judge, the institution of marriage is of absolute value for a happy human life; it is, as he says, what gives a person his positive freedom (EO II, 67n), it is the duty of every person to marry (EO II, 245). He cannot imagine not being married. It is the primary source of his contentment, his rest, his peace, his security, his happiness. We cannot imagine any higher praise for marriage.

To the contrary, A is convinced that to be married is to live the nightmare of being trapped within the temporality of finite human existence, to live the agony of not being free. To marry, he thinks, is the most burdensome act for it brings with it all of the awesome responsibilities of domestic life, of family, of work, and so forth. A is convinced that the act of getting married is a kind of paradigmatic human act insofar as it—like all other acts—brings freedom to an end. He must use his freedom to flee from such enslaving institutions.

Why is marriage a trap for A? Why is it the end of freedom? While we might expect to associate freedom with something more positive, the capacity to act, as the judge seems to, the aesthete thinks of freedom as a kind of successful avoidance. For A, however, to be free is not a matter of being able to, of having the capacity to, do something, and actually, at least on occasion, doing it; it is simply a matter of avoiding being trapped. This is the sense of freedom at work in our description of wild animals as free: to be free is just to be uncaptured! It is this negative sense of freedom that A wants to achieve and to maintain. Accordingly, he must avoid marriage at all costs, for in his imagination, the act of getting married is the most deadly human trap. His negative conception of freedom leads the aesthete to take the act of getting married to entail an implicit consent to an unfree life of deadening monotony. He is sure that to get married is to resign oneself to a life of boredom; he is sure that to get married is to exchange the extraordinary for the ordinary, the exciting for the uninteresting and the mundane.

A and the judge agree on this much: to praise marriage is just to praise time, finitude, the world, the ordinary, the human. In ridiculing marriage, the aesthete knows quite well that he is also ridiculing the whole human enterprise, or at least what he takes to be its dark and deadly liabilities: its temporal uncertainties, its deadening ordinariness, its anxiety-fraught contingencies and vulnerabilities, its delicate fragility, its routinized repetition.

The disagreement comes, however, at the point at which the judge judges that the aesthete has discarded the blessings of marriage in order to free himself from its liabilities. As the judge thinks of it, A's life lived in a perpetual pursuit of negative freedom, in a perpetual escape from human existence, in a frantic flight from the ravages of temporality, finally comes to grief in an unhappy faithlessness (EO II, 14). Lacking faith, the aesthete is robbed of the blessings of positive freedom, the blessings of responsible action, the blessing of the temporal, its joys of marriage, of duty, of work, of friendship.

The aesthete's ridicule of marriage reveals his deep misanthropy, his deep self-contempt, his deep despair. But A sees no way out. He may agree with the judge that marriage is the human institution par excellence, that being human and being married are deeply connected; he may agree with the judge that the affirmation of marriage entails the affirmation of temporality, and affirmation of the finite, of the human; but so much the worse for the human! A simply hasn't the faith for marriage, for the embrace of the other, for the embrace of his own humanness. And A is shrewd enough to know that he cannot ridicule and reject marriage without implicitly ridiculing and rejecting all the rest as well. Yet, he is ready for this, he is ready to have nothing further to do with the historical actuality, with his own humanity.

The aesthete's objection to marriage is altogether too familiar. He thinks that marriage will kill the excitement and passion of romantic (first) love. The aesthete prefers the erotic excitement of the moment, of the new, of the prospect of conquest, of the engagement to be married, and so forth, to what he takes to be the lifeless life of everydayness and ordinariness that always seems to occur in the ongoing relation of monogamous marriage. He is sickened by the thought of being continually with the same person; he is sure that familiarity breeds not so much contempt as boredom; he fears that continuity inevitably reduces to monotony and that monotony annihilates the erotic passion of romantic love. The aesthete is sure that the covenant of marriage is a covenant with death.

I suspect, however, that as a matter of fact, the deeper motive of A's ridicule of marriage is his recognition of its fragility. A knows how easily promises are broken—he is quite an expert in this himself; he knows that marriage often blunts the excitement of engagement, that the hope of marital happiness ends, more often than not, in the agonizing disappointment of separation and divorce; he knows how easily love fades, how easily passion wanes; he knows how subject a marriage is to the slings and arrows of outrageous fortune. It is better, he thinks, never to have been married than to have been married and lost; and in the end, every marriage ends in loss.

Judge William is out to show that a major premise of the aesthete's argument is incorrect. Contrary to A, the judge claims that marriage does not destroy romantic love, first love, erotic love; rather, marriage preserves the erotic, the romantic. But it does not just preserve it, marriage brings the happiness of first love to its full fruition. The judge asks whether the marriage ceremony halts first love and answers, "Not at all—but it allows what was already in motion to appear in the external world" (EO II, 93). Herein lies the aesthetic validity of marriage.

Marriage, Judge William asserts against the aesthete, is not merely a civil matter, nor is it a matter of convenience; indeed, it is not a matter that can be reduced to any external explanation. The constituting element, the substance of an authentic marriage, the judge claims, is found in nothing less than the passion of (erotic) love—that very love that the aesthete frantically pursues but never finds. As William puts it, "marriage is the transfiguration of first love and not its annihilation, is its friend and not its enemy" (EO II, 31). Because the aesthete eschews marriage, he misses just what he is looking for.

The judge argues that the reason that real love eludes the aesthete's pursuit and comes to its fruition in marriage is that it is the teleological nature of first love to become *historical* (EO II, 47). The aesthete thinks of first love as alive only in the accidental moment—a kind of frozen first moment in which his eyes meet hers across a crowded room. "You love the accidental" the judge says to A; "A smile from a pretty girl in an interesting situation, a stolen glance, that is what you are hunting for, that is a motif for your aimless fantasy" (EO II, 7). The judge does not deny that first love has within itself such an immediate unhistorical dimension—an instant without continuity in which everything stands still in a kind of eternity. He says, however, that that instant longs to become historical, to come into time; this is its telos.

The aesthete, however, thinks that if first love gained a history, the passion of it would be killed. He is therefore fixated on the unhistorical character of love—this, he thinks, is what love is in its full passionate reality. He pursues the moment; he continually seeks to capture and recapture this instant of erotic excitement, this unhistorical rush of chemistry and emotion. But as the judge sees all too clearly, he finally comes to grief on the contradiction that what he wants to last—the instant—cannot last; immediacy cannot endure.

As the judge sees it, however, first love longs to become historical. And this is exactly what happens to first love in an authentic marriage. "Therefore it is marriage that first actually gives a person his positive freedom, because this relationship can extend over his whole life, over the least as well as the greatest" (EO II, 67n).

The teleology of first love is like the teleology implicit in the individual: the telos of both is to develop historically, to develop a history (EO II, 118). William says, "A human being's eternal dignity lies precisely in this, that he can gain a history" (EO II, 250). What he gives voice to is the rhetoric of existential faith: a human being gains his eternal dignity only when he, in freedom, chooses and, in self-consciousness, takes responsibility for his own given historical actuality. To quote William:

> [An individual] can give this history continuity, because it gains that, not when it is a summary of what has taken place or has happened to me, but only when it is my personal deed in such a way that even that which has happened to me is transferred from necessity to freedom . . . (250). The individual, then becomes conscious as this specific individual with these capacities, these inclinations, these drives, these passions, influenced by this specific social milieu, as this specific product of a specific environment. But as he becomes aware of all this, he takes upon himself responsibility for it all. . . . He has his place in the world; in freedom he himself chooses his place—that is, he chooses this place. He is a specific individual; in the choice he makes himself into a specific individual: namely, into the same one, because he chooses himself. (EO II, 251)

An individual is not an instant, but develops in a temporal succession.[8] But to be *this* individual, that is, to be the individual he already is, he must choose

---

8. The existence of the aesthete, as A has suggested in vol. 1 of *Either/Or,* is essentially musical; and his conception of first love finds its absolute expression in music. (See my discussion of *Don Giovanni* in *Word and Spirit,* chapter 3.) The judge seems to agree with A's interpretation of the musical. He says, "Music has time as its element but has no continuance in time; its significance is the continually vanishing in time; it sounds in time, but it also fades and has no continuance" (EO II, 136). For A, first love is musical in just this sense: it has time as its element, it is a moment, or a succession of discrete moments. Yet, as the judge points out, such a musical succession does not add up to historical continuity; as a vanishing moment, first love is perpetually dying—and therein lies its erotic intensity. Only marriage can provide first love with its life, for only in marriage does first love gain

himself as such. He must choose himself in time "as a complex specific concretion"; but this implies that he must choose himself "in his continuity" (EO II, 251).

(Again, this is the rhetoric of existential faith. The questions, however, are as follows: Has the judge made the movement of existential faith himself? Has he chosen himself? his wife? their life together? their marriage? Or more generally, can one choose in any existential sense, if one has not existentially faced the possibility of doing otherwise? Does the judge freely embrace marriage, his wife, or does he merely grasp it, as one clutches a liferope, or as a child holds on to his mother's hand when frightened, or she the child's hand when danger is sensed?)

And the judge goes on extolling the virtues of marriage. So it is, he says, with first love; it must gain a history if it is to gain its existential reality and power. To gain this, first love must be transfigured from the abstract into the concrete. Marriage accomplishes this. It brings love down to where it longs to be, down to earth; it places it within its most comfortable home, the ordinary, the concrete historical continuity of dailiness; it rescues it from its own destruction in the loftiness of the vanishing eternal instant; it brings love into time. The covenant of marriage, its vows, its promises for the uncertain future, provide just that perfect context of temporal continuity, of steadfastness, of faithfulness, that first love needs in order to come forth in its existential reality and power.

What the judge does not understand is how marriage and time could be the enemies of love. The judge sees the married man as follows: "[He is] content in his home, and time runs smoothly for him. He cannot understand how time could be a burden for anyone, or be an enemy of his happiness; on the contrary, time seems to him to be a true blessing" (EO II, 305). The aesthete, however, does not think of time as a blessing, as the context in which first love blossoms into its full maturity as marital love. He thinks rather of time as his ruination, that the temporality of the everyday in marriage would be ruination of the blissful eternity of first love. Paralyzed in a cataleptic stupor,[9]

---

historical continuity. As the judge says of marital love, "It is faithful, constant, humble, patient, long-suffering, tolerant, honest, content with little, alert, persevering, willing, happy. . . . All these virtues have the qualification of time, for their veracity consists not in this, that they are once and for all, but that they are continually" (EO II, 139).

9. See Martha Nussbaum's discussion of the cataleptic impression. Such an impression she says, "compels assent by its own intrinsic character . . . [the person struck by such a cataleptic impression] has an absolutely indubitable and unshakable grasp of some part of reality" (LK, 265n). Nussbaum develops this idea of a cataleptic impression in relation to Marcel Proust's leading character (Marcel) in his novel *The Remembrance of Things Past*. In the novel, Marcel is struck by such a cataleptic impression when he receives the shocking news of Albertine's departure. He had just a mo-

the aesthete is at a standstill alone with himself: "[H]e has, so to speak arrived in eternity ahead of his time. He sinks into contemplation, stares fixedly at himself, but this staring cannot fill up time. Then it appears to him that time, temporality, is his ruination; he demands a perfect form of existence. . . . He has not chosen himself; like Narcissus, he has become infatuated with himself. Such a condition has not infrequently ended in suicide" (EO II, 231).

Is there something to the aesthete's worry about the ravages of time and something suspect about the ease with which the judge embraces time as a blessing? Here we arrive at what I think is the heart of the matter.

The aesthete sees more clearly than the judge, I want to claim, the dangers of a temporal existence. The aesthete knows more deeply than the judge of the anxiety and suffering that life within contingency entails. This is why he does not want first love to gain a history—time, he thinks, will ruin it. As he thinks about it, placing the moment of first love in time would destroy its bliss. And so he withdraws from time, this world, the historical actuality. He knows that time defines human existence. Why can't the aesthete bear the dangers of a temporal human existence, its vulnerabilities, its being subject to a future of uncertainties, anxiety, fortune, and so forth? *The simple answer is that he lacks faith* (EO II, 11). And so he ridicules time and seeks his escape in the moment; and for the sake of the happiness of this moment of eternity, he is prepared to forswear his temporal life, and he is prepared to accept the consequence of his escape from temporality, he is prepared to sacrifice his own humanness.

How is it that the judge feels no need to escape from human existence within the temporal? How is it that he is able so easily to praise time, the ordinary, the everyday, marriage, work, the finite, the human? How does he cope so easily with the contingencies of human existence? Where is the fear and trembling that the aesthete and the knight of faith know so well to be inextricable elements within the human? What is the source of the judge's security? Why does it appear that the ethical knight senses no threat to his embrace of the human, no threat to his happy marital embrace of his nameless wife? How does the judge manage such an easy embrace of the human, of marriage? Or is his embrace an illusion?

---

ment before come to the "rational conclusion" that he did not love her. Now he is overwhelmed by the emotion of love; now he knows with absolute unshakable certainty that he loves her. "The impression comes upon Marcel unbidden, unannounced, uncontrolled. Because he neither predicts nor governs it, because it simply gets stamped on him, it seems natural to conclude that it is authentic and not a stratagem devised by self-assuaging reason" (LK, 267). Such a cataleptic impression is also and essentially a blinding moment, "It is not a progress or a sequence; it is not a relation evolving over time. In fact, it's because it is not a relation at all—it has really nothing to do with the other, it's a chemical reaction in oneself—that it can have this instantaneous character" (LK, 277). I will come back to this issue in Part 3.

To answer these questions, we must turn to a discussion of the relation between the particular (the individual) and the universal.

The Universal and the Particular

As it turns out, Judge William is married more to the institution of marriage than he is to a particular person. Although he speaks high praise for "his wife," she remains nameless. Indeed she seems more important to the judge in her wifely office than in her particular personhood. Moreover, the judge's praise of his wife often gets transposed into a praise of womanhood—for example, his praise of woman as having a secret rapport with time and with the finite (EO II, 307). His wife is a perfect instantiation of the universal woman, his own marriage a shining example of the eternal validity of the institution of marriage. Yet, the particulars of his own marriage to *this* particular woman seem to the judge almost incidental. While he continually praises his wife, she, as a particular person, as a unique other *I* with a proper name, never appears in the judge's defense of the virtue of the institution of marriage.

To put this in a slightly different way, we can say that the absolute commitment to marriage that the judge shares with his nameless wife is not a commitment made in his (or her) own first person. What is missing from the judge's defense of marriage is the sense that at some particular time and place he actually said in his own name to some other particular person with a proper name and face-to-face: "I, William, take you, (calling her by name), as my wife." Their commitment, their marriage, then, seems not to each other, but to the ethical duty of marriage, or to the institution itself, or to its universal principles of faithfulness, loyalty, steadfastness, comfort, and honor.

What this comes to is that, for all of William's praise of the particular, of the historical actuality, and so forth, notwithstanding, the real premise of his critique of A, the deeper premise operating from the beginning to the end of his two letters, is the principle that the universal is higher than the particular. It is just this premise, I want to claim, that exposes his praise for the human, for marriage, work, and all the rest, as faint and ultimately damning; it is just this premise that shows his praise for the particular to be empty rhetoric, a mere illusion of faith. And what is revealed in all of this is that the judge's truest and deepest commitment is to the absolute value of marriage, much more than his commitment to his wife. The judge is so absolutely committed to the value of marriage that he has no critical distance on it. He is blind to what the aesthete sees as its dangers, its liabilities. He is perhaps even blind to his own wife, at least, as a real other. And as I read it, this makes the judge's rhetoric of existential faithfulness a mere illusion of faith.

True to his rhetoric, the judge says that the universal and the particular must be unified. He thinks marriage does this, or at least love does; in marriage the universal is possessed in the particular (EO II, 90). But truer to his deepest commitments, the judge operates with a notion of the particular as an *instance,* an *occasion,* in which the universal may (happily) or may not (unhappily) be realized. He is quite clear that the task of the individual is to become the universal, the universally human. He says, "What is required of me is the universal; what I am able to do is the particular" (EO II, 263).

We are reminded that Taciturnus has told us that the requirement of the ethical to become the universal is so infinite that the individual always goes bankrupt. Surely we can't wonder why. If the universal has its validity at any time and place and for any human being; if it is, as we might say, fixed in a kind of eternity, or at least in a kind of eternal validity, prior to particular situations in which it is realized, then how can a particular individual ever realize it, that is, be an instance of it, without forfeiting his own particularity, that is, himself? The judge flounders on this, and desperately tries to claim that it is possible to realize the ethical task of transforming the self into the universal without having the universal consume the particular (EO II, 261). The judge, at least Taciturnus thinks, is faced with an impossible task; the judge is in despair; or more generally, the ethical task is impossible; the ethical modality is despair.

Accordingly, William does not manage to move significantly beyond the aesthete that he criticizes, or beyond the religious forms of resignation and refusal that he also criticizes (mysticism and monasticism—forms of religiousness A). In the final analysis, the judge's defense of ethics, of the human, of time, and so forth, comes down to another clever, very clever, technique of refusing it all, at least when push comes to shove. Therefore, it would be a mistake to think that he has "come very close to faith," as is the usual interpretation.[10] In fact, this ethical knight—once all is said and done—turns out, as much so as the aesthete, or the knight of infinite resignation, to represent an alternative to existential faith. All, in their own way, lack the re-

10. For example, Ronald M. Green says, "Judge William is no straw man set up to be demolished but represents a position close to Kierkegaard's own conception of moral responsibility" (KK, 92). While I agree that the position of Judge William is no straw man, my argument here is that his position is simply another, more subtle form of refusing the human embrace—a kind of serious version of the playful erotic embrace that Don Juan pursues in order to refuse.

sources to appropriate the basic premise of the knight of existential faith, the premise that the concrete, historical particular is higher than the universal.

Let us consider further the judge's unbridled praise for the universal and his faint praise for the individual. In connection with his discussion of monasticism, he says the following: "In our day the market value of the monastic life has fallen; we seldom see a person *break altogether with existence, with the universally human*" (EO II, 328, italics added). Notice that the judge has virtually identified human existence with "the universally human." Obviously there is certainly something odd in this identification of the human with the universal, at least if human existence is essentially temporal and historically particular, and if the universal is essentially ahistorical, that is, eternally fixed across time and place, and general, that is, if it applies to any and every person.[11]

The judge draws us into some very slippery arguments here. Consider his claim that "[t]he genuinely extraordinary person is the genuinely ordinary person" (EO II, 328). For the judge, there is both a good and bad sense of *extraordinary*. The former good sense of the term is determined by the extent to which an individual has actualized the universal within the context of ordinary human existence; the more this is accomplished, the more extraordinary the ordinary person.

The latter bad sense of the term is marked by the extent to which the ordinary individual has been unable to actualize the universal within the ordinary, and so has withdrawn from the ordinary (in monasticism, for example). Such a person is thus *extra*-ordinary, in the sense of being outside of the ordinary; but for the judge, this is the bad sense of *extraordinary*. As he puts it, "The more of the universally human an individual can actualize in *his life* [the ordinary, the existential], the more extraordinary a human being is. The less of the universal he can assimilate, the more imperfect he is. It is true that he may then be an extraordinary person [that is, outside the ordinary like the monk], but not in the good sense" (EO II, 328, italics added).

The upshot here is that the judge thinks that the ordinary existence of an

---

11. Kierkegaard, it is fairly safe to say, does think that to exist, is to have come into history (see *Philosophical Fragments*, trans. David F. Swenson, rev. trans. Howard V. Hong [Princeton: Princeton University Press, 1962], 91); and the judge does seem to think that the universal in itself, for example, the purely universal human being, that is, the human being apart from his concrete historical particularity, is a phantom, a nonentity, an ahistorical abstraction, lying, like the Archimedean point, outside of the world (EO II, 265).) The question is, however, whether the judge's dogged insistence that the universal must be united with the particular finally shows the universal to be essentially concrete, essentially bound up with historical particularity, or, as I think, that his unification project is achieved at the expense of the particular's historical particularity.

individual is praiseworthy, indeed, is extraordinary, directly in proportion to the *extent* to which it *assimilates* the universal. The perfection of the particular individual is measured by the *extent* to which he becomes the universal while remaining within the ordinary.

We know that the judge does not think it is a mark of human perfection if a person, when he encounters difficulties in this assimilation, in fulfilling his task—and everyone's task—of expressing the universal in his own individual ordinary human existence, seeks an escape from existence in the monastery or elsewhere; and we know that the judge thinks that it would be an especially heightened imperfection for such a person to become conceited about his exceptional status vis-à-vis the ordinary. But does it follow that the judge is simply a moralistic perfectionist ready unequivocally to condemn every human effort that falls short in its task of actualizing the universal? Not quite.

Some people are fortunate enough simply to succeed, or to succeed to a rather great extent in fulfilling their task of actualizing the universal within the ordinary. Such a person is extraordinary insofar as her ordinary worldly life has been assimilated to the universal. But for the judge, there is more than one way to succeed in the task of actualizing the universal in one's life. Ironically, the judge suggests, it is possible to succeed in failure. (Though I might add here, it does not seem that the judge himself has ever failed at anything.)

What the judge, in his usual dialectical cleverness, asserts is that success at actualizing the universal to some extent—the greater the extent, the more extraordinary—is not the only route to being an extraordinary person. The judge allows that one may become extraordinary, in another good sense, what he calls an intensive sense. In such a person, the universal is raised to its proper inward heights, that is, raised higher than the particular, not because the person has reached some degree of success in his task of actualizing the universal in the particular, but precisely because he has failed at this task. As William says, "What he lost in extensiveness he may win in intensive inwardness" (EO II, 331).

For the judge, a person may be ennobled by his inward and intensive love of the universal, even though that love is frustrated by failure. William remarks as follows: "If it so happens that the universal he is unable to actualize is the very thing he desired, then in one sense he will, if he is high-minded, rejoice in the circumstance. He will then say: I have struggled against the particular; I have transferred my desire to the side of the enemy; to make it complete, I have made the particular the universal. It is true that all this will make the defeat harder for me, but it will also strengthen my consciousness and give it energy and clarity. At this point, then he has emancipated himself from the universal" (EO II, 330).

This "emancipation" from the universal via a defeat of the universal by the particular is a tricky matter. The person "defeated" by the universal, if she is high-minded, may still testify to the principle that the universal is higher than the particular. She positively testifies to the universal in her failure insofar as she continues to rejoice at those who succeed at actualizing it, but more importantly by the intensity of her inward grief over her own failure. Such a person says, "If it is the happy fate of others to testify to the universally human by actualizing it, well, then I testify to it by my grief, and the more deeply I grieve, the more significant is my testimony. And this grief is beautiful, is itself an expression of the universally human " (EO II, 330).

For the judge, then, failure to achieve what a person chooses in freedom is not necessarily a defeat of the universal, or a defeat of the person whose task it is to actualize the universal. Indeed, as the judge sees it, failure at the task of actualizing the universal may testify to the nobility of the universal, but only if that failure brings with it an intense inward grief over not being able to actualize the universal. This grief will show that such a person desires (inwardly) the right thing, even if she cannot actualize it, even if she has abandoned even trying.

Moreover, the judge seems to think that recognizing that one cannot actualize the universal also brings an awareness of the positive importance of the particular. Each of us is an exception insofar as each of us is subject to the accidental limitations, circumstances, contingencies, and so forth, intrinsically attendant to our particular existential situation. The fact is, no one is free to do anything he wants. Even though "every human being develops in freedom," no one is able to "create himself out of nothing" (EO II, 332).

Too much success in our pursuits to actualize the universal may cause us to overlook the particularity of our existential situatedness. Failure can function positively, if it causes us to come to terms with our individual uniqueness, with the fact that we are all exceptions. In trying to do the right thing, that is, in trying to do what any rational human being ought to do, regardless of the circumstances, I run the danger of overlooking the particular unique facts of *my* situation here and now. Failure reminds us of the fact that we are all exceptions. Failure teaches us that it is "equally true that every human being is the universally human and also an exception" (EO II, 332).

The judge shows himself here to be no naive moralist for whom the task of actualizing the universal will always meet with success if we just try hard enough. The judge wants to acknowledge the difficulty of the ethical task; he wants to find a place, an important, an instructive place, for the exception. He therefore does not sit in judgmental condemnation of those who fail to meet the harsh demands of actualizing the universal. "I love life and being a human being too much," he says, "to believe that the way to become an extraordinary person is easy or without spiritual trials" (EO II, 332).

The judge's praise of the exception, however, is faint and damning. The reason is that for the judge, the particular, the exception, is always measured in terms of its relation to something higher, the universal. Hence, his praise for the particular always turns out to be a disguised praise for the universal. The consciousness of being an exception, a particular human being born in these circumstances, with these gifts and these limitations, from the judge's perspective, is praiseworthy and noble, only to the extent that it brings with it a consciousness of the fact that "every person is an exception" (EO II, 332). Being an exception is thus itself transformed, in the judge's imagination, into that which is not an exception, into that which is the universal human condition. In the judge's analysis of the ethical life—his praise of the particular notwithstanding—the particular ends up being swallowed by the universal.

The judge would strenuously object to this charge that his praise of the universal overshadows his praise of the particular, to the charge that he ends up with a conception of the universal that engulfs the particular. He protests:

> The task the ethical individual sets for himself is to transform himself into the universal individual. . . . But to transform himself into the universal human being is possible only if I already have it within myself. . . . In other words, the universal can very well continue in and with the specific without consuming it; it is like the fire that burned without consuming the bush. . . . Every person, if he so wills, can become a paradigmatic human being, not by brushing off his accidental qualities, but by remaining in them and ennobling them. But he ennobles them by choosing them. (EO II, 263)

Far from advocating a position in which the particular, the accidental, the exceptional, gets consumed in the universal, the judge champions these elements of historical contingency as necessary in the ethical life. He insists that the ethical individual does not deny the particular; rather, he learns how to subordinate it to the universal; but this subordination preserves the particular, it does not annihilate it. Or does it?

In spite of the judge's objections, I maintain that Kierkegaard means to say that the ethical life lived in accordance with the judge's principle that the universal is higher than the historical particular does not allow the particular (or the universal, for that matter) to appear in its existential reality and power. And accordingly, the ethical *alternative* to aestheticism that the judge represents is no radical alternative at all. Or more positively, I think Kierkegaard intends to present the judge's vision of the good life as falling—as much so as A's—outside of existential faith. And moreover, this is so precisely because only in faith is the existential reality and power of the particular vested with its rights; only in faith is the concrete particular more valuable than the abstract universal. In faith, I do not become a paradigmatic human being, I become my (unique, concrete, historical, individual) self.

For the judge, there are two possible resolutions to conflicts between the universal and the particular that are praiseworthy: one negative, one positive. We have just been discussing the first of these. As I have said, the judge realistically admits that when there is a conflict between the universal and the particular, sometimes the particular triumphs, or appears to. William sees such "defeats" of the universal as actually testimony to the nobility of the universal, if and only if, such defeats, or negative resolutions, produce an inwardly intense grief in the person who has fallen short. Such a grief concerning the triumph of the particular over the universal, he says, may actually be a negative, an indirect, triumph of the universal. Indeed, this defeat may testify to the nobility of the universal. In this light, the judge's praise for the particular is undermined. In the final analysis, the particular for him is the source of our deepest grief.

The fact that the judge thinks that particularity, when it is placed higher than the universal, is the source of our deepest grief is evidence that his ethical duties do not in fact allow for an existential embrace of the particular. Again, the judge's praise of someone who has not managed to actualize the universal is proportional to the intensity of that person's inward grief in his failure. Granted, this person reminds us of the fact that we are all existentially situated in particular circumstances, and that as such we are sometimes not able to transform this particularity into the universal, but, is this not faint and damning praise of the particular?

Perhaps an example will help here. Let us amend the story of Agamemnon and Iphigenia to suit our purposes. As the story actually goes, Agamemnon has been commanded by Zeus to avenge a breach of hospitality by the Trojans. Agamemnon forms an expedition to fight for a just and noble cause. But he is faced with the conflict between his civic duty to carry out his military expedition (the universal) and his love of his daughter Iphigenia (the particular). The gods have becalmed the seas and the mission has been stalled. The gods have told Agamemnon that the seas will remain becalmed unless he sacrifices his daughter. If he does not, everyone, including Iphigenia, will die. Moreover, if he does not make the sacrifice, he will ipso facto abandon his duty to the gods and his civic duty to his countrymen. (I might note here that, even though we do not know her name, we do know that the judge has one and only one daughter; she is three years old [EO II, 78].)

Suppose we change the story so that Agamemnon has the choice of saving Iphigenia, but at the price of everybody else, himself included. Let us also suppose that Agamemnon cannot bring himself to sacrifice his daughter. Let's say he has realized that she is more important to him than anything else; or that he simply does not have the courage, the will, the resources to raise the knife; or alternatively, that he has the courage, the will, etc., not to raise the knife. Yet, let us also stipulate, he is convinced of what the right thing to do is, of what every human being in these circumstances ought to do: he is convinced that it is his duty to sacrifice her for the sake of the others, the mission, the will of the gods, etc. Nevertheless, he simply cannot (will not) do it; he loves her.

Here is a clear case where the demands of concrete particularity—the demands of this particular person's love for his daughter, for this person named Iphigenia—have triumphed over the abstract universal demands of civic and social duty. What would the judge think about this? Would he praise Agamemnon's choice in our amended story?

I think that the judge would have to say that this would depend on the inward grief in Agamemnon over his failure to actualize the universal. If he simply dismissed his civic and social duty, if he simply acted idiosyncratically, if he had no remorse for his failure to do his duty, the judge would condemn his action as immoral. However, if he felt sufficient grief, then the judge would simply say that it was a matter of Agamemnon's moral weakness (his akrasia) that kept him from carrying out what he knew inwardly to be the higher course of action. If Agamemnon felt sufficient grief over his *choice* of the particular over the universal, he would not thereby testify to the idea that the particular is higher than the universal, but only to his moral weakness in not being able to choose what is higher.

If the judge thinks that embracing the particular brings with it an intense inward grief at not being able to embrace the universal, at not being able to sacrifice the particular for the universal, then surely he must think of the particular as an unfortunate, albeit inescapable, obstacle to the ethical task of actualizing the universal. This is no full embrace of particularity. If anything, it betokens a hidden resentment toward existence, a kind of *resignation to* our inescapable human condition.

As I see it, the judge's praise for the particular comes down to a claim that our existential embranglement in particularity is inescapable. My task is to become the universal, but I may have to resign myself to being able to do only the particular (EO II, 263). To resign oneself to the inescapableness of something, as I see it, is to imply a bankrupt desire to transcend it. If indeed, particularity is inescapable, and yet our secret desire is to transcend it, then no wonder that the judge thinks that our failure to embrace the universal as higher than the particular can cause us only grief.

This places the judge at absolute odds with the knight of faith. In faith, the most horrible human grief is generated by the loss (actual or threatened) of the particular; the prospect of this loss produces anxiety; it produces the knight's profound fear and trembling. For the judge, the deepest human grief is caused when the choice is to embrace the particular over the universal; for the judge, what strikes the deepest fear and trembling in the human soul is the prospect of falling short of the universal.

The positive resolutions of such conflicts fare no better. Just as the grief at not realizing the universal indirectly testifies to the principle that the universal is the higher, the unequivocal joy, delight, and happiness felt when the universal triumphs over the particular testifies directly and loudly to the glory of the universal, and hence to the idea that particularity always stands in need of being transformed into something higher. Again, we can put this matter in terms of the conflict between love and duty.

First, however, in fairness to the judge, I must again acknowledge that I am not contending that the judge does not give a rhetorical place to the particular, that he does not claim that it has an essential place in the ethical life. My claim is that his efforts to subordinate it to the universal ultimately end up turning the particular into something negative, something to be overcome, to be transcended. But, even though William's vision of an ethical existence has it that the happy resolution of a conflict between the universal (duty) and the particular (love) entails the triumph of the universal over the particular, the judge sticks firmly to his concern to give the particular its due.

The dialectical preservation, yet subordination, of the particular within the universal is contained, the judge argues, in the very notion of duty. He says that duty is what is required of me, as it is universally required of every human being, but *my* duty is bounded by what I am in fact able to do, and this is a function of my particular circumstances, talents, liabilities, inclinations, etc. As the judge puts it, "I never say of a man: he is doing duty or duties; but I say: He is doing *his* duty; I say: I am doing *my* duty, do *your* duty. This shows that the individual is simultaneously the universal and the particular.

Duty is the universal, it is required of me. Consequently, if I am not the universal, I cannot discharge my duty either. On the other hand, my duty is the particular, something for me alone, and yet it is a duty and consequently the universal" (EO II, 263).

But, again, what the judge seems to founder on is conflict. What do we do when duty, *my* duty, comes into conflict with my love for some particular person? The judge's answer would have to be something like this: we choose the higher ground, what we might call the heroic path. That is, we do just exactly what Agamemnon did in the original story: when a conflict arises, we sacrifice Iphigenia; we sacrifice the particular for the universal, if we are able.

Does this mean that the model ethical individual, for the judge, is the tragic hero? Not quite. The reason for this, I suggest, is that, for the judge, the ethical hero lacks what is present in the tragic hero, namely, existential fear and trembling.

In considering what the judge would do in cases of deep conflicts between love and duty, I am going beyond what the judge explicitly considers. As Louis Mackey has pointed out, the judge more often than not thinks of love and duty as existing in a perfect harmony.[12] No really deep conflicts plague the judge's relationship with his wife; it seems that he has never been in the wrong, that he has never had to ask his wife for forgiveness; they don't even seem to argue or to bicker, or to hurt one another, or even be in conversation. For that matter, no deep conflicts seem to have come into the judge's life at all: ironically, the judge himself has never been on trial. Certainly the judge finds a place for surface conflicts, failures, spiritual trials, struggles, and so forth, but situations like that of Agamemnon and Abraham, soul-wrenching conflicts, do not figure prominently in the judge's world. He therefore does not explicitly address them. All the same, we can carry the judge's ethical principles where he himself did not venture.

Why is it true, as I speculate it is, that the judge would think of Agamemnon as a hero of the ethical life and not as a tragic hero? And from what perspective would Agamemnon become tragic? Again, the difference is fear and trembling. Let me explain.

12. See Louis Mackey's *Kierkegaard: A Kind of Poet* (Philadelphia: University of Pennsylvania Press, 1972), where he says of the judge's marriage, "[The judge's] extravagant praise of connubial love suggests in particular a closer look at his marriage. That marriage, he is quick to boast, is as nearly perfect as an earthly union can be. I have never, he says, experienced any conflict between love and duty, nor for that matter any serious martial conflict at all. . . . Even if we allow for nineteenth-century conventions about the place of woman in home and society, Judge [William's] marriage is *prima facie* suspect. . . . [H]is techniques of . . . removing to the ideal . . . run the risk of making conjugal love as abstract as 'first love' or seduction" (85–86).

Even though Agamemnon struggled with the agony of his decision at first, he finally makes the positive resolve to sacrifice Iphigenia in such a way as to dissolve the conflict, the agony, the struggle, the fear and trembling. Agamemnon's resolution of the conflict between his love and his duty, in his own interiority, was simply in favor of duty, a resolution that virtually annihilated his love for Iphigenia. As Martha Nussbaum has observed, "Agamemnon now begins to cooperate inwardly with necessity, arranging his feeling to accord with his fortune. From the moment he makes his decision, itself the best he could have made, he strangely turns himself into a collaborator, a willing victim. . . . Agamemnon seems to have assumed, first, that if an action is right, it is appropriate to want it, even to be enthusiastic about it. . . . Agamemnon's conclusion, which from one point of view seems logical and even rational, omits the sorrow and struggle, leaving only the good" (FG, 35–36).

Agamemnon would not think of himself as tragic, and neither would the judge, for this would imply that Agamemnon's act was tainted, essentially flawed in some way, and hence the source of remorse, grief, agony, and so forth. But as Agamemnon sees what he has done, and as the judge would no doubt see it, something bad has been transformed into something good; Agamemnon has realized the universal in the particular; he has, in effect sacrificed the particular for the universal. And, for the judge, this is unequivocally the good, the very model of the ethical life.

What would make Agamemnon a tragic figure? Simply this: that his positive resolution of the conflict between love and duty had not so easily transcended the agony, the fear and trembling, of his decision. Indeed, this is just the complaint of the Chorus against Agamemnon, just the grounds upon which they condemn his act; not that he did the wrong thing, but that he was able to do the right thing with such ease, without any sense of fear and trembling. Consider what Martha Nussbaum has said about the sacrifice scene:

The Chorus does not so much blame the fact of the action. . . . What they impute to Agamemnon is the change of thought and passion accompanying the killing, for which they clearly hold him responsible. He dared to become the sacrificer of his daughter—not just *became,* but endured to become. He put up with it; he did not struggle against it. Their description of his behavior in the execution bears out this charge. Her prayers, her youth, her cries of 'Father,' this father 'counted as nothing,' treated his daughter, from then on, as an animal victim to be slaughtered. . . . After the usual prayer, Agamemnon commands the attendants to lift Iphigenia 'like a goat' in the air above the altar. His only acknowledgment of her human status is his command to stop her mouth, so she will not utter inauspicious curses against the house. And even this command uses animal language; they are to check her voice 'by the force and voiceless power of the bridle.' . . . Never, in the choral narration or subsequently, do we hear the king utter a word of regret or painful memory. No doubt he would endorse the glib summary of his career by Apollo in the *Eumenides* trial scene: 'He made good bargains, for the most part.' (FG, 36)

But even if Agamemnon had been a tragic hero, he would not have been a knight of faith. But, he would have been different than the judge, but not because he finally managed to raise the particular to a position of being higher than the universal, but because he was not able to subordinate the particular to the universal as easily as the judge. Because the tragic hero feels the agony, the suffering, the struggle, the fear and trembling, in his choice of the universal, a choice that crushes the particular, he shows that he acknowledges the value of the particular. Yet he has not yet risen to the point of existential faith, to the point at which the particular is chosen as higher, as more valuable, than the universal; he does not embrace the particular. The tragic hero can't and doesn't make the sacrifice; Agamemnon can and does; Abraham can and does not.

Let us turn then again to existential faith. Let us turn to see what happens to both the particular and to the universal when the particular is given its place as higher. In faith, Abraham fully and freely embraced the historical particular as higher, as more valuable, but only on the far side of the existential realization that he could have done otherwise, that he could have abandoned the particular. But let us also see how the ethical attempt to transcend human particularity continues to figure paradoxically within faith.

The Paradox of Faithfulness

For Kierkegaard, if I am to exist as a human being in any fully authentic sense, I must exist in existential faith. To exist in faith, moreover, is to act, and to act presupposes the presence of others before whom I am called to choose, to affirm, to embrace responsibly my own and other's concrete historical particularity in the first person. In such personal acts of faith, in the presence of others, the unique particular self that I already essentially am comes to its existential realization. But, again, this can happen only to the extent that I am willing to say, "I" in good faith before some other—some other who is also an "I."

The desire to escape from, or the refusal of, the historical particularity of concrete first-person, responsible action is tantamount to a desire to transcend our human condition. Such a wish for transcendence, for a technique of resignation or renunciation, is the mark of every version of aestheticism; it marks off the fundamental difference between the aesthetic and the existential; indeed, it marks the essential difference between all of the various versions of the alternatives to faith.

The aesthete seeks his escape in the technique of hovering. Lacking faith, but possessed of a knowledge of the dangers of existing, he is terrified. He flees from historical action, from its continuity, its repetition, its responsibility. Although the aesthete hovers in the flux of tempo—what I have elsewhere called the musical flux—he does not exist within, indeed he flees from, time in its essential sense, that is, time as historical continuity. He simply does not have the faith to enter into the historical realm of human affairs; he hasn't the faith to act; and without faith, action, as he knows, is much too dangerous; and so for the sake of safety, he keeps his distance.

The knight of infinite resignation, hurt by the disappointments and vulnerabilities of historical particularity, or perhaps only threatened by the possibility of being hurt, escapes to the monastery, or into a mystical union with the divine, or otherwise into some other world, into a worldless realm outside of historical time, into eternity. This religious knight resigns *from* existence; he gives up the world for god; he sacrifices the human for the sake of the divine.

The ethical knight's refusal of the human comes out as a different and more subtle form of resignation. What appears sometimes as high praise for the human, turns out to be praise for something else, something thought to be much higher, namely, the universal. But in the final analysis, the pursuit of the universal shows itself to be just one more technique for transcending history and human particularity. Such an ethical technique does not have as its telos a *resignation from* the human, but finds its peace and relief from the anxiety—the struggle, the fear and trembling—of concrete historical existence in a different form of resignation: a heroic *resignation to* our human condition of historical particularity. Resigned to the fact that we cannot escape our human condition, we nevertheless can take the sting, the fear and trembling, out of it, if we will continually and heroically transform the particular into the universal, or at least try to.

But there is something troublesome in this task of removing the stinger from historical existence: or rather with the ease of it, with the ease with which the ethical knight subordinates the particular to the universal, the ease with which he is able to transform, to transcend particularity. This suggests no real attachment to it, no real reckoning with it, no struggle, no agony, no fear and trembling. Using Judge William's logic, the measure of how much one cares about something, the measure of how important something is, is the measure of the grief one feels at the prospect of its loss: the more the grief at the loss of the particular, the more its reality and value in one's life.

The tragic hero is acquainted with the existential grief entailed in the loss of the particular. In this regard, he values the particular more than Judge William; he considers existentially the idea that the particular may be higher than the universal. The fear and trembling, the struggle, the anguish he feels when he is called to sacrifice the particular to the universal, reveals his deep attachment to particularity. The extent that the tragic hero cares about the particular attachment he is to give up, the extent to which particularity is real and important to him, is shown in the depth and agony of his struggle, of his anguish, of his grief. And yet, even the tragic hero has not managed to move beyond the principle that the universal is higher than the particular. He reluctantly sides with the universal.

Let us therefore turn to the alternative to these forms of transcendence; let us turn to faith, to the commitment to the particular as more valuable than the universal, to its refusal of all of the various techniques of refusal, to its full and faithful embrace of our concrete human existence.

This brings us to the heart and soul of Kierkegaard's critique (via the Priest from Jutland) of the ethical found in the closing "Ultimatum" of *Either/Or II*. Suppose, the Priest asks the judge to consider, a real ethical conflict arose between a lover and his beloved, how could this conflict be resolved? Suppose further that the lover believed himself to be in the right and the beloved in the wrong. Will he stick to his principles against his beloved? will he do his duty? will he be obedient to some abstract ethical ideal come what may? If the lover acts out of principle only, then he shows that it is ethical rectitude that he loves, not the other in her concrete particularity. If it is really this concrete other person that the lover loves, then he will be willing to be in the wrong vis-à-vis the ethical principle, for her sake, for the sake of their love. Love, marital or otherwise, is, or ought to be, a relation of radical particularity. As the priest puts it, "Might it actually be this way? Why did you wish to be in the wrong in relation to a person? Because you loved. Why did you find it upbuilding? Because you loved. The more you loved, the less time you had to deliberate upon whether or not you were in the right; your love had only one desire, that you might continually be in the wrong" (EO II, 349).

I do not take this willingness to be in the wrong for the sake of the other, for the sake of the relationship, simply as a form of self-deprecation. Rather, I take it that the priest is attempting to speak from the point of view of faith, from the point of view that sees the particular as higher than the universal. In faith, in an authentically existential modality of existence, one's ethical task is to be responsive to, and hence responsible to, the concrete needs of this other who is a unique, particular individual with a proper name who stands before me here and now. This is quite different from understanding one's ethical task solely in terms of being in the right (or the wrong) relative to one's ethical duty.

Existential faith has its ethics, call this the ethics of responsiveness to the other, to the concrete other right here before me, to her needs here and now. The ethics of faith is an ethics of the particular, the historical, the human, not an ethics of the general, the abstract, the eternal. What are the differences?

First, I must make it clear that an ethics of the particular, an ethics of faith, does not leave the universal out. How could it? Rather, it places the particular higher than the universal, but it does not throw the universal out. This is what the aesthete proposes, what he desires, the particular as completely independent of the universal—call this the bare particular. At the same time, in making the particular higher than the universal, and yet including the universal in its ethics, it effects a radical transformation of the universal itself. And this is a major difference that I will presently come to between the ethical modality and faith: in the former, the universal is abstract in the sense of being prior to a particular time and place; in the latter, the universal is concrete, derived from particular times and places. In the ethical modality, essence precedes existence, in faith this is reversed.[13] But first, some preliminaries.

Because concrete human existence is essentially historical, it necessarily unfolds temporally; human existence develops in time; it is a concrescence. Human historical existence is therefore intrinsically, and as a matter of principle, open, unpredictable, irreversible, contingent, surprising, inexhaustible. In historical existence, possibility is vested with its existential reality and power.

13. It is interesting to note here that Sartre is an aesthete, in my way of thinking, and as such, not a proper exemplar of his own definition of existentialism. For Sartre, existence does not precede essence, it precludes it. In this respect, Kierkegaard, and an ethics of particularity, are closer to Sartre's definition of existentialism than Sartre himself.

It is the radical contingency of historical existence, its inexhaustible portent of future possibilities, that short-circuits any attempt to formulate a set of absolute duties or rules fixed in advance to cover every conceivable eventuality; for the fact is, not every possible eventuality is conceivable in advance. The flow of historical existence is, for good and/or ill, richer than this; therefore, no set of absolute ethical duties can cover every situation.

In the ethics of the ethical modality, the judge's ethics, the universal (duty) is manifested in the particular, but only by raising the particular to a higher power, indeed to an absolute power. The judge embraces not the historical (relative) particular, rather he embraces an absolutized particular. He absolutizes the institution of marriage, for example. As he puts it, it is the duty of every person to marry; or to capture the absoluteness of this, no person is free not to marry. Or what this comes to, in an ethics of the ethical modality, is this: I am in bondage to the law, to duty. That is, in this ethical bondage (of marriage, for example) I am not free, something A realizes more than the judge, something that justifies his flight from duty-as-bondage, his flight from marriage. In an ethics of faith, by contrast, if we are not free not to marry, or say, if we are not free to divorce if we are married, then we are not free to marry, or to remain married. In an ethics of faith, the relative is relativized. A faithful marriage is a bond not a bondage, not even a welcome, happy bondage that brings security, peace, and rest, as it seems to be for the judge. In an absolute duty, there are no alternatives, there is, in short, no freedom. In the ethics of existential faith, I can always do otherwise; in an ethics of faith, I am always faced with alternatives, alternatives that tempt me, that call me to decision; in existential faith, I am free indeed.

But I am not left alone in an ethics of faith. I do not abandon, as the aesthete does, the universal altogether, I simply relativize it. Universals are helpful guides in making ethical decisions, but in an ethics of particularity, such duties and rules must always give way to the art of judgment, to what Martha Nussbaum has called a *discernment of perception* in the concrete situation,[14] to what Michael Polanyi has called *personal knowledge,*[15] and to what Aristotle has called *practical wisdom.* From these points of view, the concrete particular is higher than the abstract universal; example is more instructive than formula; practice is richer than theory; personal engagement in discerning all of the relevant emotional features of the particular context truer than a

14. See Nussbaum's "The Discernment of Perception: An Aristotelian Conception of Private and Public Rationality" (LK, 54–105).
15. Michael Polanyi, *Personal Knowledge: Towards a Post-Critical Philosophy* (New York: Harper Torchbooks, 1954) (hereafter PK).

detached calculation; the qualitative incommensurability and singleness of *this* case is more valuable and important than quantitative commensurability and sameness. As Polanyi puts this, "Rules of art can be useful, but they do not determine the practice of an art; they are maxims, which can serve as a guide to an art only if they can be integrated into the practical knowledge of the art. They cannot replace this knowledge" (PK, 50).

Further, Polanyi says that the development of such a practical knowledge is a matter of *connoisseurship*: "Connoisseurship, like skill, can be communicated only by example, not precept. To become an expert wine-taster, to acquire a knowledge of innumerable different blends of tea or to be trained as a medical diagnostician, you must go through a long course of experience under the guidance of a master"(PK, 54).

And commenting on Aristotle's view of learning, Martha Nussbaum says something very similar: "[T]eaching and learning [on Aristotle's view] . . . do not simply involve the learning of rules and principles. A large part of learning takes place in the experience of the concrete. This experiential learning, in turn, requires the cultivation of perception and responsiveness; the ability to read a situation, singling out what is relevant for thought and action. This active task is not a technique; one learns it by guidance rather than by a formula" (LK, 44).

So if making an ethical judgment is an art in which the focus of attention is on the particular, including the richness of its concrete historical context, if it involves a developed sense of connoisseurship and perceptual discernment, then what becomes of the universal? Well, the long and the short of it is that the universal in such an ethics of particularity becomes concrete; or what amounts to the same thing, the universal becomes historical, it becomes relativized.

In Judge William's view, the universal is eternal in the sense of being prior to my choices and in the sense of being absolute. Even though he would maintain that it applies at every historical moment, it is nevertheless fixed in advance of any such actual moment. And even though he would say that the embrace of the universal is a matter of freedom, there is really, for himself, no real alternative. For the judge, the embrace of the universal, because it is absolute and because it can cover any situation that may in fact arise, is the source of his great security, his sense of peace and well-being, his lack of a deep-seated sense of anxiety. Whatever may come up, the judge is sure that we will never be thrown back onto our own selves to decide something, to decide it existentially in the way that Abraham had to decide, that is, in fear and trembling.

Ironically, given the judge's praise of choice, such a reliance on a set of ethical duties and rules would have the effect of relieving him of the responsibility of choosing. It would certainly relieve him of the fear and trembling that would necessarily accompany a choice that was his to make. If I am convinced that it is wrong to lie in any situation, I do not have to choose whether to lie or to tell the truth, even in the famous case where the Gestapo ask me if Anne Frank is hiding in my attic. What do I do here? If it is left up to me to discern what is the best course of action in this case, if ultimately I must make the decision and bear the responsibility for it, then immediately I am cast into the anguish, the fear and trembling, the anxiety, of existential choice.

Again, let me make it clear that in an ethics of particularity we are not simply thrown back solely on our own individual resourcefulness without the help and guidance of universals of any sort. Rather, the historical, concrete universal functions very differently than abstract ideals and duties. As we might put this, the concrete universal develops within history; it is a concrescence based on the particular. And when I say, "based on the particular," I mean that the universal is not fixed in advance of particular cases, but to the contrary, is established by them and always subject to being corrected, amended, or even abandoned, by future unforeseen particular cases. Or what amounts to the same thing, when I say that in faith the particular is higher than the universal, I mean that the particular must come first—call this the existential priority of the particular.

In this light, we could put the contrasts between the various stages as follows: (1) The aesthete wants to have the particular without the universal and so abandons the historical particular for the momentary, the accidental; the aesthete is not free to marry, since he thinks marriage will destroy his freedom; (2) the knight of infinite resignation abandons the historical particular altogether for a universal that is elsewhere; this knight gets himself to a monastery; (3) the ethical knight tries to harmonize the particular within the universal, but ends by absolutizing the particular, thus transposing it into the universal, and, as such, making the universal the measure of the concrete historical particular, which amounts to an abandonment of it, or at least a denigration of it, for in relation to this universal as absolutized particular, the actual finite historical particular always and inevitably falls short; the judge is not free to marry, since he is not free not to marry, that is, to divorce; and (4) the knight of faith, in contrast to all the rest who are not free, relativizes the universal by freely embracing the concrete historical particular as its measure, that is, by freely embracing the historical particular as higher than the universal without absolutizing either; this knight is free to marry, and is free not to, that is, he is free.

But this is not all that unusual a point of view. It seems as a matter of fact to be the very point of view of Anglo-American jurisprudence. Here the law is thought to evolve, to develop in history on the basis of particular cases. In this historical evolution, close attention is given to the complexities of particular cases and precedents are established, precedents that themselves are subject to being overturned by other particular cases.

When a precedent is established, for example, when it is determined that a person was justified in taking another person's life in these particular circumstances, then that precedent is put forth as having what Polanyi has called a universal *intent* (PK, 311). I put the emphasis on *intent* to mark the difference between it and something that is put forth as universal in fact. That is, Polanyi's notion of the universal is a relativized notion, not the universal as an absolute.

This point is sometimes put in terms of universalizability. If we put forth our case, again say the case of justified homicide, as a precedent, we put it forth with universal intent, with the claim that it is universalizable. What this means is something like this: it was rational for this person in these circumstances to do what he did; he was justified. And if some future judge or jury determines that some other case is sufficiently like the precedent, then either or both must let the decision of the precedent case stand. If not, if the situation is not quite the same, some new precedent must be established; or if the situations are relevantly similar but complexities of this case are noticed that were unnoticed before, the precedent may have to be overturned. In any event, the point is that the law—the universal—is conceived in this system as subject to the correction of particular cases, just as much as every particular case carries with it a universal intent. It is not absolute.

Polanyi's notion that our judgments are made with universal intent leaves them open, rather than fixing them. No truly historical universal can, without contradiction, be closed off from development. If history is one-way, irreversible, unrepeatable, and so forth, then, strictly speaking, we never really can say that two similar sets of circumstances, two similar acts, two similar motives, two similar persons, and so forth, were *exactly* the same. Historical existence implies intrinsic differences.

Historical universals are very helpful in making our ethical decisions if, and to the extent to which, we can establish that our circumstances are sufficiently like those of a model case in which we discern that a good judgment was made. I might, for example, admire what Kierkegaard did in breaking his engagement to Regine, and in the way that he did it, as an act of unselfish love for another, and be guided in my own situation, in my own relation to some other, by my conviction that Kierkegaard did what he did with a universal intent. And it may be that my own situation is sufficiently similar. Yet I would be unwise, if I did not also perceive and acknowledge that my own situation is, after all, uniquely my own, that I am not Kierkegaard, that my lover is not Regine. Historical universals can go only so far; and, in the end, it is I who must, with universal intent, decide what is the best course of action in my case.

It is always I alone who ultimately must choose in the particular decisions I face in my life; it is I who must rely on my own resourcefulness, accredit my own powers of judgment, and so forth. But this does not in any way entail that I am called to act in a vacuum, that is, to act outside of a tradition, outside of the presence of others, to set aside the fact that I exist in an ongoing and lively conversation with my fellow human beings. Practical wisdom requires that we finely attune ourselves to all of the voices that call us, warn us, encourage us, advise us, and guide us. And yet the decision is finally and irreversibly my own.

But what does all of this have to do with being faithful? I want to say that an ethics of particularity is impossible outside of faith; or more positively, I want to say that only within faith it is possible to embrace the particular as higher than the universal. I have tried to reflect this intimate connection between faith and an ethics of particularity by insisting that, for Kierkegaard, faith is the only modality of human existence that fully embraces the human, the only modality that puts the human being in a position, as it were, to value, care for, and to love and robustly embrace his own and others' concrete existence in the world.

The major reason that an ethics of particularity requires faith is that its premise—namely, that in our existential choices the particular is higher than the universal—drives us toward a confrontation with our own concrete, unique, situated existence as this free and responsible "I" with this name, called to this particular here and now, to this situation, before these others. An ethics of particularity drives me to an existential confrontation with my own freedom and responsibility, not in any abstract universal sense, but in the most concrete sense. In such an ethics, my question is not simply a matter of considering what any sane, rational person would do, my question is always, "What am *I* to do?" Or more concretely, my questions are, "Who am I to be?" "Whom am I to be like?"

Such a confrontation with our unique historical human particularity, with our uniquely human call to personal freedom and responsibility, produces, not surprisingly, a profound anxiety in us. This anxiety is intrinsic to our consciousness of particularity: the more consciousness of particularity, the more anxiety. This anxiety, however, cannot be faced outside of faith. And since this anxiety is intrinsic to our consciousness of our historical particularity, we cannot embrace our own particularity, our own human existence, without also embracing the anxiety. What the various life-possibilities that are the alternatives to faith have in common is the wish to transcend this anxiety, even if it means transcending our own humanity.

What, again, is the source of this anxiety and how does faith make it possible to embrace it as an intrinsic element of our historical particularity? In a word, *contingency*!

Contingency is inextricably connected to a consciousness of possibility, and hence to the consciousness of freedom and to the historical consciousness of the future. Contingency, as double-edged as possibility, naturally generates a double-edged anxiety. We can be anxious in a positive or negative sense: we are anxious in the positive sense for the celebration to begin; we are anxious in the negative sense about the examination; we are anxious, perhaps in both senses, about the arrival of our beloved; and just so can possibilities bring good and/or evil. The idea that *anything is possible* strikes in us both excitement and dread.

Faith embraces positive freedom, and so contingency, and so anxiety. Faith appreciates anxiety, both sides of it, as intrinsic to human existence. This embrace, however, does not put it to rest, or choke its essential unrest out of it. This would not be an affirmative embrace of anxiety, it would be a technique of escaping, avoiding, or subduing it. So how does faith positively embrace anxiety, and hence make possible a positive embrace of positive human freedom? Here is where the paradox of faith shows itself.

Faith, I assert, annuls the possibility of escaping from, or otherwise refusing, the anxiety intrinsic to human historical particularity; it annuls the possibility of fleeing into some worldless realm of extrahuman security. Faith says "no" to the human temptation to transcend history, freedom, and responsibility; it courageously embraces the human vulnerability to loss and suffering intrinsic in its concrete attachments of particularity. Faith annuls the possibility of resignation from, or refusal of, our own humanity.

Faith, by continually annulling this possibility of transcending our humanity, invests possibility with its existential reality and power. As such, faith recognizes resignation and refusal, and so despair, to be real human possibilities; we really have a choice here. And the consciousness of this fact that we have a real choice, the fact that we possess the power, the freedom to give up on, resign from, or otherwise renounce our human existence in the world among others brings with it the consciousness that to exist as a human is to choose such an existence—continually to choose it.

How does faith annul the possibilities of transcendence and yet continue to acknowledge them as real? I submit that what faith finally comes to, if not for Kierkegaard, at least for this Kierkegaardian, is this: *faith annuls the human possibility of transcending the human by self-consciously choosing concrete human particularity as worthwhile in itself; it believes (trusts, hopes) that there is nothing higher; and it believes this in the face of the existentially realized possibility—as evidenced in the suffering, loss, pain, and anguish of life—that human existence may not be worthwhile; yet faith continually annuls this possibility and thereby also acknowledges it as real and as threatening.* Faith thus takes its stand on the worthwhileness, the goodness, of human existence in the midst of fear and trembling, for at every moment it feels the anxiety of the possibility that it may not be; and yet it believes.

Faith does not annul anxiety, it embraces it, as only faith can. It does not annul the possibility and the actuality of the pain, the suffering, the agony and anguish of personal freedom and responsibility, the vulnerability to loss entailed by our concrete human attachments of particularity; and certainly, it does not annul the possibilities of life's joys, its loves, its hopes, its blessings. Faith takes the whole human package, and believes that all of its equivocal elements contribute to making our human particularity worthwhile; it believes that this whole human package contains the conditions for our happiness.

What faith does annul is the real and threatening possibility of trying to find a way out of all of this, or at least out of taking only a part of the package, of trying to find a technique to escape or avoid the equivocal elements of human existence. It annuls the life-possibilities presented in the various versions of the aesthete, Don Juan, Faust, as well as the religious version in the knight of infinite resignation, and the ethical version in the resignation of Judge William and even in the tragic hero. At the same time, faith acknowledges these possibilities and takes them seriously as real; it takes them as presenting us with a real threat, with a real choice, with a real either/or. The embrace of the human does not do away with its alternatives; rather, existential faith paradoxically includes them within itself, as the conditions of its possibility, we might say.

But I would be remiss if I did not speak a word of explanation here about what may appear as the glaring fact that I have not mentioned God in my discussion of faith. My understanding of faith, I must admit, is not as explicitly theological as is Kierkegaard's. Yet I contend that my interpretation of faith is nevertheless essentially Kierkegaardian and that, as such, it opens naturally to God.

As I see it, the hidden theological premise of faith's affirmation of our human existence as good and worthwhile is the premise that it has been *given* to us as such: faith embraces human existence as a good and perfect gift. That is, faith's basic posture toward our human condition is one of gratitude; faith is thanksgiving; it is eucharist. But this posture makes sense only if there is a transcendent Giver, a God who has created our condition, a source and ground of our human being. If faith is right in thinking of the whole package of human existence as a good and perfect gift, in thinking that this gift contains all that we need for a full and complete human happiness, then it has good reason for thanksgiving. This posture of gratitude opens naturally onto the belief that there is a God-Giver; but it also opens onto the belief that this Giver cares about our well-being, about our happiness. Such a God certainly seems worthy of our praise.

In my view then, God is the creative ground of Kierkegaardian faith. The individual is higher than the universal, we might say, because God made it so; this was God's gift to us. But I do not think that this is a kind of existential deism: the God of faith does not give us this gift and then abandon us; God is not so aloof. Rather, the God of faith is always with us, continually whispering into our ears, in the language of human history, the worthwhileness of the divine gift given to us, the gift of our existence. This suggests a different kind of theology, call it a theology of radical incarnation. But I will leave it to the theologians to work out the details of such a theology of faith.

But I would also be remiss if I did not come back to the issue of marriage, to the question of whether it is possible to embrace the other in marriage in any authentically faithful way; or what is the same thing, to the question of whether marriage has a place within existential faith. And further to this question, If so, what would such an authentically faithful marriage be like?

One might well wonder if marriage is thought to have, by Kierkegaard, any place within the existential modality of faith, especially when we know that he himself broke his engagement with Regine, that is, refused marriage. Did Kierkegaard himself come to the conclusion that every marriage would turn out to be like the judge's, that is, a mere illusion of faith? In some sense, I am thrown back on speculation here.

In my opinion, we do not find much help on this question of what a faithful marriage would be within existential faith, if we simply rely on what some think of as Kierkegaard's major work on love, I mean *Works of Love*.[16] Here Kierkegaard's focus is on contrasting Christian love (agape), love of neighbor, with preferential love (eros), love of spouse or friend, for example. His argument in this work is that Christian love supplants (while not doing away with) preferential love. Agape loves without distinction, without preferences. God, Kierkegaard claims, commands us to love every human being equally, as oneself. In this respect, we can read this work as a call to embrace the human, and so consistent with my interpretation of existential faith. In this work, we find Kierkegaard's appreciation of the human qua human. And we can certainly read his interpretation of God's command to love as not a call to rise above the human, but to embrace it as such, refusing to allow distinctions to keep us from the embrace of every human being.

Nevertheless, if *Works of Love* were all that we had to go on, we might well wonder if Kierkegaard himself had not finally succumbed to the temptation to transcend the human. I come back to his focus on transcending earthly distinctions in Christian love. Christian love, he says, is blind, but not in the same way that romantic love is, indeed, in an opposite way: it is blind to earthly distinctions (WL, 79). He is careful to say that this love does not deny earthly distinctions, the value of the particular, but that Christian love nevertheless lifts us above these distinctions, these preferences. As I see it, this is all too close to the judge's insistence that the universal is higher than the particular.

But when we return to the human exemplars of faith, and of faithful love, I see clearly that Abraham's existential anguish is connected to the fact that the one he is called on to sacrifice is his son, his only son, the son he loves so dearly. He is not called on to sacrifice a stranger, even a neighbor. This is his son. And when he finally embraces him, Isaac has not been transformed into Abraham's neighbor. He is still, indeed all the more so, his son, his only son. To be sure, in *Works of Love* Kierkegaard wants to let earthly distinctions stand, but for me, putting the importance of the particular this way seems too much a concession, a resignation to, rather than a existential embrace of, the historical actuality, every inch. I find the so-called second ethics of *Works of Love* profoundly disappointing.

Fortunately, I have not set as my task here the defense of Kierkegaard's conceptual consistency. Rather, my focus has been one of building on his

---

16. Søren Kierkegaard, *Works of Love: Some Christian Reflections in the Form of Discourses*, trans. Howard V. Hong and Edna H. Hong (New York: Harper and Row, 1962) (hereafter WL).

characterizations of faith and its alternatives in the figures that he uses to represent the various modalities of existence.

But let me return to the question of what a faithful marriage would be (like). Since I have ruled out the judge's marriage as a paradigm of an authentically faithful marriage, where do we turn to find a model of such marriage? Or does faith have no place for marriage? Based on a single remark Kierkegaard made regarding his relation to Regine, I venture to say that he thought faith was essential for marriage, a necessary condition for it. In a journal entry, he said, "Had I had faith I would have remained with Regine." I take this to mean that he would have married her, had he had faith, from which it follows that existential faith not only has a place in it for marriage, but that faith is essential for an existentially legitimate marriage.

If so, what would such a marriage be like?

Following the lines I have been suggesting, it would be appropriate to think of a marriage within faith, a faithful marriage, in terms of embrace. But not every embrace is a matter of the intertwining of arms; there are simpler, more symbolically charged, embraces. What I have in mind here is the mutual embrace of hands. After all, the hand is what is asked for, and what is given in marriage. The holding of hands is an integral part of the wedding ceremony, and, as every single person knows, it is the hand that bears the sign, the ring, that tells others that we are married. I suggest then that an appropriate metaphor for an existentially legitimate marriage is the mutual embrace of hand in hand.

What I like about this metaphor is that it acknowledges the freedom of the two whose embrace of hands brings them together. This togetherness is then a matter of a mutual consent and therefore a mutual acknowledgment of the separateness of the two who are in fact together in this embrace. Each is free to let go, each knows that about himself or herself, and about his or her partner. Marriage does not solder hands or rings together; the connection of hand to hand is not like this, not this secure, we might say. Indeed, sometimes we are tempted to let go, sometimes it would be easier to let go, sometimes we do let go. But what we always know is that we can.

As I will put this in more detail in Chapter 4, following Stanley Cavell, in a legitimate marriage, divorce is always a real possibility. The legitimate marriage faces this threat head on, and if lucky, is able to refuse it, continually to refuse it. A legitimate marriage continues (as long as both partners continue to hold the other, as long as both continue to honor the mutual promise to have and to hold the other) from this day forward, till death do they part. On the one hand (so to speak) this embrace seems so fragile, so likely to break asunder; on the other, nothing seems stronger, more secure. In a good marriage, one that acknowledges its fragility, neither principalities, nor powers, nor anything in the world can prevail against it, can separate the bond of love in and through which the two are united. What makes the security of such a marriage different from the judge's is that it is a security established within the full awareness of the possibility of divorce. As I see it, divorce is, for the judge, not even a remote possibility, not to mention a real and wrenching existential threat. A legitimate marriage continually annuls this possibility, this threat. Judge William's seeming refusal of this possibility, I read as a refusal of possibility, a refusal of freedom, a refusal of marriage in any existential sense, that is, a refusal of faith, that is, despair.

In conclusion, let me say a last word about the implications of my interpretation of existential faith for making sense of the biblical story of Abraham's sacrifice of Isaac. I read the biblical story as a myth of a human existential possibility. God's call to Abraham in the first person and his first-person response is a representation of Abraham's consciousness being re-awakened to his own particularity and at the same time to the existential possibility of resigning from it. This possibility of resignation is focused when Abraham realizes that it is within his power, his choice, to renounce all of his precious attachments to this world, the whole package of which is symbolized in Isaac. He really raises the knife, and yet his faith enabled him to say "no." And in this, he realizes that even God does not demand this, that, in fact, God wants to tell him that there is nothing higher, nothing more worthwhile than our existence in this world. Yet, the story also suggests that we cannot come to this realization, to the point of being able to choose our existence, apart from coming to the point of realizing that we have the freedom to do otherwise.

As I interpret the story, God did not ask of Abraham that he take a course of action that is higher than human fatherhood, the course of obedience to a heavenly father's command to murder his son. What God's call was designed to re-awaken in Abraham was not something higher, it was, as I see it, a call to realize the human possibility of sinking into something lower than the human, namely, into the murderous, the bestial! The story then turns out to be something very akin to Martha Nussbaum's reading of what Walter Burkert says about animal sacrifice in general: "[it expresses] the awe and fear felt by [the] human community towards its own murderous possibilities" (FG, 37). The refusal to sacrifice the human, and the substitution of an animal, testifies to the truth that " '[h]uman sacrifice . . . is a possibility which, as a horrible threat, stands behind every sacrifice' " (FG, 37). Abraham realizes in a moment of revelation that he is not required to sacrifice his son; he realizes, by God's grace, that he has the power to say "no" to this inhuman act, that God does not require *this* from him. And in distancing himself from such a murderous act, he "at the same time acknowledge[s], the possibilities for human slaughter that reside in human nature" (FG, 37). It is just these inhuman human possibilities that Abraham's faithful embrace of the human continually annuls.

Two

CAVELL

Pursuits of Knowledge and Happiness

Three

KNOWLEDGE
AND DISAPPOINTMENT

That Stanley Cavell was influenced by Søren Kierkegaard is clear; what that influence finally comes to, however, is less clear, perhaps even to Cavell himself. Although he devoted an early article—an article that has now become rather well known among Kierkegaardians—to a discussion of a not-so-well-known piece by Kierkegaard, *On Authority and Revelation* (CE, 372–93), Cavell's acknowledgment of Kierkegaard comes mostly in the way of passing references.[1]

While some might make the cynical claim that Cavell's use of Kierkegaard is no more than a polite gesture to his mentor, Wittgenstein, for whom Kierkegaard was important, I think there is more to Cavell's attraction to Kierkegaard. As I would put it, Cavell seems to be attracted to something in Kierkegaard's way of thinking, or of doing philosophy. In fact, I propose to show that Cavell has adopted, knowingly or not, a Kierkegaardian way of thinking, especially in what he says about skepticism and about marriage.

---

1. One such reference that is particularly relevant, a kind of cryptic summary of my project here, is as follows: "And this is the Kierkegaard whose Knight of Faith alone achieves not exactly the everyday, but "the sublime in the pedestrian." I do not quite wish to imply that Kierkegaard's (melo-dramatic) sense of the pedestrian here, with its transfigurative interpretation of the human gait of walking, is matched in Wittgenstein's idea of the ordinary. Yet it seems to me that I can understand Kierkegaard's perception as a religious interpretation of Wittgenstein's. In that case an intuitive sense is afforded that the everyday, say the temporal, is an achievement, that its tasks can be shrunk from as the present age shrinks from the tasks of eternity; a sense, I would like to say, that in both tasks one's humanity, or finitude, is to be, always is to be, accepted, suffered." *This New Yet Unapproachable America: Lectures After Emerson After Wittgenstein* (Albuquerque, N.M.: Living Batch Press, 1989), 39 (hereafter UA).

When I say that Cavell has adopted a Kierkegaardian way of thinking, I mean that his thought is informed at critical junctures by the peculiar dialectic that also informs Kierkegaard. This peculiar dialectic I am calling *the dialectic of paradox*. The fact that this dialectic lies at the center of Cavell's philosophical reflections (about, I might add, philosophical subjects that also preoccupy Kierkegaard, that is, knowledge, love, and marriage) is what leads me to think of his philosophical position as a variation on a Kierkegaardian theme.

In the present chapter, I will consider the paradoxical relation that Cavell asserts between knowledge and skepticism—a relation that leads him to defend the truth of skepticism. In the next chapter, I will take up the matter of marriage and divorce, or more specifically, Cavell's claim that divorce plays a paradoxically positive and indispensable role within a legitimate marriage.

I do not want to be read as reading Cavell's work as a variation on a Kierkegaardian theme only because it is driven, like Kierkegaard's, toward an affirmation of the human. The deeper theme, the deeper connection, is found in the fact that both make the claim that a full and complete affirmation of the human is possible only on condition that it is made within a dialectical context of paradox.

This context of paradox is created when we existentially realize that the full affirmation of our humanness is possible only if, and to the extent to which, we come to terms with the fact that we have the power, the freedom, existentially to repudiate our humanness. Or as we may put the paradox, both Kierkegaard and Cavell want to tell us that the human urge to escape from, or refuse, the human is an essential ingredient in our humanness, so much so, that a full affirmative embrace of our humanness must dialectically include precisely what it excludes, the ubiquitous human urge to transcend our humanness. ("Only what is human can be inhuman."[2])

Kierkegaard thinks that the question of the place of the human urge to transcend its own humanness, the urge to some sort of aesthetic flight from, or ethical refusal of, or religious resignation from, existence, history, the world, and so forth, is particularly acute within modernity. He traces this to the legacy of the impact of Christianity on human consciousness.

As I see it, the human urge to transcend the human condition is at the very core of the human pursuit of knowledge, but especially so in modern

---

2. *The Claim of Reason: Wittgenstein, Skepticism, Morality, and Tragedy* (New York: Oxford University Press, 1979), 418 (hereafter CR).

epistemology. Since Cavell does not say much about the historical roots of this urge to transcendence, or the issue of why it is particularly evidenced in modernity, I will take a moment to present a Kierkegaardian brief to the effect that Christianity brought the issue of human transcendence acutely to the fore and in so doing set the modern epistemological problematic.

I have argued elsewhere that modern culture—in its basic philosophical assumptions about the world, human existence, value, and so forth, what I call the modern world-picture—is, in large measure, an indirect product of the impact of biblical faith on the human imagination, an impact that the advent and eventual triumph of Christianity turned into a world-historical force.

The impact of biblical faith/Christianity on modern culture was not direct insofar as it did not provide, nor did it intend, the substance of the modern world-picture. The biblical world-picture did have an indirect impact in shaping modernity however. It had this indirect shaping impact insofar as it provided the existential and conceptual innovations that made the modern world-picture—its practical and conceptual framework—possible.

As it turns out, there could be no greater divide than that between the biblical and the modern world-pictures. As I might put this point, the modern world-picture is simply a profound derangement of, and thereby parasitical upon, the biblical world-picture. (I employ here as an axiom of my thinking the principle that a sense of derangement comes into existence by virtue of a prior sense of arrangement. It is in this way that modernity is parasitical upon the innovations of biblical faith.)

Kierkegaard's incisive, and I believe correct, assertion, made indirectly through Author A, is that Christianity was the first to posit a picture of the human being as spirit/flesh, as having a radically dual nature, as being both radically transcendent and immanent. In this picture, the human being as spirit/flesh stands in both opposition to, and as incarnate within, the world. This model of the dual nature of human being was, of course, the historical Jesus, who became Christ.

From the Christian perspective, Christ is the knight of faith in its most perfect expression—its dual, double, nature; he is the perfect model of a fully human existence; he is the touchstone of what it is to be a self, to be spirit/flesh; he is the measure of what it is to realize and to embrace existentially one's own incarnate transcendence.

I say that Cavell does not say much about these matters, but he is not silent either. He reads Descartes, I think correctly, as both the cultural Christian and the modern philosopher par excellence, at least in this respect:

Descartes sees and sets the modern problematic as the issue of coming to terms with the radical duality of human existence. Cavell puts it as follows:

> [Descartes's] sense of himself as composed of his contrary natures (of what he means by mind and body, the one characterized in opposition to the other, each essentially what the other is not) is the idea of a double nature, symbolized centrally in the culture we share with him (but perhaps now only in literature) as the figure of Christ. So the thing of incarnation, the mysterious meeting of heaven and earth, occurs in Descartes' thought not alone in the inspirer of Christianity but in each individual human being. From here you may conclude that the human problem in recognizing other human beings is the problem of recognizing another to be Christ for oneself. (CR, 482–83)

Descartes's failure, as I see it, was not in seeing the radical duality of human being (this is the sense that he was a kind of conceptual, or at least, cultural, Christian), it was in his failure to see connections, or to see connections properly (the sense in which he was the father of modern philosophy). That is, I do not accept the usual criticism of Descartes to the effect that the radical duality that he saw in human existence is the cause of his failure to make proper connections, a criticism that usually leads to some form of reductionism in which the need for connections has vanished. But this is another story.

To carry the Kierkegaardian framework further, we can say that the Christian proclamation was the good news that the radically transcendent God of the Bible, whose faithful word brought the world into existence, has now provided the ultimate affirmation of the creation by declaring his presence *within* it. Christianity began, we might say, in a scandalous proclamation: God loves *this* world, *his* creation, he is connected and committed to it deeply and intimately—to what is radically *other* than he is—so much so, that the best picture we can have of him, of his transcendence, is the incarnate transcendence that was once and for all manifest in the Son of Man, in the life of that faithful human being who was the Christ, that human being who walked among us, conversed with us, suffered with us, died with us, became the model for every human being who would realize his or her (our own implicit) dual nature.

This contribution of Christianity to world-consciousness, Kierkegaard claims, was innovative since the existential reality and power of spirit as incarnate transcendence was unknown in antiquity. He says, in that remarkable essay, "The Immediate Erotic States," (EO I, 47–135) that the idea of spirit was completely foreign to the Greeks and only intimated by the Hebrew antecedents to Christianity.

Radical transcendence, that is, incarnate transcendence, was certainly intimated in the Hebraic image of God. According to this picture, God as creator radically transcended the creation; and yet as its creator/ground, this God was also embrangled in his own creation. (The second-century Gnostics saw in the Hebrew Scriptures' doctrine of creation this intimation of incarnation. That is why they sought to dismiss the Hebrew Scriptures, its doctrine of creation, its picture of the spirit of God as thoroughly implicated in the muck and mire of existence.)

The Hebrew imagination pictured God as desiring to express the promise of spirit within the world. This is shown in the biblical companion to the doctrine of creation, the doctrine of *imago dei*. In this doctrine, the flesh and blood human beings that God raised up out of the earth and breathed life into were vested with the promise of becoming like God, of becoming spirit, of becoming an "I am." Again, however, the full realization of this first-person incarnational transcendence had to wait for its proper time before it would become a world-historical force.

It found such a time in the first century, and it gained its expression in the Christian doctrine of the incarnation, in the idea that the absolutely transcendent God who created the world out of nothing is decisively revealed within a human life of faith.

What the Christian doctrine of the incarnation expresses is the idea of first-person incarnational transcendence, that is, the dual reality of transcendence *within* immanence, *within* the historical actuality, *within* the world. Christianity brought this understanding of transcendence to its most decisive expression and made it a, if not the, primary driving principle that would, after the delay of the Middle Ages, profoundly and irreversibly shape the development of modern sensibility.

The modern picture of the self as essentially transcendent *from* the world, albeit temporarily confined to or within it, is very different from that found in Plato's philosophy. Even though the soul is pictured as trapped within the body and animated by a desire to escape it, for Plato, this desire for escape is not radical; it turns out to be a desire to escape from a surface immanence (the shadows seen by the eyes) to a deeper immanence (the Logos perceived by the mind's eye). Plato simply lacked the modern dynamic, temporal, sense of radical transcendence. As Kierkegaard would put this matter, the ancient Greek sense of transcendence, and Plato's in particular, was psychically, not pneumatically, qualified (EO I, 61ff).

And as Cavell points out, Aristotle, as well, had a very different framework from Christianity, and from those moderns who operate from within that Christian framework, moderns not only like Descartes, but like the other modern philosophical giant, Kant. Cavell makes this difference out in terms of animation and incarnation. He puts it as follows: "Kant, if I understand . . . reverses the Aristotelian field and thus redirects the problem of connection. He regards the human being as a species of the genus of rational beings, to wit, the species that has the distinction of being animal, i.e., being embodied: the human being is the animal rational. Hence the human being is no longer the highest among creatures but the lowest among hosts. The direction to the human is not animation but incarnation. . . . This still sounds as if their aspiration was to be God" (CR, 399).

Modernity (Descartes, Kant) takes from this Judaeo/Christian world-picture its notion of transcendence—call this, transcendence *from the world*—but not the incarnational grounding of this transcendence *within* the world, *within* the historical actuality. That is, modernity takes as its basic presupposition the idea that transcendence is essentially and exclusively alien to, and essentially and exclusively disconnected from, immanence, or finitude, or the world, or whatever one may call the historical actuality of the here and now. It defines the task of being human exclusively in terms of disconnection, in terms of transcendence *from* the world. Such a task, modernity came to think of as man's quest to become god—an ironic reversal of the biblical idea of incarnation. In this subtle but enormous twist, the stage was set for the emergence, indeed, the eruption, of a phenomenon that is most distinctive of modernity: what I have earlier called, following Hannah Arendt, *world-alienation*. The modern age was ushered in when human beings began to picture themselves as transcendent gods without any mooring within immanence, as disembodied, disconnected, ghosts.

This picture of the self as a discarnate, dynamically transcendent god, has thoroughly shaped modern epistemology. What can be known is shaped for the modern by the conviction that an ideal knower would be one who is able to achieve an Archimedean "standpoint" wholly outside the earth. Such a "standpoint" of infinity, a "standpoint" of transcendence from the world, is a "standpoint" that is other than, that is alien to, disconnected from, our natural, human, embodied perspective within the world. To achieve this disembodied "standpoint," that is, to be in a position to know, one must escape the human condition and find that "point of view" that we imagine a disembodied, omniscient God to have.

This picture of knowing shapes our ideal of objectivity in modern science. At the same time, our modern scientific world-picture acknowledges the inescapability of our human *predicament,* our finitude. Transcendence in knowledge thus becomes an *ideal* transcendence, an ideal we must ever pursue, but an ideal that is unrealizable in fact and in principle.

No philosophers in modernity bear witness to this picture of the self as discarnate (but confined) transcendence more clearly or more decisively than Descartes and Kant, the two preoccupations of Cavell's philosophical agenda.

I want to focus, as Cavell does increasingly in his later work, on Kant. For Kant, to know things as they really are in and of themselves would require a radical transcendence of the human perspective—a godlike perspective—that we humans simply cannot, as a matter of both fact and principle, achieve. We therefore cannot know *things;* we as humans have no access to them. As a trade off, however, Kant offers us the possibility, against Humean skepticism, of a limited knowledge: if we cannot know things, then we can at least know phenomena.

Cavell's reflections on such a Kantian response to skepticism bring the issue of the so-called limits of the human condition and the urge to transcend those limits clearly into focus. He says:

> It is as if Kant were saying: . . . 'the whole of things' *cannot* be known by human creatures, not because we are limited in the extent of our experience, but, as we might say, because we are limited *to* experience, however extensive. Put this way: to know the world as a whole, or the world as it is in itself, would require us to have God's knowledge, to know the world the way we more or less picture god to know the world, with every event and all of its possibilities directly present. And this simultaneous, immediate intuition of the world is not merely beyond us in fact or in extent; it is not a matter of having more or less of something we now have a little of. It is beyond us in principle; human knowing is not like that.[3]

Let us turn then to Cavell's discussion of such a Kantian response to skepticism—a response to what I shall call the human disappointment with its own humanness.

Objectivism, Skepticism, and the Kantian (I)deal

A life-long preoccupation of Stanley Cavell has been the problem of philosophical skepticism. He has wrestled with this problem as far back as his

---

3. *Pursuits of Happiness: The Hollywood Comedy of Remarriage* (Cambridge: Harvard University Press, 1981), 75–76 (hereafter PH).

graduate school days at Harvard, where he submitted a dissertation (roughly on Wittgenstein) in which the problem of philosophical skepticism was of central concern.

This early interest shaped his philosophical agenda. His dissertation (submitted in 1961) was finally published (with further implications and applications added) in 1979 under the title *The Claim of Reason*. Here he brings to term his unique and long-developing interpretation of (Wittgenstein's treatment of) skepticism. In subsequent publications, right down to the present, he continues to develop this unique reading of skepticism, especially as that reading has applications to the themes of romanticism, or more particularly, as the themes of romanticism appear in American philosophy, film, and literature.

According to Cavell's unique interpretation, philosophical skepticism is not in need of refutation. He argues that Wittgenstein never tried to refute it and we shouldn't either. What then was Wittgenstein trying to tell us about philosophical skepticism? Cavell offers a startling answer: what Wittgenstein wanted to show us was the truth of philosophical skepticism—that we need to acknowledge that skepticism is always at play in our every pursuit of knowledge.

What does this mean? Does this make sense? How can it be that any pursuit of knowledge that does not acknowledge the truth of skepticism will fail? It is in answering this question that Kierkegaard's dialectic of paradox becomes relevant. But I will postpone a consideration of this issue until the concluding section of this chapter. For now, I must set the stage.

At the outset, I need to make sure that the term *philosophical skepticism* is clearly defined. We must distinguish philosophical skepticism from ordinary skepticism, even though both have it in common that they involve a repudiation of knowledge claims.

Ordinary skepticism is directed to specific knowledge claims that we simply are not able to accept. Such a skepticism is thought perfectly reasonable if there are appropriate grounds for doubt. Indeed, such reasonable skepticism is essential to the responsible pursuit of knowledge. In certain circumstances, it is the failure to be skeptical enough that is suspect.

"She says she loves me, but I have my doubts; I don't see love in her eyes; I don't hear it in her voice." Such ordinary doubts or reservations of this sort do not imply philosophical skepticism, a skepticism about whether, for example, I can ever really know how anyone feels about anything. And herein lies the basic distinction between philosophical skepticism and the ordinary garden variety: philosophical skepticism is a reservation or doubt about the legitimacy of a whole segment of knowledge claims; or, in its most ecumenic form, as for example we find in Descartes, philosophical skepticism involves a doubt about the legitimacy of any knowledge claim whatsoever; it is not directed (like ordinary skepticism) at questions of the plausibility or legitimacy of some particular claim within some particular field in which knowledge is pursued. Or more cryptically: the doubt of ordinary skepticism concerns the legitimacy of *this* particular claim *to* knowledge; the doubt of philosophical skepticism concerns the legitimacy of this segment of claims, or the legitimacy of every claim, to *knowledge.*

Now back to Cavell. The background that led to his thesis that the pursuit of knowledge must incorporate within itself, if it is to be honest, the truth of skepticism, is found in his dissatisfaction with the standard attempts to refute it. As he points out, the standard lesson in the philosophy classes we all have taken is that skepticism is in need of refutation, at least if knowledge is to be saved. So we set out to refute it. Moreover, there is a fairly standard such refutation. Cavell puts that standard refutation of skepticism as follows:

> [S]kepticism's repudiation of knowledge is merely a function of having set the sights of knowledge too high; *of course* if you impose the idea of absolute certainly on knowledge, you will not find that we know anything (except perhaps mathematics, together with what, if anything, is given to the senses); *of course* if you try to turn induction into deduction, induction will seem wanting; *of course* if you demand that in order to see an object you have to see *all* of the object, then we can never really or directly or immediately *see* an object. . . . So skepticism is just the cause of the disappointments of which it complains. (QO, 139)

Cavell found that he was not satisfied with this argument. After all, why would a philosopher set his or her sights so high as to ensure self-defeat? He concludes, "What I am to conceive is that the self-defeat of skepticism is precisely the point of it—But does this make sense to me? Or is its *not* making sense something I should further regard as its point?" (QO, 139).

Before we explore further why Cavell is not satisfied with this refutation of skepticism, before we see why he claims that there is a truth to skepticism that tells something important about knowledge, allow me to present Cavell's version of one such refutation: the critical philosophy of Immanuel Kant. But again, I must set the stage for this.

Under the suasion of his immediate philosophical training, Wolff, Baumgarten and Meier, locally, and Descartes, Leibniz and Locke globally,

Kant had come to think that he could (that this is the business of philosophy) make contact with reality, with things as they really are, things-in-themselves. He accepted what we may call the objectivist ideal of knowing, the ideal that says that if we are to obtain true knowledge, we must transcend our human condition, put ourselves in the position of an omniscient, transcendent god. Moreover, for a while at least, he thought this possible. And even though Hume awoke him from his dream of omniscience, awoke him to the realization that any such attempt to transcend the human condition is destined to fail, there is some question as to whether, or to what extent, he ever got over his objectivistic dream.

Certainly we can find such an objectivism alive and well in modern science. This is clearly shown in the scientist's insistence that the decisive mark of the objectivity of some scientific claim, the extent to which it captures the true essence of some entity, the extent to which it penetrates into that reality and finds out what it is in and of itself, is just the extent to which it has been established, as much as is (humanly) possible, in radical independence from what is taken to be the intrusion of a human knower. Karl Popper articulates a modern version of this ideal of scientific objectivity as follows: "Knowledge in this objective sense is totally independent of anybody's claim to know; it is also independent of anybody's belief, or disposition to assent or to assert, or to act. Knowledge in the objective sense is *knowledge without a knower*: it is *knowledge without a knowing subject.*"[4]

Objectivism of this, and other sorts, has become virtually the epistemological common sense of modern science. Its assumption is that what is (really) real, whatever it is, is a self-contained, fully determined, complete package that is in no way dependent on a human for its actuality; here, the human knower has no ontologically constitutive effect on the known. In fact, according to most accounts of scientific method, the human knower is thought to be an obstacle to knowledge. For the scientist, the task of being objective is the task of purifying any and all human elements (perspective, commitment, values, bodily "limitations," and the like) from the scientific investigation. It is these human elements that are thought to contaminate or distort objectivity, that is, thwart the achievement of true knowledge. As it turns out, if this were ruthlessly pursued, the effect would be to eliminate the scientist from science![5]

---

4. Karl Popper, *Objective Knowledge: An Evolutionary Approach* (Oxford: Clarendon Press, 1972), 109.

5. Compare what Michael Polanyi has to say on these matters. For instance, he says that science proceeds "from a misguided passion—a passion for achieving absolutely impersonal knowledge which, being unable to recognize any persons, presents us with a picture of the universe in which we

Even though objectivism is widespread in the practice of modern science, it would be unfair and simply untrue to say that modern science has not been chastened by Kant, by the realization that the objectivistic ideal of knowing is merely an ideal, an ideal that cannot be fully realized by human knowers. But it would also be untrue to say that modern scientists are not disappointed with this Kantian concession to skepticism—call this a disappointment with the concession to the inescapability of our human limitations, our confinement within space and time. Modern science is just as disappointed with Kant's deal with skepticism as Kant was with the failure of objectivism, and just as disappointed, surprisingly, as many modern romantics are with Kant's bargain.

In general, modern romanticism (or what I could just as well have called modern subjectivism) would have us think that it offers an alternative to the ideals of scientific objectivism, ideals they perceive, rightly enough, as threatening the complete devastation of the human. And yet, as I see it, modern romantics—at least of a certain sort—are equally committed to the vision of detached, godlike transcendence as the epistemological ideal par excellence. In this respect they occupy the same boat as the scientists, the boat romanticists think is taking the human to its ruination.

While some romantics would take us further from the earth, into ourselves perhaps, others seek to bring us back to earth, to sober us, as it were, from the intoxicating dreams of transcendence that science seems to foster—dreams of conquering and mastering the universe, of going beyond all limits, of going beyond the human senses, beyond the human standpoint, of obtaining godlike objectivity. Some romantics focus our awareness on the agonizing struggles of finitude, the confinement of its limitations, on our feelings of being trapped within the world, within ourselves, within our own subjectivity; others remind us of the joys and blessings of finitude, of the sublime within the lowly, of the extraordinariness of the ordinary.

The strategy of romanticism, its celebration of the human as its response to skepticism, must seem to the scientist defeatist, pessimistic. Why should we celebrate (romanticize) the fact that we are human, that we are confined within our limited human subjectivity, as we of course are? The scientist, at least insofar as she is chastened by skepticism and agrees to the Kantian settlement with it, will come to the same conclusion that we cannot get out of our subjectivity and obtain a godlike objectivity; but she does not

---

ourselves are absent. In such a universe there is no one capable of creating and upholding scientific values; hence there is no science" (PK, 142).

celebrate this, rather it is a source of her deepest disappointment, her deepest grief. And yet she remains undaunted by this disappointment, by this concession. She wants to keep trying to get as close as is possible to such a perspectiveless transcendence, while recognizing the impossibility, in fact and in principle, of ever realizing this ideal.

The romanticist celebrates our humanness by accepting our confinement within our subjectivity, as though this is the only way for us to continue to claim uniqueness, nobility, as though our only claim to being human is to be found in what he might call our imperfections, our limitations (to err is human). This is worth celebrating, the romanticist may claim, for at least here within ourselves we are safe from the leveling effects of scientific reduction. It is precisely these human limitations and imperfections that machines cannot duplicate that are celebrated in the lofty heights and depths of poetry and romance, and celebrated just because they have the essential virtue of being beyond the reach of scientific leveling.

Yet even here, I would say, the sense of world-alienation, however disguised and subtle, comes through. While the romantics celebrate the fact that we human beings are neither machines nor beasts, what shows through in their protests against those who would dehumanize us (mad scientists, let us call them), what shows even in the celebration of the fact that we human beings are irreducibly human, with all of the nobility and agony that this implies, is a deep and dark suspicion (concession?) that we human beings are, and disappointingly so, *all too human*!

While the romantics protest at the prospect of being reduced to machines or beasts, and while they celebrate the fact that we are human beings, the haunting suspicion is that behind this protest there lurks a deep disappointment that we human beings are so limited, that we are not angels, at least not yet, or not in this finite world. Perhaps here, no less than in science, the modern notion of transcendence drives the human to quest for that which is other than, or in some way beyond, the human, beyond the world.

The disappointment inherent in the modern epistemological ideal conceals a deep-seated misanthropy: what is contemptible in human knowing is its humanness! In the face of the wish to transcend the human condition, the dream of finding an Archimedean "standpoint" outside of the world from which passively to behold the real ends in a concession of impossibility. This failed transcendence breeds resentment, disappointment, and a contempt for our own humanness.

This godlike ideal of knowing is just the sort of example that Cavell has in mind when he speaks of an epistemology that sets itself up for disappointment. In setting its sights too high, in requiring human knowing to be, per impossible, nonhuman, such an epistemology invites its own collapse.

It was Hume who would respond to this invitation with a vengeance. Hume awoke Kant from his epistemological presumption. What Hume discovered was that human knowing is always subject to an essential fragility, the core of which lies in the fact that human claims to know often are, perhaps always are, mistaken. Hume's Cartesian assumption is that only what is indubitable can be known. But, when it comes to the empirical world, the world of sense, we are always liable to be mistaken; nothing here qualifies as indubitable—something that Descartes knew and proclaimed as well. Hence, we cannot know anything in this world, not even that a causes b. More generally, he concluded that we do not (really) know, that we are not in a position to know, and that we in principle cannot be in such a position to know, that there is (really) an external world, others, and so forth, "out there"; perhaps indeed, there is nothing, perhaps we really know nothing; or more Socratically, perhaps all that we know and can know is that we know and can know nothing.

Kant's *Critique of Pure Reason* begins by accepting Hume's refusal to accept the possibility that human beings can ever come close to meeting the demands of godlike knowing—a refusal based on, I would say, Hume's acceptance of those demands as defining real knowledge. To put this differently, Kant begins with disappointment; or as we might put it, in the grip of the skepticism that he wishes to overcome.

It no doubt appeared to him that Hume had, in Samson-like manner, pulled down the pillars of the divine house of knowledge human beings were trying to construct and move into. With the heavenly mansion of knowledge in shambles and his pietistic faith threatened as the result of his encounter with Hume, Kant begins to pick up the pieces, or better, to construct a new epistemological edifice. This new house is more modest, it is more limited in its pretentiousness, it is more clearly a human dwelling place, and hence more clearly separated and divided from the divine. It has two main rooms, clearly divided, clearly separate, but not clearly equal in value: one room is for limited—and thereby secured—(scientific) knowledge, call this the library, or perhaps the laboratory; the other a room for a limited—and thereby secured—faith, call this the living room, or perhaps the chapel.

What Kant accomplished can be easily summarized: he demonstrated conclusively, in favor of Hume, or let us say more broadly, skepticism, that we cannot ever really know what things really are in and of themselves (that is, he limited knowledge); and against Hume and skepticism, that nevertheless we can know something (that is, he secured knowledge). What can we *not* know and what *can* we know? We cannot know things, but we can know phenomena.[6]

What are phenomena? They are, of course, appearances, but Kant's interesting reading of appearances is that they are human constructions. For Kant, and contra the objectivistic insistence on the passivity of the knower, the critical knower has an ontologically constitutive role in the construction of phenomena, indeed phenomena do not exist independently of the knower's constructive participation. Moreover, all we have (to go on) is the phenomenon; we are limited to appearances. But at least appearances are indubitable and hence can be known.

(The irony of Kant's settlement: he managed to turn what the older objectivistic tradition had thought of as the licit and morally praiseworthy pursuit of things as they really are into a moral perversion. Under Kant's new interpretation, the wish for transcendence is now thought of as a wish for transgression—a wish for an illicit peak over the edge of our human limits. The once admired pursuit of godlike knowledge is now thought to be the sin of wanting to be god. But human beings, being what we are, that is, jealous of our freedom, and often perverse in our attempts to protect it, do not take kindly to prohibitions. In fact, Kant's proposal to draw limits to human knowing produced an exaggerated temptation to cross those limits.)

If phenomena are not things; if they are not things-in-themselves, and if phenomena are all that we have, then what, for Kant, has become of things? They did not, for Kant, go away completely. Rather, the reality of things (in-themselves) has now been removed to a new realm, the noumenal world, a super-(sub?)-sensible world, a world beyond (above? below?) our human access. Such a noumenal world is essentially beyond the limits of human knowing, perhaps even, off limits—a notion that again brings to mind the sense in which the wish to know things becomes a temptation to an illicit, to an immoral, transgression of our humanness.

Kant concedes: human beings must accept our humanness; we should not yield to the all too human temptation to try to transcend our humanness,

---

6. Cavell puts Kant's argument in the first *Critique* as follows: "(1) Experience is constituted by appearances. (2) Appearances are of something else, which accordingly cannot itself appear. (3) All and only functions of experience can be known; these are our categories of the understanding. (4) It follows that the something else—that of which appearances are appearances, whose existence we must grant—cannot be known. In discovering this limitation of reason, reason proves its power to itself, over itself. (5) Moreover, since it is unavoidable for our reason to be drawn to think about this unknowable ground of appearance, reason reveals itself to itself in this necessity also" (*In Quest of the Ordinary: Lines of Skepticism and Romanticism* [Chicago: University of Chicago Press, 1988], 30 (hereafter QO).

to try, that is, to be gods. We must forego this temptation if we are to avoid falling into skepticism. The price we pay for resisting this temptation, the price we pay for being able to know anything at all, is that we must abandon our human craving to know things as they are in themselves—call this a natural human desire for a *connection to things,* for an intimacy with the world. We may not be able to know face-to-face, as perhaps we are known, but we can at least see through a glass darkly: we can know what *appears* to us through the clouded spectacles of space and time, through the human grid constructed by understanding and reason.

We have arrived at the core of Kant's philosophy: *human knowing is inherently limited and we must accept this if we are to secure knowledge and avoid being dragged into skepticism.* We must face the fact, Kant might say, that human knowing is limited by the very fact that it is human, by the fact that it is limited to and by human (always structured) experience; and we must accept the fact that for human beings, things, things-in-themselves, are off limits. They exist to be sure, but as a kind of forbidden fruit—and hence as a temptation.

The objectivistic ideal failed to see that the fruit of the tree of knowledge was forbidden. It thought, naively, it possible for us to have our eyes opened and to see things as a god does—it did not think of the pursuit of knowledge as a transgression of a prohibition. But neither did it reckon with the fact that knowledge exposes our vulnerability (QO, 49), that its attempt to transcend the human condition, to be a god, was destined to fail.

Kant warns us to resist this temptation not to be human, for yielding to it will inevitably lead to skepticism and the loss of faith. It is as though Kant were preaching to us from his pietistic pulpit: "You may be disappointed that you can't be gods, but it is time to grow up, to give up that wish, to accept your limitations, your humanness. Amen!" But as the congregation files out, they are comforted, but also deeply, strangely, disturbed by a secret wish to transgress, to demonstrate their freedom, to prove to themselves that they are not as limited as the parson says they are.

Along these lines Cavell remarks on a possible romantic use of this Kantian paradox: the paradox that limitation carries within itself both a sense of comfort and confinement: "It appreciates the ambivalence in Kant's central idea of limitation, that we simultaneously crave its comfort and crave escape from its comfort, that we want unappeasably to be lawfully wedded to the world and at the same time illicitly intimate with it, as if the one stance produced the wish for the other, as if the best proof of human existence were its power to yearn, as if for its better, or other, existence" (QO, 32).

We must be clear on what Kant is rejecting here: Kant's critique and rejection of the human temptation to be god does not entail his rejection of the objectivistic ideal of objectivity. In fact, my claim is that the deal he cuts seems to trade on this ideal. The ideal is not abandoned; rather, Kant simply rejects our capacity, in principle, to realize it, to be gods. In a heroic effort to save knowing from skepticism, and faith from the ravages of the new science, he settles for a conditioned human knowing; in the face of his own disappointment at not being able to be a god, and yet in the grip of the steadfast pietistic belief that there is such a god who does indeed see all things as they really are, he accepts what he takes to be the limitations of his human condition.

As Cavell remarks on this issue, we are inclined to say to Kant who makes a bargain with skepticism by taking away with one hand the possibility that we can know things as they really are in order to give us the possibility of knowing something, that is of avoiding complete skepticism, "Thanks for nothing" (QO, 31, 53). And further Cavell says, "Kant, however, really does take the mind as *confined* in what it can know, takes it that there are things beyond the things we know, or something systematic about the things we know, that we cannot know, a realm of things-in-themselves, noumenal, open to reason, not phenomenal, not presentable. . . . Is this really confinement? Is our freedom checked? From what are we withheld? I do not of course deny the presence of a *sense* of confinement here" (PH, 78).

Allow me to suggest an analogy for what I take to be Kant's less than radical settlement between the wish of the objectivistic ideal of knowledge and the disappointments of skepticism. I propose that we think of Kant's notion of limited human knowledge as analogous to what I will call the modern conception of human freedom. Such a notion, I would say, is of freedom as essentially limited. I take it that at the basis of this conception of limited human freedom there is a humanly unrealizable ideal (a picture) of perfect freedom, just as there is for Kant an ideal (a picture) of pure knowledge that is outside our human access. Again, god (what is other than human) is at the center of this picture, the standard, as it were: in the case of knowledge, we picture the ideal knower as a disembodied, omniscient god; in the case of freedom, we picture true freedom as possible only for a disembodied omnipotent god.

My contention is that the modern claim that human freedom is *limited* comes to the claim that it is, of necessity, embodied—structured by time and space. Such limitations, it is widely thought, keep us from doing anything and everything we want, keep us from omnipotence, or from a certain picture of omnipotence. It is thought unreasonable to think otherwise than that our freedom is so limited. But, the secret wish is, "Wouldn't it be nice if we could be a god, say for a day, and even for some noble purpose, to bring about world peace, for example?" But reality dawns, and we realize that such an ideal is intrinsically unrealizable, for human beings at least. Yet we continue to harbor a secret disappointment, a secret desire to cross the lines of finitude; but, if we are grown up about it, we learn to accept and be content with our human limitations, with our humanness.

The modern, however, hardly ever questions this basic definition of freedom, hardly ever sees that it is completely negative: freedom just is *freedom from*. According to this negative definition, pure freedom would be possible only on condition that every obstacle, limit, and restriction to freedom, potential or actual, is cleared away. What counts as an obstacle, restriction, or limit to freedom? Again, the short answer here is embodiment. Embodiment, however, has numerous dimensions.

The most obvious level of embodiment is the fact that we human beings have bodies. But not only are we embodied in an organic structure, we are also embodied in a culture and history none of which is of our own choosing. It is these structures of embodiment that limit our freedom, keep us from being totally free.

As the argument goes, we are limited by our natural gifts, our intelligence, our physical coordination, our heritage, the particular circumstances of our birth, and so forth. I am not free to choose to be a brain surgeon if I have a severely limited IQ; nor can I choose to be a professional basketball player if I have no muscle coordination. (And it will not do to say here, well I could choose to be, say, a rocket scientist, I just could not be one. As I will argue below, this does not capture what we ordinarily mean by having and making a choice.) On this view, embodiment limits our freedom, and at least as long as we remain embodied, total freedom is an impossible dream.

This ideal of freedom as *freedom from* is ubiquitous within modern sensibility. I venture to say that it is so much a part of the *common sense* of modernity, that if you ask anyone if he thinks that he is "totally free," the universal answer will be "of course not." If you pursue this line of inquiry, you will likely find out that the reason nobody thinks that he is "totally free" is that he thinks that his situation in time and space, his situation among others within a culture, and so forth are restrictions to his freedom. But what would a state of release from the body and the world be like? That is, what would disembodied freedom be?

This is particularly problematic if freedom is acknowledged to have a positive sense, namely, as the power to act, the power *to do* this or that. Freedom in this positive sense involves two dimensions, what I call *option and fulfillment.* In order to be capable of performing an action freely, one must be able to choose a particular course of action from among various possibilities. But this dialectical moment of option in the free act is not sufficient to add up to a complete free action. One must also have the capacity to carry out the intention, to perform the course of action chosen. Without this latter moment of fulfillment, no action, indeed, no choice has occurred. Here, the choice simply failed. I don't mean that the choice was made and failed to be fulfilled, rather that the lack of fulfillment, or follow-through, entails that there was no choice, that, in a parody of J. L. Austin's speech-act, the choice-act failed to succeed.

Consider the following bit of freedom-from rhetoric. A rebel for "freedom" is captured by the establishment and imprisoned. He laughs at the authorities and says defiantly, "You can put me in prison, but you can't imprison my spirit; you can't keep me from being free!" Now what could this mean? When asked, the rebel replies that he means that these four prisons walls do not a prison make precisely because these walls cannot contain his free thought. He can think as he chooses and choose what he thinks. But is such a disembodied freedom of thought really freedom? After all, the prisoner may be able to choose to eat pizza for supper, but he has no way to fulfill his choice. This, I think we would all agree, is no freedom at all. Would anyone be thrilled to be told that he could choose to have any gift of his wildest imagination, but that he would actually receive nothing? Such is the incoherency of the freedom-from ideal of freedom: *total freedom (from) is achieved only when the conditions of positive freedom (to) are absent.*

Well, perhaps the moral in all of this is simply that we ought to set our sights lower, or better, to define our terms in terms of the kind of being that we human beings are, as opposed to defining them in terms of a nonhuman god. Perfect freedom would then not be defined as an unconditioned, unlimited, fantastic power to do anything at all we might wish to do—a kind of childish wish for omnipotence. Freedom in its positive (say its grown-up sense) needs a setting, it needs embodiment, structures of time and space, for its perfection; indeed, it is imperfect without conditions, limits, and so forth.

If I am given a choice between two or more courses of action, and it is really possible for me to take one or more of these options, and I take one (or more) and carry it (them) through, then how could my freedom in that situation be more perfect? What would this choice lack? Is it only a limited freedom? In fact, one might ask, would a disembodied god be so capable? Might such a god envy human freedom? Might he/she see the blessings of what we curse as our human limitations?

And couldn't similar things be said for knowing? for knowing things, indeed, things-in-themselves, things as they really are, others as they really are? Why does perfect knowledge require that I know as a god? Why can't human beings know things as they really are? and know this as human beings?

The usual answer here is that human knowing is essentially unreliable because it is intrinsically subject to mistake, and hence, essentially fragile. Human pretensions to know simply do not produce certainty, and nothing short of certainty can count as really knowing. But, isn't this true? Of course it is true if we define knowledge in terms of indubitability. But why do this? Why must we say that human knowing is imperfect, intrinsically flawed, and so on just because every claim to knowing is subject to being mistaken? Since when does being subject to being mistaken amount to being mistaken? Or is the claim here deeper? Is the claim actually a claim that we can never know because we can never know when our claims to know are mistaken and when that are not? But is this claim true? Or is it always true?

How did we ever come to think that merely being subject to mistake is the mark of imperfection? How did we ever come to want to extirpate even the possibility of mistake, the very possibility of doubt, from our claims to know? My surmise is that a picture of knowing has captivated our imaginations; a picture of perfect knowing based on a picture of god's knowing, as such a god would be imagined to know within the perfect being theology that developed in the wake of the impact of biblical faith on Western consciousness. In such a picture, human knowing is doomed to imperfection; in such a picture, real (that is, absolutely secured) knowledge of things as they really are, can only be obtained by a being that is completely beyond, completely immune to, and hence not threatened by, doubt, or by the possibility of mistake. Well, we are not gods, hence, our knowing is imperfect.

Yet we may ask, indeed, we must ask, why, granting that human knowing carries in itself an intrinsic liability to mistake, to doubt, does this fact make human knowing intrinsically imperfect? Is it imperfect just because skepticism, of the ordinary and the philosophical sort, is always a possibility within the human knowing situation? But why should being subject to skepticism entail skepticism? Perhaps the liability of human knowledge claims to mistake has another moral? Perhaps the liability of human knowing to skepticism simply tells us what kind of thing human knowing is. And what is this? Well, perhaps the kind of thing that has within it a intrinsic element of risk, of vulnerability, of fragility. Could it be that if knowing did not involve this element of risk, this possibility of being wrong, that we would not count it as knowing? (And couldn't we even think of god's knowledge as such?) This view of knowing would not entail that whatever we know we also in fact doubt. Rather, it would only entail this: we can only know what we *can* doubt, but, insofar as we risk the claim to know it, we would say that we do not in fact doubt it. The one who claims to know takes his stand (in courage?) before the possibility of doubt, and before others, and boldly asserts, "I do not doubt this, take my word on it!" As I might put this, in the human knowing situation, doubt is always included within knowing, but included as excluded, that is, included as an *annulled possibility*.

This, of course, is a far cry from the Cartesian and Kantian (Humean, Enlightenment) picture of perfect knowledge: in this picture, doubt is always an imperfection, the door to skepticism, the door that must be closed if knowledge is to be secured. For Descartes in his way, and Kant in his, and for the subsequent tradition of positivism and phenomenalism to follow, doubt is always and intrinsically possible concerning things (themselves), but not so when it comes to what appears. While I may not be able to know the real thing, say the pain itself (whatever that may mean) that you profess in your words and behavior, I cannot doubt that you appear to me to be in pain. We cannot know things themselves, but we can know how they appear to us; we cannot know that the flower is in fact yellow, but we can know that we experience it as such. And we can know this precisely because we cannot doubt it. The line between appearances and reality is once again clearly drawn. And so it goes.

Kant does not take the route of rethinking the idea of human limitations—that is, he does not consider the possibility that what he takes to be human limitations do not in fact keep human beings *from* something. Rather than rethink the idea of knowing, recognizing that its inherent risks, vulnerabilities, and doubts do not entail its imperfection, or its limitation, Kant simply resigns himself to the accept fact that the human pretension to know things themselves cannot succeed. He offers in place of this pretension, a more modest proposal, call this, his offer of limited knowledge, a knowledge limited *to* appearances.

And to put this in terms of our larger theme, Kant does not finally bring himself to embrace his humanness. Or perhaps the way to put this is that his pretension to embrace it is actually (like Judge William's) a resignation *to* it, a begrudging, reluctant embrace. His soul, we might say, continues to want to be elsewhere, as though while embracing his lover he thinks of another. But this would be a romantic flight; Kant is too sober for that. Or is he?

The recent film *Shadowlands* may be a kind of popular expression of such a Kantian resignation to our humanness. The story of the film centers on C.S. Lewis (Anthony Hopkins), the Oxford Don philosopher/theologian, who is faced with the sickness, suffering, and death of his dearly beloved and newly wedded wife Joy Gresham (Debra Winger). In the denouement of the film, as the two seek shelter from the rain, a shelter that overlooks his child-hood vision of heaven-on-earth, she tells him something to the following ef-fect: human existence has to be accepted with its bitters and its sweets, with its delights of love and happiness—the things Joy had brought to his dull (dead) academic life—as well as with its chance, its vulnerability to loss, its risk, its pain and suffering, its death. And in a heroic and perhaps Stoic *resig-nation to* this condition, accepting in her own way a kind of settlement be-tween the noble, but failed, dream of transcending the human condition of mortality on the one hand and complete skepticism—call this despair—on the other, she says , "The pain then [when she dies] is part of the happiness now. That's the deal!" In the concluding epilogue of the film, after Joy had died, Lewis repeats her words, almost. But he reverses the time, the *now* and the *then*. He says, off camera, "The pain now is part of the happiness then. That's the deal!"

I am not sure about this, but this deal may itself be a form of despair. The existential embrace of the human need not be thought of as a deal—at least if the deal is thought of as a reluctant resignation to the human condi-tion, a reluctant regret that we cannot be something other than what we are. Such a deal is certainly not existential faith.

Every such Kantian kind of "embrace" of the human condition, of human knowing as limited, is fed, I think, by a silent, eternal wish: the wish that things were different, the wish that we could in fact transcend our human condition, the wish that we were gods. This is not a *resignation from* our hu-manness, but it is a *resignation to* it. Resignation, in any form, however, is not faith; it is not Abraham's existential embrace of finitude every inch. As I see it, there is a vast difference between the acceptance of, or the resignation to, human fragility and the faithful, existential embrace of this fragility as the source of human beauty and human value. Surprisingly, it may be that it is just the fragility of the human that makes it so wonderful, so very precious.

Rethinking the Human Condition

As Cavell points out, the word *condition* means "talking together."[7] "Add to this," he goes on to say, "that conditions are also terms, stipulations that de-

---

7. Since only human beings are capable of talking together, we can only wonder whether the modification of *condition* by the word *human* is not somehow redundant; could there be an animal condition?

fine the nature and limits of an agreement, or relations between parties, persons, or groups." And he concludes by saying that what sets the conditions of our knowledge (and conduct) is language (QO, 39).

As soon as human beings are thought of as dual or double in nature, as I think with Kierkegaard and with Christianity that we are, then, the problem of connection arises.[8] As Kierkegaard puts it, we human beings are a synthesis (or as Emerson says, an antagonism of opposites[9]), at least insofar as the existential reality of our duality has been posited, that is, insofar as we have come to picture ourselves as spirit/flesh—as sons and daughters of God.

What is it that connects us? What is it that connects our transcendence and our immanence? What is that connects us to the world, others, ourselves, God? If Cavell is right, and I think that he is, the connection is language, or, as I prefer to say, speech. What connects us is our capacity to talk together, to enter into agreements, covenants, if you will. This is the human condition. (The biblical tradition, I aver, has grasped this more firmly than any other; as is shown by the central place it gives to the metaphor of the word: it is the word that ties Creator to creation, the word that forms the covenants that tie creatures to fellow creatures, to the creation, and to Creator; it is the word that figures the God-Man, that figures our own *imago dei*.)

The wish then to escape from, to refuse, or otherwise deny, the human condition finally comes down to a wish to transcend speech—as though its

8. I do not wish to be read here as saying that Kierkegaard is a Cartesian dualist. Certainly he is not. What I do want to say is that the problematic of both Descartes and Kierkegaard, call this, the modern problematic, or even the inheritance of a certain (Platonized) form of Christianity, is the issue of connection: the connection of the body and the soul, the connection of one to another, to the world, to nature, to history, and all the rest. In the end, this is where Descartes failed. It is, I think, fair to say that in the end, he abandoned any real connections of the self to itself, to its body, its world, others (can we think of Descartes as a kind of Platonic idealist?). Kierkegaard, by contrast, comes down (shall we say to earth?), all of his emphasis on spirit notwithstanding, to a robust embrace of our embodiment in nature (the particularity of flesh and blood embodiment), and in history (the particularity of time and place among others). Kierkegaard invokes no pineal gland solution to the mind-body problem; he does not need to, since for him, spirit and flesh, while distinct, are always inextricably (albeit dialectically) related (like time and eternity, and freedom and necessity) within what he calls a synthesis. But the very idea of a synthesis implies a radical distinction (call this a distinction of opposites) between the inseparable components of the synthesis. As he once says, via A's voice, "The basis concept of man is spirit, and one should not be confused by the fact that he is also able to walk on two feet" (EO I, 65). As well, clearly Cavell is no Cartesian. His work, like his mentor, Wittgenstein, is always directed against the Cartesian attempt to find a way of transcending the human condition. He certainly would agree with Wittgenstein's famous remark—something I might take to solve the mind-body problem in a nutshell: "The body is the best picture of the soul."

9. Cavell quotes Emerson as follows, "[Man is] a stupendous antagonism, a dragging together of the poles of the universe. . . . The secret of the world is the tie between person and event . . . the copula is hidden" (QO, 36).

criteria, grammar, conventions, rules, and so forth limit or confine us. And this wish, for Cavell, is the central motive that animates skepticism. Skepticism is just the fantasy of attempting to speak "outside of language games" (QO, 57). "The wish underlying this fantasy covers a wish that underlies skepticism, a wish for the connection between my claims of knowledge and the objects upon which the claims are to fall to occur without my intervention apart from my agreements" (CR, 352–53).

What gives rise to this fantasy? One thing that Cavell, interpreting Wittgenstein, suggests is a deep-seated dissatisfaction with words, a sense of disappointment with words, a fear that words cannot say, or get to, or express what we would like them to, a fear of inexpressiveness. As Cavell puts the matter, "The dissatisfaction with one's human powers of expression produces a sense that words, to reveal the world, must carry more deeply than our agreements or attunements in criteria will negotiate" (QO, 60).

The fear of inexpressiveness is played out in slightly different ways in the two great modern responses (of disappointment) to the Kantian bargain with skepticism: science and romanticism. These two responses correspond to the two separate worlds the Kantian settlement with skepticism bequeathed to us—call these the worlds of nature and spirit.

From the point of view of science, language, ordinary human prose, is inadequate to express what the world (of nature) *really* is; it is impotent to reveal what things *really* are in and of themselves; and this is so precisely because it is not precise enough, not objective enough. Ordinary speech is too subjective, too ambiguous, too equivocal, too subject to what the subject means, too much a victim of interpretation, too fraught with metaphor, idiosyncratic particulars, and so forth, to be able to express objectively the true nature of things—things as they are independent of our intrusive structuring of them. Language, for the scientist, doesn't allow us a proper disconnection from appearances so as to allow us access to things. Language confines us to appearances; it is a wall that separates us from things.

The fear of inexpressiveness, the sense of the inadequacy, the impotence of words, turns science from verbal language to mathematics. The vision here is that mathematics offers us a way to cross the Kantian line, to know things, not just phenomena. The vision is almost Platonic: ordinary human life is confined to shadows, to a cave, to the world; it is confined to the limitations of the images conveyed in the words of our daily discourse. Mathematics offers us a way to transcend our human confinement to and by language; it offers us an access to things as they really are.

And what are these things? Well they are surely not what appears to us;

they are nothing like what is reflected in our ordinary conversations. We *say* of things, for example, that they are solid, fragrant, resistant, tall, heavy, green; of other human beings that they are in pain, in love, sad, happy; and so forth. But these are just metaphors, the scientist claims; they structure and reflect how things *seem to us*. Mathematics digs "deeper," beyond these "secondary qualities" to the real thing, to "primary qualities"—measurable length, depth, and breadth, or more summarily, mass. At last, we are in contact with things as they really are, things-as-mass. Mathematics has rescued us from our human condition, crossed the Kantian line, and entered into the noumenal world; it has given things back to us.

The problem, at least from the point of view of romanticism, is that even though the operation was a success, the patient died. The price the scientist pays for rescuing things is their death. These things-as-mass are not alive; they are not part of *our* human life; they are not the things that make up *our* human world; they are, in short, alien to us, inhuman, dead.

Again, the romanticist would say to the scientist (who offers to return things, or the remains of things, to us) the same thing that he says to the Kantian (who has puts things off limits), "No thanks!" He would say that science's attempt to escape the confinement of language into the lofty heights of abstract mathematics has effectively killed the world, human beings included. And he questions the value of what science proposes to give us back: the world as mass in motion, ourselves as robots, zombies. Has the dream of making contact with things turned into a nightmare? Has the fantasy of escaping words and into mathematical symbols turned our ordinary existence into a night of the living dead?

The romanticist says to science's proposal to put us back into contact with things (things-as-dead) in no less uncertain terms than it had said to Kant's proposal to limit our access to things, "Thanks for nothing." The romantic protest is that things are alive, that we are alive, that we can have (restore) an intimacy with things, with the world. We and the world throb with life much more so than we, in our naive ordinary existence, ever thought. We can recover our (lost) intimacy with the world, with things, with others, with ourselves. But we must breathe new life into our ordinary existence, to the extent that it has become "silent melancholy" (Emerson), or "quiet desperation" (Thoreau), or "everydayness" (Heidegger), or "bewitchment" (Wittgenstein) (QO, 9). How can we do this?

From the point of view of romanticism, we must transform language (prose) into something higher, more expressive—call this poetry, or better, lyrical poetry, or more strictly speaking, music, or speech-as-music: the very highest expression of the human spirit. Language, as it is, ordinary language, is inadequate precisely because it is not ambiguous enough to express the depth of human feeling; it is not subjective enough: language objectifies. For the romanticist, the thought is that words cannot penetrate into the interior of the other; they cannot convey my own depths, say in the way that poetry or music can. If I am to know fully and completely, per impossible, the agony or ecstasy of the other, or if I am to convey my own such feelings, then it would be necessary in the first case to merge with that other, to disappear in his or her feelings, and in the second for you to merge into me. Language cannot achieve this subjective merger; it stands between us; it is again an obstacle, a confinement, a limitation.

We can know things, the romanticist insists, if we can transcend the (merely) ordinary—that is, what is left of its after the ravages of science, call this its banality, its horror, our sense of disconnection from it. We can recover from the death of the world, we can recover a lost intimacy with things, but again, only if we can find a way to escape the confinement of ordinary language. Poetry and music, or perhaps, poetry-as-music, serve the romanticist in the same way that mathematics serves the scientist: they are techniques for transcending what are taken as the limitations of our ordinary language, its rules, its conventions. For the romanticist, the hills, our habitat, will indeed come alive again with the sound of music (or poetry) if we have ears to hear. But again, what is the price of the romantic prescription for this recovery? As Cavell says, the price may be a return to animism:

> Romanticism's work here interprets itself, so I have suggested, as the task of bringing the world back, as to life. This may, in turn, present itself as the quest for a return to the ordinary, or of it, a new creation of our habitat; or as the quest away from that, for the creation of a new inhabitation. . . . But romanticism in either direction makes its own bargain with the concept of knowledge and the threat of skepticism, one which a philosopher may feel gives up the game, one that accepts something like animism, represented by what seems still to be called, when it is called, the pathetic fallacy. (QO, 52–53)

As I would put it, the price of the romantic prescription for recovery may be the embrace of the demonic. The romantic negotiation comes to this: I (and you) can come alive again, only if everything does. The price of (my) life is the reanimation of everything. The consequence of this, however, is the horror of the demonic: the world is no longer dead, it is haunted, inhabited by ghosts, demons, spirits, as it were. For the romanticist, the hills, the forests, even the dead are alive. For the sake of recovering his own life in the midst of the death of everything, he closes his eyes to the horror his magic effects; with a stroke of his romantic sorcery, he transforms death into life, but the magic turns out to be black, ghostly, demonic. The romantic restores life to the house of the world, a house once inhabited, once teeming with human life, then abandoned. But there is something he does not notice, or perhaps something he thinks it worth keeping his eyes closed to: what brings the house to life again is not a re-inhabitation, but a haunting. Human beings have not moved in again, say to restore that old run-down place and make it what it once was; rather, demons, spirits, ghosts, have entered the abandoned shell: the house (the world) has become haunted, but at least alive.

The move of romanticism opens to and invites superstition, the irrational, the occult, sorcery, fanaticism, dogmatism, the wish to transcend the intelligible. For those who prefer the intelligibility of the human condition, its terms of agreement as set forth in our ordinary speaking together—I for one—such a return of (life to) things at the price of intelligibility is not worth it. While the romantic says "Thanks for nothing" to the Kantian bargain with skepticism, our human desire for intelligibility leads us to want to say to the romantic, "No thanks for everything" (QO, 53).

Is there an alternative in all of this? Is there a way not to have to live in either one or the other of Kant's two worlds, romanticism or science? Is there a way to embrace our human condition, the terms, the language, the agreements, that enable us to talk together, to establish and maintain connections to the world and to others, without feeling that our language traps us, or limits us, and hence that it needs to be transcended or escaped if our freedom is to remain intact? I suggest that there is. The key to this alternative conception of language is found in Cavell's interpretation of Wittgensteinian criteria.

What, according to Cavell, are Wittgensteinian criteria? The short answer here is that criteria provide us with ways of counting something *as* something, what Cavell often calls the means that enable us to "word the world together" (QO, 126). A longer answer will require that we distinguish criteria from symptoms.

"The idea is, I take it," Cavell says, "that a symptom does not make it a part of the very meaning of my words" (CR, 68). He gives the following example. It is a symptom of a stable government that the people governed are cheerful. And this is so despite the fact that the government may be very unstable; after all, the fact is the people could very well be cheerful in an unstable government, in which case their cheerfulness in the face of adversity would be testimony to something else, say to their staunch character, or perhaps even to their thoughtlessness.

Clearly this cheerfulness of the people is no criterion of stable government, of what counts as a stable government; it is not part of the meaning of term *stable government.* "But when I present the criteria in terms of which I assert this concept of a government, and the government does meet them, then that *is* (what I mean by; what I mean in calling it) a stable government" (CR, 69). And Cavell goes on to say:

> If I'm not fully prepared to call it one [a stable government], that may be either because I haven't fully articulated my criteria of the concept for myself, or because the government doesn't fully satisfy one or more of them. In the former case . . . there is an uncertainty, but it is in me: "I'm not sure whether I'd call that stability or tyranny"; " . . . whether instability or tolerance". In the latter case . . . I may hedge my claim, but not because of any uncertainty in the situation: "It's really not what I would call stable, but it's more so than others; anyway there are good reasons for saying it is"; "It is far from a perfect example of what I had in mind; but up to a point I wouldn't mind calling it one". (CR, 69)

Criteria then, tell us something about what counts as something being something, a government's being stable, for example. Having or possessing a concept of something is being able to relate other concepts to the concept of that something. The test of whether or not I possess the concept of what it is to know something is my "ability to use the concept in conjunction with other concepts, [my] knowledge of which concepts are relevant to the one in question and which are not"(CR, 69), etc. In particular, to be in possession of the concept of what it is to know something I must also be in possession of the concept of what it is to doubt something, of what it is to be wrong (or right) about something, or what it is (merely) to believe it, and so forth.

This web of relations among concepts forms the grammar of the term. And, as Wittgenstein tells us, "It is grammar that tells what kind of object anything is" (CR, 76). Cavell remarks on this grammatical conceptual matrix, what he calls a "grammatical schematism," as follows: "To think of a word as embodying a concept is to think of the word as having a grammatical schematism . . . the schematism marks out a set of criteria on the basis of which the word is applied in all the grammatical contexts into which it fits and will be found to fit. . . . In this sense a concept is the meaning of a word. . . . To have a concept is to be able, so to speak, to keep up with the word. . . . The schematism is the frame of the world, and to exit from it should mean to exit from our mutual attunement" (CR, 77–79).

Criteria then are a part of a system of connections, connections among concepts, between concepts and things, between me and others. This web of connections is what my language establishes when I am in it, speaking it, living within it. As W.H. Auden once remarked, "a sentence uttered makes a world appear." Our talking together brings forth what Arendt calls a space of appearance (HC, 175ff). But this space is not only the space in which I appear before you, and you before me, though it is that, it is also the space in which things appear to me and to you, the space in which things become the things that they are and would not be otherwise.

This being so, it is simply false to think that my language, my lively speech-acts before some other, separates me, or abstracts me from things. My words do not form a matrix that stands between me and the world as an obstacle, or as a veil between me and things as they really are. The grammatical schematism that my words embody does not function for me as a filter or grid that confines my access to the world by reducing my world to phenomena, to appearances; words do not conceal things or turn them into noumena; they do not disconnect things from me or me from things.

Rather, and to the contrary, as Cavell has put it, my speech-acts enable me to word the world. Or as he also puts it, words are our access to things, our primary connection to the world. The grammatical matrix that our speech-acts form produces the space in which things appear to us as what they are, as what we call them.

What a thing is, I would say, is what it is called; knowing what a thing is, is knowing what to call it, knowing its name, having the criteria for the correct application of a term. Acquiring a language, learning to speak, is just learning what things are by learning what they are called. (We do not decide these names, we inherit them.) To learn what things are called is to acquire a fabric of criteria for employing the terms that name them, a kind of coming to terms with things.

Coming to terms with things, moreover, implies an ability to recognize differences as well as similarities, a sort of basic Sesame Street ability to discriminate: this thing is (or is not) like the other (thing). As distinctions get refined, which is to say, as I master the concepts that my words embody, the world takes its determinate shape. This is what it is to word the world: it is to call it into being.

Language gives us the terms, the criteria, rules, grammar, conventions, and so forth, all of which set the grammatical schematism within which we can make ourselves intelligible to one another; language sets the conditions, the rules, for what we can and cannot mean, what it makes sense and does not make sense to say; language sets the conditions in which things and others appear to us, the conditions in which we appear in the world before others.

Kant told us that we must settle for this human condition, this condition of intrinsic human limitation, otherwise we have no way to secure knowledge against the threat of skepticism (and hence no way to make room for faith). Kant's bargain with skepticism comes at the price of a loss of things, of an intimacy with the world. It has generated two sorts of response, what I have called the protests of science and romanticism against the Kantian settlement.

Both protests have dared to suggest that limits were made to be broken, to suggest a route of escape from the human condition; both have dared us to cross the Kantian line, both have offered to restore things to us: the first gives us things as dead, the other things as demonic.

But common to this whole Enlightenment mentality is the assumption of skepticism, the assumption that the conditions of being human, as set by the terms of the language we speak, constitute a limitation, our particular human limitation, the human condition of being limited. On this view, words form a kind of prison that keep us confined to mere appearances, locked out from things, others, the world. And when the human condition is thought of this way, as a prison, it naturally leads to the wish to escape it, and in particular to escape that which conditions us, that is, our language. And this wish is just the wish that defines skepticism. As Cavell remarks, "I have read Wittgenstein's portrait of skepticism, as the site in which we abdicate such responsibility as we have over our words, unleashing them from our criteria, as if toward the world—unleashing our voices from them—coming to feel that criteria limit rather than constitute our access to the world" (CH, 22).

If what Cavell implies here is right, namely, that language does not disconnect us from things, but precisely the opposite, then we are open to rethinking the human condition, to rethinking language. Such a rethinking may well lead us to see that the skeptical idea that words lock us out from the world is profoundly mistaken; such a rethinking may well lead us to see rather that words are the very means of our connection to things—to see that words provide us access to things, things as they really are, things in themselves.

But if this is right, where does this leave the wish to transcend language, the wish to escape the human condition? Where does it leave skepticism? Is it simply madness? Can it simply be dismissed? Has it been refuted? Or is the wish to transcend the human an intrinsically human wish? Is there a truth to skepticism that must be preserved?

Agreement and the Truth of Skepticism

If I understand, the common assumption of the Enlightenment mind—in all of its various manifestations, in modern science, in Hume's skepticism, in Kant's response to Hume, and in romanticism's response to Kant's bargain with skepticism, and so forth—is the idea that to be human is to be limited, confined, kept from something, call this the world, or reality, or things, or others, or God. The other side of this idea, or what this idea generates, is a desire to transcend our human confinement, a desire usually followed by a resignation to (and resentment of) the reality of the inescapableness of our human condition, even while the desire to transcend it continues to be pursued as an impossible dream, as an approachable but unreachable ideal.

Or as Cavell has put these matters, the central preoccupation of modern philosophy has been with skepticism, or more particularly, with the problem of how to answer it, or its threat. And skepticism turns out to be "an argument of the self with itself (over its finitude)" (QO, 5). And moreover, this argument comes down to being "a kind of argument of language with itself" (QO, 5).

The alternatives for the modern, as far as coming to terms with what it means to be a self in a world among others, seem to be exhausted in one or another form of a resignation to or from our human condition.

There are, however, faint voices—and growing fainter—that still call us to existential faith, Kierkegaard's voice for one, and, as I read him, Cavell's for another. Both call us to existential faith insofar as both call us to a full and unequivocal embrace of our finitude, our humanness; both tell us that the gift of our human condition is gift enough to warrant our full embrace, to warrant our gratitude for it as good and worthwhile. This means that this call to faith is not a call to a settlement; it is not a call to a resignation to (or from) our inescapable condition, it is a full and unequivocal embrace of it as not only enough for our happiness, but just what our happiness requires, warts and all.

When I say *warts and all,* I mean to point out that the call of faith is a call to embrace *all* of our human finitude, its joys and blessings, as well as its vulnerabilities, its sufferings, its losses, its griefs, its mortality. The call to faith is a call to receive the whole human package as good and worthwhile, to raise our glass to it, robustly to say to it all: *L'Chaim!* This is not a call to suppress the desire to transcend our humanness, or at least from the unsavory parts of it, as though it could be thusly broken up; it is a call to say an unequivocal "no!" to that temptation.

As has been the theme of these discussions, this rejection of the human temptation to transcend its humanness is dialectical through and through. This is perhaps clearer in Kierkegaard than in Cavell. But it is, I submit, also at work in Cavell. In particular, we find this Kierkegaardian dialectic of paradox at work in Cavell in his argument for preserving the truth of skepticism.

I find the clearest statement of Cavell's wish to preserve the truth of skepticism in the following two statements:

(1) . . . skepticism is a place, perhaps the central secular place, in which the human wish to deny the condition of human existence is expressed; and so long as the denial is essential to what we think of as the human, skepticism cannot, or must not, be denied. This makes skepticism an argument internal to the individual, or separate human creature, as it were an argument of the self with itself over its finitude. (QO, 5)

(2) The way I work this out in relation to the *Investigations* starts from the thought that we share criteria by means of which we regulate our application of concepts, means by which, in conjunction with what Wittgenstein calls grammar, we set up the shifting conditions for conversation; in particular from the thought that the explanatory power of Wittgenstein's idea depends on recognizing that criteria, for all their necessity, are open to our repudiation, or dissatisfaction (hence they lead to, as well as lead from, skepticism); that our capacity for disappointment by them is essential to the way that we posses language; . . . (If we could not repudiate them they would not be *ours,* in the way we discover them to be; they would not be our responsibility.) (QO, 5)

I will spend the rest of this section trying show how these remarks, which I take to summarize and penetrate to the heart of Cavell's defense of the truth of skepticism, suggest, and can be clarified in terms of, the Kierkegaardian dialectic of paradox.

I accept Cavell's broad definition of what skepticism is, which is, as he puts it, "the very raising of the question of knowledge in a certain form, or spirit" (CR, 46). The skeptic's problematic always takes the form, roughly, of the following question: " 'So we don't know (on the basis of the senses (or behavior) alone); then (how) do we know?' " (CR, 46).

And this brings us back to the issue of criteria. In order to employ the word (concept) *know,* I must have some idea of what will or will not count as knowing. Knowing how to use (properly, with sense) the words *I know,* means that I have some good idea of (say an ear for) when it makes sense to say "I know?" Moreover, I must be able to relate this concept to a number of other relevant ones: I must know that it is possible to *say* "I know" and not know; I must know what would cause me to have to retract my claim to know; I must know how knowing is different from believing; I must know that if I know something I cannot also, at the same time, doubt it; and so forth.

We learn these criteria as we learn to speak, although not explicitly. Criteria form a grammatical fabric of meaning, our human skin, we might say. This grammatical skin grows on us, or rather we grow within it, as it expands and contracts; it is a flexible skin that moves with us, and yet contains us, both accommodating and chastening our wills. Pictured as such, it is misleading to say that we are *taught* criteria; rather, they develop as part of our natural history; we learn them as we learn to speak; we grow up together. Indeed, we can be human only inside this nexus of meaning, only inside a world that is worded together; this is our form of life, what makes it human.

If we attend, as Wittgenstein, Austin, and Cavell do, to the ordinary, the everyday contexts of our talking together, our human condition as it is, we notice—or at least, we are able to extract, or abstract, or otherwise make explicit—some of the criteria that we (most of us, most of the time) rely on in our employment of the term *know.*

One such thing that we notice is that when we say "I know," we mean to say something different than what we mean to say when we say "I believe." If I do know, then I can't be wrong—at least and still know. And yet, I can be wrong, and if it turns out so, I must retract my claim; I must say, "I thought I knew, but I didn't know." Whereas, when I say "I believe," I can be wrong, although of course so long as I continue to believe, I think that I am not. And if it turns out that I am wrong, I stop believing, but without the humiliation of having to retract my claim to believe: it would rarely make sense to say, "I thought I believed." I really did believe, but alas falsely. This of course, makes believing a safer, more guarded claim than knowing, but also less comforting.

And why less comforting? Precisely because the claim to know is usually designed to settle something, to calm some doubt, or answer some question; and saying "I know" in the face of a doubt is a much stronger claim than simply " I believe." But this tells us something about the relation of (the concept of) knowing (and believing) to (the concept of) doubting. But let us leave believing and concentrate on knowing.

Wittgenstein has made a remarkable contribution to our understanding of what it is to know by calling attention to the fact that we, normally, use the term in a context of possible doubt: where there is no room for the possibility of, the intelligibility of, doubt, there is no room (no illocutionary space) for the claim to know. For example, in Wittgenstein's famous discussions of a person's relation to his own sensations, most famously, one's own pain, he points out, and quite uncontroversially, that it simply makes no sense to say, "I *doubt* that I am now in pain." But then he goes on to say, that *therefore* it makes no sense to say, "I *know* that I am in pain," a claim that shocked the Cartesian pants off of the philosophical community.

And why was this so shocking? Since the father of modern philosophy had declared it so, the common assumption of the philosophical community—an assumption that has by now been absorbed into modern common sense—is that whatever the criteria of knowing that we employ in our ordinary (unsophisticated, naive) lives, it is not good enough, or it is simply wrong. For Descartes, the criterion that we should employ is simply one of certainty, that is, indubitability. What comes out of this criterion shift is this: we can only know, we ought to say "I know," only when doubt about the matter is unintelligible.

Since doubt about the matter of whether we are in fact right now in pain is unintelligible, then no wonder our Cartesian sensibility was offended when Wittgenstein said we can't know it either. As Descartes would no doubt say, "If we can't know that, we can't know anything," thereby launching us on the road to skepticism.

As Wittgenstein sees it, ordinary usage shows that the term *know* is essentially connected to the term *doubt*. In my terms, the connection is paradoxically dialectical. Following the idiom for expressing this that I have adopted from Kierkegaard, I will say that the insight of Wittgenstein is that knowledge includes doubt within itself as an *annulled possibility*.

This works out as follows. For Wittgenstein, the possibility of doubt about something, its intelligibility, does not entail that one actually is in doubt about it. Just because I do not in fact doubt something doesn't mean doubt is senseless. He says:

> But that is not to say that we are in doubt because it is possible for us to *imagine* a doubt. I can easily imagine someone always doubting before he opened his front door whether an abyss does not yawn behind it, and making sure about it before he went through the door (and he might on some occasion prove to be right)—but that does not make me doubt in the same case.[10]

---

10. *Philosophical Investigations,* trans. G. E. M. Anscombe, 3d ed. (New York: Macmillan, 1998), par. 84 (hereafter PI).

> "I know . . . " may mean "I do not doubt . . . " but does not mean that the words "I doubt . . . " are *senseless*, that doubt is logically excluded. . . . One says "I know" where one can say "I believe: or "I suspect"; where one can find out. (PI, 221)

> But, if you are *certain,* isn't it that you are shutting your eyes in face of doubt?—They are shut. (PI, 224; CR, 431)

The point in all of this is that, for Wittgenstein, when I claim to know that x, I don't imply, as the Cartesian assumes, that doubt about x is not possible (intelligible). On the contrary, it is possible, or better, the claim to know x is possible only if doubt about x is also possible, although not (now) actual. When I say "I know that x" to some other, normally in the face of some doubt about it, some doubt about it in the other (perhaps even in me), I am giving assurance to the other (perhaps to myself) that x is the case: you have my word on it! Although x is dubitable, I give you my authority for saying with confidence that x is so (when of course it may not be). In saying "I know" I acknowledge the possibility of doubt about x, but at the same time, I annul that possibility—I take a leap across it, as it were, but I do not deny the dangers of the leap. Knowledge includes doubt within itself as an *annulled possibility.*

Is this the truth of skepticism, that doubt always includes within itself the (annulled) possibility of doubt? Not quite. Even though the dialectic of paradox is at work here—at this level of existence, call it—we are not yet at the point of being able to see the truth of skepticism. That truth dawns at another level, the level of criteria not existence.

Seeing that knowledge and doubt are dialectically related—that doubt is always included within knowledge as an annulled possibility—does not yet get us to Cavell's claim that there is a truth of skepticism that must be preserved. In fact, one might even read this dialectic as grounds for thinking that skepticism is simply false. Skepticism is in fact based on a denial of the inclusion of doubt within knowledge. Wittgenstein has shown that skepticism is simply wrong about this, or at least, at variance with the way we normally use the word *know.* So where does the truth of skepticism lie? What is the truth contained in Descartes's project?

The truth of Descartes's move is found in the fact that he was able to make it, that he was able to repudiate our ordinary criteria and provide his own. This Cartesian move was a repudiation of the agreements, the covenants, that constitute the intelligibility of human intercourse and define the human condition. His project was to set new criteria, criteria of his own devising. He was, as it were, attempting to improve on the ordinary, attempting to seal up all of its holes, its vulnerabilities, its anxieties, its fragility. He wanted security, certainty; he was unable to live with anxiety, with contingency; Descartes lacked faith.

But the fact that he could propose this, or wish to transcend the human condition, or propose to get outside of the language games and forms of life that define it, shows something important and essential about human beings. If we are to be fully human, we must agree to, intend to, and choose to, participate in the human conversation. Our call as humans to be human is the call to make this conversation our own, to possess our language, our knowledge, ourselves; we human beings, unlike any other creature, must decide to exist. "I am a being who to exist must say I exist, or must acknowledge my existence—claim it, stake it, enact it" (QO, 109).

The truth of skepticism is found in its reminding us that we need not so decide, that we need not be human, that we need not participate in the human condition; if the agreements, the covenants we enter, or find ourselves in, are ours, then it must be open to us to repudiate them. To the extent that our lives are bounded by agreements is the extent to which the possibility of skepticism is a permanent feature of our lives.

Two caveats are in order here. Both have to do with how we read Cavell's reading of Wittgenstein's idea of agreement, his idea that human beings agree in the language they use. We need to guard against reading *agreement* (or *decision*) too superficially, or too formally, or too conventionalistically, as though agreements were simply formal contracts, or deals, or matters of conscious choice, like the choice of which hat to wear.

The key to seeing the depth of our human agreement is shown by Wittgenstein's follow-up remark to the effect that our agreements in the language we use is not a matter of agreement in opinions but is a matter of our agreement in a form of life. Cavell sees this as saying that our human agreements range over the whole gamut of the ethnological end—the biological, the social, and the natural. Cavell's way of putting this is to say that agreement has both a horizontal (a social) dimension and a vertical (biological, or natural) dimension, or more accurately, a mutual absorption of each.

In this mutual absorption of the ethnological and the biological, it is the latter that provides the depth, that guards against superficiality. Only when we acknowledge that our agreements have a vertical dimension, only when we are able to think of *forms* of life as forms of *life,* will the dangers of a conventionalized reading of agreement be dispelled.

The biological or vertical sense of form of life recalls differences between the human and the so-called "lower" or "higher" forms of life, between, say, poking at your food, perhaps with a fork, and pawing at it, or pecking at it. . . . My idea is that this mutual absorption of the natural and the social is a consequence of Wittgenstein's envisioning of what we may as well call the human form of life. In being asked to accept this, or suffer it, as given for ourselves, we are not asked to accept, let us say, private property, but separateness; not a particular fact of power but the fact that I am a man, therefore of *this* (range or scale of) capacity for work, for pleasure, for endurance, for appeal, for command, for understanding, for wish, for will, for teaching, for suffering. . . . [E]verything that human beings do and suffer is specific to them . . . like running in place or hoping, as well as patterns we share with other life forms but whose human variations are still specific, like eating or sniffing or screaming with fear. (UA, 41–42, 44, 48)

And the second caveat is related to the first, it has to do with my place as a player in the agreements that we enter: the fact is, we are speakers long before we come to a consciousness of our moral accountability, our capacity for moral choice. We inherit our language, our criteria. Hence, I (alone, or even in consultation with others) do not simply decide that this is what will count as this or that, a chair, a pain, a case of knowing, and so forth. I do not decide or agree to criteria in this sense; I am a victim of meaning.

Yet while I am not called on to decide what counts as this or that, I am called upon to decide what I will count. As such, I am free to discount what ordinarily counts as this or that. I am, in short, accountable. This is the sense in which our agreements in criteria are subject to repudiation, this is where I come into play as more than a mere victim of meaning. "Of course people can confirm for me that the world exists and I in it, but only on condition that I let them" (UA, 52).

But is such a repudiation really possible? Can we refuse to be human? For example, is it really possible for us to refuse to speak? Well there is "speaking" and there is speaking. This is part of what Cavell is getting at in his discussion of Emerson's distinction between saying and quoting. Emerson says, "Man dares not say . . . but quotes" (QO, 113). As Cavell reckons, surely every saying is a sort of quoting in this respect: "language is an inheritance. Words are before I am; they are common" (QO, 113). But the deeper point is that there is always a question when we speak or when we are spoken to: "Is she (am I) saying these words, does she (do I) own them or possess them, is she (am I) speaking as herself (myself), or is she (am I) quoting them, reciting a line as if from a play written by someone other than herself (myself). This question, Cavell says, comes to "the same question as the question of whether I do or do not exist as a human being"(QO, 113).

We can only *possess,* or *own* our criteria, our language, ourselves, if we have criteria of what counts as possessing or owning something, if we know what it is to possess, to own, something. And so we encounter the connection of possession and ownership with loss, or the possibility, or threat of, loss. The fact is, it makes sense (to say) that something is ours only if, and to the extent that, we are vulnerable to its loss, that we can in some way be separated from it. (It is this very point that Kierkegaard makes so much of: self-possession, for him, implies the possibility of not being a self; it is just this possibility that faith annuls, and thus dialectically presupposes.) As Cavell remarks, "The criteria Wittgenstein appeals to . . . are always 'ours,' the 'group' which forms his 'authority' is always, apparently, the human group as such, the human being generally. When I voice them, I do so, or take myself to do so, as a member of that group, a representative human. . . . there is a background of pervasive and systematic agreements among us. . . . The 'agreement' we act upon he calls 'agreement in judgments,' and he speaks of our ability to use language a depending upon agreement in 'forms of life' " (CR, 18, 30).

Yet when we realize that our human life, human language, are grounded in agreements, call these covenants, then we immediately see what our relation is to our own humanness: as a matter of consent, it must also be a relation of possible repudiation.

Cavell comes back again and again to the notion of possession, of owning, in order to show the intelligibility of repudiation, the intelligibility of the skeptical wish to transcend what is taken as the limits of our language, the confinement of our criteria, of our human condition. I assemble some of his comments as follows:

> [D]iction, is what puts us in bonds, that with each word we utter we emit stipulations, agreements we do not know and do not want to know we have entered, agreements we were always in, that were in effect before our participation in them. Our relation to our language—to the fact that we are subject to expression and comprehension, victims of meaning—is accordingly, a key to our sense of our distance from our lives, of our sense of the alien, of ourselves as alien to ourselves, thus alienated. (QR, 40)

"They (my eyes) are shut", as a resolution, or confession, says that one can, for one's part, live in the face of doubt.—But doesn't everyone, everyday?—It is something different to live *without* doubt, without so to speak the *threat* of skepticism. To live in the face of doubt, eyes happily shut, would be to fall in love with the world. For if there is a correct blindness, only love has it. (CR, 431)

But in *Walden* the proof that what you have found you have made your own, your home, is that you are free to leave it. (QO, 175)

The issue of consent becomes the issue of whether the voice I lend in recognizing a society as mine, as speaking for me, is my voice, my own.[11]

What justifies what I do and say is, I feel like saying, *me*—the fact that I can respond to an indefinite ranges of responses of the other, and that the other, for my spade not to be stopped, must respond to me. . . . The requirement of purity imposed by philosophy now looks like a wish to leave *me* out, I mean each of us, the self, with its arbitrary needs and unruly desires. (CH, 77)

When we see the centrality of agreement and hence the possibility of the repudiation of these agreements in our lives, we begin to see just how deeply the issue of our being human is a matter of freedom and hence a matter of responsibility. We would not be human beings if we could not choose not to be; we would not be human if we could not take the responsibility for being. We *can,* it is essential to our human being that we can, live as angels (gods) or as beasts; we can refuse to participate in the human conversation, refuse to be human, live aesthetically, or ethically, or in religious resignation. It is precisely these possibilities that the choice to live a human existence excludes and thus presupposes. It is this refusal that reminds us of our responsibility of deciding.

And there is proof enough that we do have the power of repudiating our own humanity; this repudiation is certainly more than just a human possibility. We do not need more proof than we already have of our own inhuman possibilities, our own potential for the monstrous, aesthetic detachment and

---

11. *Conditions Handsome and Unhandsome: The Constitution of Emersonian Perfectionism* (Chicago: University of Chicago Press, 1990), 27 (hereafter CH).

indifference, the demonic: "Users of language, humans are creatures of language, exist only from it, as equally it exists only from us. If one is perverse so is the other. If we cannot speak . . . we are inhuman. If the responsibility for speaking is suffocating, you might think of enacting a deed so horrible that speech seems impossible; you might choose to become a monster" (QO, 140). Madness, the inhuman, angelism and/or beastialism, are ever-present, inexpungable possibilities *within* human existence; and unfortunately too often historical actualities. The extent to which we human beings can succeed at being fully human is just the extent to which these possibilities can be faced and yet annulled.

We come then to the truth of philosophical skepticism, the truth about ourselves, we might say, the truth of the human condition. This truth is that our knowledge (our life together) is ours, ours to live, ours to repudiate. Our knowledge is grounded in nothing more and nothing less than the authority and consent that we as human beings grant it. The truth of skepticism whispers into our ears the truth that every claim we make to know makes sense only from within a context of agreement, a context that is as such always subject to refusal or repudiation. Skepticism teaches us about contingency, about choice, about responsibility, about human fragility.

As such, skepticism plays, I suggest, a similar role in the pursuit of knowledge that despair plays for Kierkegaard in faith. Both despair and skepticism teach us about human possibilities, about historical contingencies, about anxiety, about human vulnerability, about human fragility, but in a dialectical sense.

Despair is an annulled possibility within faith. Despair tells us of the great gulf between who we are and who we pretend we are; it tells us that we most often are not willing to be, or will not to be, the self that we really are; it tells us that if we are to come to ourselves in faith, we must take the risk, take the leap of faith. Despair is therefore a dialectical element within faith in that it provides the abyss over which faith must leap.

Philosophical skepticism operates within a similar dialectic. Skepticism opens a fault, a crevasse, that looms before the would-be knower, an abyss between the human and the inhuman. It warns us of the fact that our humanness is fraught with vulnerability, doubt, fragility, contingency, and informs the knower of the risk of joining the human conversation. And it tempts us with the possibility of finding our lives elsewhere; it reminds us of the fact it is in our power to refuse to be a human being.

Claims of knowledge bridge the abyss of skepticism, as much as faith bridges the abyss of despair, not by denying skepticism or despair their place, but by annulling, and thus acknowledging them as ever-present human possibilities. Neither knowledge nor faith presume to heal the rift or erase the threat posed by skepticism and despair—they presuppose them. As such, knowledge dialectically takes up skepticism within itself (as faith takes up despair within itself) as an annulled possibility.

And this finally is the truth of skepticism: in awakening us to the temptation to transcend the human, it also, like despair, awakens us to our humanness, to the fact that it is *ours*. Paradoxically, skepticism, like despair, in tempting us to transcend it, invites us to embrace our finitude, all of it; it invites us to see it as world enough for our human happiness. In perhaps the most ironic of human ironies, skepticism, like despair, invites us to fall in love with the world.

MARRIAGE AS REMARRIAGE

In his more recent writings, Stanley Cavell has turned his attention to film, or rather to the philosophical reading of film. The first venture in this direction was *The World Viewed: Reflections on the Ontology of Film.*[1] This was followed ten years later by *Pursuits of Happiness: The Hollywood Comedy of Remarriage* (1981). And most recently, the publication of his *Contesting Tears: The Hollywood Melodrama of the Unknown Woman* (1996).[2]

1. *The World Viewed: Reflections on the Ontology of Film* (Cambridge: Harvard University Press, 1979).

2. *Contesting Tears: The Hollywood Melodrama of the Unknown Woman* (Chicago: University of Chicago Press, 1996). I was not aware of the publication of *Contesting Tears* until after the completion of this book, but let me comment briefly on it. In the melodrama of the unknown woman, the story line is of the woman who is searching for a story, or a right to tell her story, that is, the woman's search for her own particular feminine mode of experience; and a man's desire to know what this is, and his not wanting to know (as though knowing might spoil the mystery of the feminine).

The genre of the melodrama is a companion to the genre of the remarriage comedies in the sense that the former is derived from the latter. Here the particular derivation is via negation, or dialectic: the melodramas negate the central features of the remarriage comedies. For example, the father (or husband) or older man is not on the side of the woman; and the mother of the woman is always present—in one way or another; and the woman is always shown as a mother and her relation to a child is explicit; and the past is thought of differently: in remarriage, it is something fun, something shared; in the melodramas, it is thought of as mysterious, forbidden, etc. The chief negation, however, is the negation of marriage itself.

Both genera present the woman as wanting a marriage of shared equality, mutual education, transfiguration, playfulness, etc. Neither could have a marriage of irritation, condescension, silence, etc. It is just that in the melodramas, the woman chooses solitude and unknowness to such a failed farce of a marriage. This reminds us again of Nora in Ibsen's *A Doll's House,* who refuses to stay one minute longer in that marriage which is no real marriage. This is the melodramatic refusal of marriage.

Cavell's historical premise, correct I think, is that modern American popular film stands to modern American culture as Shakespearean drama stood to Elizabethan England, as tragedy stood to the golden age of the Greeks. His philosophical premise is that popular film is, for us Americans, *our* medium, *our* literature, *our* unique way of publicly confronting, addressing, solving, or in some way dealing with the philosophical problems that are part of the common sense of our culture.

In American culture, one popular access to these philosophical problems has been via stories of marriage and remarriage. (Shakespeare had also done this in, e.g., *The Taming of the Shrew.*) In his *Pursuits of Happiness,* Cavell isolates a genre of films he calls the Hollywood comedy of remarriage, a genre of some seven talkies from the thirties and forties.[3] The central theme of these films is the issue of the legitimacy of marriage, a question raised by the fact of, or at least the threat of, divorce.[4] As Cavell puts it, "If we express

---

In the melodramas, the education of the woman is still at issue. But unlike the comedies of remarriage the man in the melodramas is out to educate her to her own mystery and distance from him. He wants to show her this but he doesn't like it anymore than she does—he resents it, he resents her! He plants the seed: perhaps she can never be known; perhaps we are separated beyond recognition; he raises the question of madness, or at least of despair. Well, in some sense we are isolated, we are alone. Moreover, if this distance is not fully realized, marriage is not possible. That is, this awareness of our not being together, our separateness, our isolation, is the condition of being together, that is, a condition of marriage. Marriage requires crossing an enormous gap; the melodramas represent this gap as uncrossable—they are thus tragic; the woman lacks the resources of faith to cross the gap; the man lacks the resources as well. But we cannot fault these women for a lack of faith only, for the men these women are with are not worthy of their faith. While it may be true that it is not good that man/woman should be alone, the fact is, many are, and this is reason enough for tears.

The tears of the melodramas contest the laughs of the comedies of remarriage. Without this companion genre of the melodrama of the unknown woman, we might get the impression from the comedies of remarriage that every pursuit of happiness, of a happy marriage, will be successful. But finding a happy marriage is largely, but certainly not completely, a matter of luck. We are lucky if we find it and have the resources of faith to embrace it. Many are not so lucky. But even the unlucky, who decide not to marry rather than to be in an unhappy marriage, who decide to live alone, need not abandon the ideal, though, in bitterness, of course, some do. The women of the melodramas, however, continue to value marriage, even if they finally are forced to decide against it, as they do. In so deciding, these women do find integrity. This integrity is found in not being willing to settle for an unhappy marriage just to fulfill the romantic fantasy of marriage. And in this, they find a measure of happiness. And for them, as it is for me, this is ample reason for a smile through the tears. (See also Joseph H. Smith and William Kerrigan, eds., *Images in Our Souls: Cavell, Psychoanalysis, and Cinema* (Baltimore: John Hopkins University Press, 1987).

3. These films include *It Happened One Night* (Frank Capra, 1934), *The Awful Truth* (Leo McCarey, 1937), *Bringing Up Baby* (Howard Hawks, 1938), *The Philadelphia Story* (George Cukor, 1940), *His Girl Friday* (Howard Hawks, 1940), *The Lady Eve* (Preston Sturges, 1941), and *Adam's Rib* (George Cukor, 1949).

4. Clearly the issue of marriage/divorce is of great importance to Kierkegaard. The break of his engagement to marry Regina (a kind of premarital divorce) was an ever-present preoccupation in

the condition of marriage as one in which first a kinship is to be recognized and then an affinity established, we have a possible explanation for a genre of romance taking the form of a narrative of remarriage: a legitimate marriage requires that the pair is free to marry, that there is no impediment between them; but this freedom is announced in these film comedies in the concept of divorce" (PH, 102–3).

The themes of marriage, divorce, and remarriage ramify in multiple directions. The following sorts of issues come up, perhaps couldn't help but come up in any full treatment of marriage: the issue of what it means to be free to marry, or the issue of why a legitimate marriage requires freedom, the issue of what it means to be a human being, the issue of what human happiness consists in, the issues of loss and vulnerability, the fragility of human finitude, the human wish for invulnerability and a godlike immunity from human suffering, the adult divorce from childhood and innocence and the possibility of a mature remarriage to both, the issue of the nature of the bonds that are established in conversation and covenant, both private and public, the conflict between love and ethics, and the issues of politics and power.

Before we turn to Cavell's discussion of the Hollywood comedies of remarriage, or more precisely, to my reading of these films and my reading of Cavell's discussion of them, a reading guided by the logic of the dialectic of paradox, I must address an issue that has certainly come to mind. Given Kierkegaard's idea that the temptation to live within the aesthetic modality is one form—indeed, a particularly intense temptation within the modern world—of the general human temptation to refuse our humanness, that is, to refuse our ordinary existence in the world among others, that is, to refuse to

---

his life. In his writings, especially in *Either/Or II,* marriage is not only the focus of Judge William's attacks on the despair of the aesthetic life, it is the very center of his defense of ethical existence. In his defense of marriage as the epitome of the ethical life, Judge William shows how the covenant of marriage involves a duty. It requires of the husband and wife a mutual choice and responsibility of and to one another—precisely what is needed to break the strangle-hold of aesthetic indifference. But for William, once this ethical choice is made, there is no going back, or the only thing to go back to is the despair of aesthetic indifference. While divorce may be a conceptual possibility for the Judge, it is no more of an existential possibility for him than indifference. The irony of this, however, is that the Judge is as much trapped by the burden of freedom and responsibility as the aesthete is by his flight from it. The lesson here is that an ethical existence needs a further qualification. In terms of marriage, this qualification is the existential possibility of divorce. Only when we are existentially aware of the possibility that every choice that we make in time can be repudiated at some future time does the choice become fully one's own; only then do I realize the necessity of continually choosing and hence of the continual possibility of repudiating that choice. It is Abraham, not William, who embodies this religious qualification of ethical existence; Kierkegaard sometimes calls this qualification repetition. In any case, I cannot make it OK with myself to believe that when Kierkegaard remarked, "Had I had faith I should have remained with Regina," he was wishing he had entered into a relation with her like that of Judge William to his nameless wife.

heed the existential call freely to embrace our humanness, then what place can aesthetics have within the concerns of the existential? That is, if the call to be human is the call to resist the temptation (thereby acknowledging it) to escape, or flee from, or otherwise refuse, the human, then how can attention to cinema (art, aesthetics) but work against the human project of becoming (fully, or more fully) human? Or more pointedly, what can attention to cinema, to the art of film—it is an aesthetic medium after all—tell us about the human call to resist the temptation to live aesthetically? Or what this all comes to: what can attention to the aesthetic medium of film tell us about the existential call to embrace our humanness, when movie watching seems to be itself a form of aesthetic escape?[5]

Is moviegoing what it seems to be, on the face of it anyway, that is, a form of aesthetic escape from the world? It certainly is at one obvious level: to go to the movies is to leave the light of the daily world and enter a dark (Platonic?) cave; it is to trade the reality of ordinary life for a couple of hours of fantasy; it is to rest from the demands of life; it is re-creation! And on this most obvious level, the transition from being in "the real world" to being in "the movie world" is marked by the adjustment our eyes must make upon going in and upon coming out. If moviegoing is inherently an aesthetic flight, an aesthetic hovering, a kind of detachment in the dark, a looking in on "reality" without being seen, and so forth, what can it tell us about existence in the world (outside)?

As we might put this question, what does art have to do with life? Clearly we can imagine two answers right off the bat: art is the model for life, and the opposite, life is the source of art and that which art seeks to enrich. To live aesthetically, that is, to live within the aesthetic mode, in Kierkegaard's sense, is to take the first option, to live existentially (in faith) is to take the second.

If one thinks that art is the model of life, that living life is a matter of watching it, a matter of remaining aloof from it, a matter of protecting oneself from it, a matter of being in the audience as in a movie theater, and thus fundamentally a matter of escape, then this is to see a ticket into the movies as a ticket out of existence. If living is like appreciating a work of art, or if the aim of life is to make it into a work of art, then art and existence are mortal enemies. To aim at transforming life into art is to live aesthetically, and to live aesthetically, as I have argued, is not to live a human life, but to attempt to transcend such a life.

---

5. I think here of Binx Boling, a paradigmatic aesthetic character in the explicitly Kierkegaardian novel of Walker Percy entitled *The Moviegoer.*

But moviegoing may not be this. It could be that art can teach us something about life, that this is what its aim is, or ought to be. This would be art expressing life rather than life trying to express itself as art. What an enormous difference! Here moviegoing could be seen not as providing us instructions on how to escape from life, but as providing us with expressions of life that help us to live more fully. On this interpretation, art and life are not enemies, but inalienable allies. The embrace of the human could not very well fail to embrace art; aesthetics is so deeply a part of the human. But even though aesthetics can be put to good existential use, it does not follow that existential faith simply incorporates within itself the aesthetic modality of existence. The matter is more dialectical than this.

The difference I am trying to make out between the aesthetic and the existential interpretations of the art/life relation can easily be missed. That is, the difference between the aesthetic aim of transforming life into art and the aim of putting art to good existential use in enriching our lives can easily be confused. In my opinion this very confusion lies at the center of a recent book by Sylvia Walsh on Kierkegaard, *Living Poetically: Kierkegaard's Existential Aesthetics.*[6]

As I read her, Sylvia Walsh's idea of *existential aesthetics* illustrates how easy it is to confuse the aesthetic and the existential pictures of the art/life relation. Walsh makes this mistake by conflating two independent and opposing theses about the art/life relation. In fact, the two theses are so interwoven in the text of Walsh's book that we are not sure when she is arguing for one and when she is arguing for the other. And I suspect that she thinks that to argue for one is just to argue for the other, or at least, that the two are simply two sides of the same coin, and hence that to accept one is to accept the other.

(Before I say what these two theses are, let me say that the issue that I see between Walsh and me here does not turn on which of us has the more accurate interpretation of Kierkegaard. That is, I am prepared to admit that her reading of Kierkegaard is closer and more accurate than mine. But this may just mean that Kierkegaard himself was confused on this issue, or at least that he was wrestling with it. But let me proceed.)

The two theses that I think Walsh confuses can be stated very simply:

THESIS 1: Aesthetics can be put to good existential use.

THESIS 2: The existential way of life incorporates, via a transubstantiation, the fundamental elements of the aesthetic way of life.

---

6. Sylvia Walsh, *Living Poetically: Kierkegaard's Existential Aesthetics* (University Park: Pennsylvania State University Press, 1994) (hereafter LP).

Walsh argues very persuasively and quite plausibly for thesis 1. Or what comes to the same thing, she argues well that the term *existential aesthetics* is an apt characterization of Kierkegaard's philosophical project, that is, his project of writing, producing works of art, we might say, in the service of existence. As I like to put this, she argues that aesthetics can be put to good existential use. As a writer, as a poet/artist, in his writings, pseudonymous and otherwise, Kierkegaard was trying to communicate indirectly to his readers through the use of poetic representation and imaginative projection what it means to exist: he was putting aesthetics, that is, art, to good existential use; he was using art to express life. As Walsh says, "the poetic in the forms of imagination and possibility is regarded as an essential capacity for the *projection and portrayal* of ethical-religious ideals" (LP, 3); and further, she says that the religious poet, "sees his task as providing an existential, rather than a purely poetic, portrayal of the Christian ideal" (LP, 240). So far, so good: life need not exclude art, how could it?

But, unfortunately as I see it, Walsh is not content to stop here. She also argues simultaneously for another thesis, and without in fact acknowledging that it is a separate thesis, namely, that the term *existential aesthetics* is an apt characterization of a happy human life. Here the idea is that the existential way of life, to be complete, must include within itself some of the elements of the aesthetic way of life, albeit as inwardly transformed and transubstantiated. To incorporate these transubstantiated elements of the aesthetic life into the existential life, Walsh argues, is what it means to live poetically. I quote: "For it is not the fashioning of a work of art as such but a particular way of orienting ourselves to life that constitutes the essential condition for living poetically" (LP, 60).

The problem with the second thesis is that it embraces a contradictory picture of the relation between the aesthetic way of life and the existential way of life, when, as I shall elaborate presently, all that we need is to see the relation as paradoxical. That is, if the term *existential aesthetics* is meant to express the sense in which the aesthetic way of life is incorporated into the existential way of life, it is simply an oxymoron. I take myself here to be making a grammatical remark.

As I understand the grammar of the terms, the defining element of the aesthetic way of life is captured in something like disengagement, or flight, or refusal. The aesthete employs clever techniques, including, the arts, to flee from actuality, from time, history, the concrete, and so forth; the aesthete lives in possibility by merely flirting with actuality, never embracing it. By contrast, the defining element of the existential way of life is the embrace of actuality, the choice of one's own actuality before God and neighbor. With these definitions intact, it is difficult to see how the aesthetic way of life can be incorporated, however inwardly transformed it may be, whatever this means, into the existential way of life: they simply move in opposite directions. Walsh acknowledges this difference quoting Kierkegaard as follows: "To be a [religious] poet means that one has 'one's personal life, one's actuality, in categories completely different from those of one's poetic productions' " (LP, 240).

Or as I might put this all summarily: Walsh's first thesis is true and important, helping us to come to terms with the problematic of Kierkegaardian authorship, the problem of how the existential can find expression, however indirectly, in aesthetics; the second thesis is distinct from the first and difficult to make out, especially given the idea that the aesthetic way of life is definitively characterized as a flight from actuality, while the existential way of life is definitively characterized as an embrace of actuality. As I understand, the religious poet does not live poetically, she lives; and at the same time she is free to represent, to project, to portray, in and through her poetic productions, the existential life-possibility, the possibility of embracing actuality, one's own actuality, as one's own. But this again would be incorporating aesthetics, not the aesthetical modality, within existential faith.

Certainly Walsh would agree with me that *existential aesthetics* is an oxymoron if the term *aesthetics* is restricted to characterizing the romantic's flight from actuality and into possibility. (And here I remark parenthetically that the aesthetic flight from actuality takes more forms than romanticism. I see scientific rationalism, for example, as a similar flight. But this is another matter.) The question is whether Walsh can make out another sense of the term *aesthetic* such as to make plausible her claim that the existential choice of actuality incorporates into itself the aesthetic flight from actuality. I do not think that she has made this case, or that it can be made. It does not ring true to my ears to think of the person of faith as a transubstantiated aesthete.

Nevertheless, I am in firm agreement with Walsh in her critique of romanticism. I agree with her that romanticism is an excellent example of how aesthetics embraced as a way of life is most sharply contrasted with the existential way of life. I also agree that romanticism tends to put aesthetics to bad existential use. It does this insofar as it uses art to glorify, or otherwise recommend, an aesthetic flight from actuality.

But this is not to say that I am not sympathetic to Walsh's idea that there is a relation of inclusion between the aesthetic and the existential ways of life. But her terms for inclusion are terms such as incorporation and transubstantiation, terms that seem to me suspect. Would such an existentially transubstantiated aesthetic way of life still carry, as she seems to think, something of the aesthetic modality of existence? A kind of lingering hint of flight or escape from the human? I don't think this works. Such a hint might well keep the existential embrace of the human at bay. The existential embrace of the human refuses the aesthetic flight from it, it does not incorporate it. Living poetically is a human possibility, but it is an aesthetic possibility: it is a refusal to live existentially in faith, it is a refusal to live.

Let me then offer an alternative, what I would call a more dialectical, more paradoxical, alternative. Suppose we say that the aesthetic way of life is included within the existential in the same way that despair is included within faith, namely, as dialectically excluded. On this logic—the logic of paradox—the possibility of detachment from actuality, the possibility of living poetically is absolutely necessary for living existentially. And this is so since without the possibility of disengagement from actuality, there is no logical space, as it were, for the free embrace of it. The aesthetic mode of life, as a life-possibility, is necessary for the choice of the existential mode of existence, just as the power to do otherwise is necessary to the freedom to do anything whatsoever.

But this dialectical move would take us in a different direction than Walsh wants to go. For her, the inclusion of aesthetics within the existential is a matter of incorporation via transubstantiation; for me, the inclusion of aesthetics within the existential is a matter of dialectical inclusion/exclusion. As I see it, the existential choice of actuality makes no sense apart from the possibility of an aesthetic flight from it—and so the existential includes the aesthetic. But the existential choice is a rejection of just that aesthetic possibility—and so the inclusion of the aesthetic within the existential comes finally to a paradoxical exclusion of it.

I shall read Cavell's treatment of film in the light of this logic of paradox. Film can be put to good existential use, if it aims to tell us something about living well, perhaps something that we have not seen, or fully seen. Film can often present us with just those nuances of life that we might miss in the living of it; and it can present to us, in a drama that is bigger than life, life-possibilities, life-conflicts, hypothetical resolutions, and so forth that can be instructive as we actually live. This is film, the art of film, being put to existential good use.

But just as clearly, film, like all art, can be put to bad existential use. It can encourage us to flee from existence; it can glorify the human dream of escaping from our human existence. But perhaps the most existentially pernicious use of film is to think that it is merely a source of our entertainment, that it is a distraction from existence, a ticket to escape from what is serious and real in life.

But not so with the films that Cavell isolates and studies as the Hollywood comedies of remarriage. These films, if viewed in the right way, are intended to be put to good existential use. They can tell us, are meant to tell us, something about life. But before we can turn to these films, to Cavell's treatment of them, there are some other preliminary matters to take care of. We need to set the stage for the treatment of marriage presented in these films by making the pitch for marriage that Cavell makes, namely, that marriage is a uniquely human form of being together.

Marriage as Conversation

Following John Milton, Cavell thinks that every real marriage is a real conversation. I agree. This way of putting this connection implies that not everything that goes for conversation is a real conversation and that not everything that goes for marriage is a real marriage. And moreover, the logic of this connection has it that while the presence of a real conversation is a necessary condition for the presence of a real marriage, a real conversation is not a sufficient condition for a real marriage: not every real conversation, of course, is a real marriage.

But what does it mean to call a real marriage a real conversation? Cavell quotes Milton as follows:

> And what [God's] chief end was of creating woman to be joined with man, his own instituting words declare, and are infallible to inform us what is marriage and what is no marriage, unless we can think them set there to no purpose: "It is not good," saith he, "that man should be alone. I will make a helpmeet for him" (Genesis 2:18). From which words so plain, less cannot be concluded, nor is by any learned interpreter, than that in God's intention *a meet and happy conversation* is the chiefest and noblest end of marriage, for we find here no expression so necessarily implying carnal knowledge as this prevention of loneliness to the mind and spirit of man. (PH, 87, italics added)

As I extrapolate from this quote and Cavell's approval of it, the claim is not simply that a real marriage is the only form of conversation that can keep human beings from being alone. Rather, Milton's affirmation of marriage as

God's remedy for man's aloneness, is grounded in a deeper affirmation, namely, the affirmation of real conversation in general.

As I would put Milton's insight: finding and entering into a meet and happy conversation is the chiefest and noblest (I would say, the only) way that is available to human beings to prevent or cure the agony and despair of loneliness. Marriage, therefore, although central to our human existence, is just one, though a centrally important one, among other kinds of conversation that are open to us. A real marriage can certainly serve to prevent or to cure human loneliness, but it is not the only such cure or prevention. Conversation, however, of some sort, is the only prevention, the only cure.

Milton's background assumption here, I speculate, is that being alone is the most horrible prospect that a human being can face. Perhaps he would even call this, as I certainly would, the dreadful prospect of becoming inhuman. Or to put it differently, in his recognition of the horror of loneliness, of the inhumanness of aloneness, this poet of paradise, of paradise lost, seems also to know something about hell: that the deepest human hell is the state of being alone.

On this point, Cavell agrees with Milton, and I with both, despite the obvious fact that in certain moments we all may be tempted to think that Sartre is right after all, that hell is not being alone, but the opposite, that is, being with others. In moments, it certainly does seem that hell is other people and that being alone, getting away from it all, is the chiefest and noblest of human possibilities.

Nevertheless, in our saner moments, I venture to say, we know quite well that the romantic dream of "paradise regained" defined as being alone— the dream say of being alone on an island like Robinson Crusoe, or alone in Eden, as Adam was, before God created his helpmeet—is ultimately the nightmare, the mute-brute hell, of being a nonbrute condemned to bearing relations only to the brutes. While Crusoe could talk to the animals, and Adam could name them, the animals couldn't talk back; and if Wittgenstein is right, even if they could, we couldn't understand them. The fact is, both men were alone! What a relief, what a giant leap out of this "paradise/hell" of loneliness when Friday appeared for Crusoe and Eve for Adam.

And certainly there are obvious differences here between the case of Crusoe and that of Adam. One way to put this difference is to say that the conversation of friendship is essentially different from the conversation of marriage. I suppose in every marriage worth its salt, the pair would consider themselves friends, the best of friends; but, certainly, even the best of friends would not think that their friendship amounted to a marriage. For one thing, marriage is an institution, a legal bond, friendship is not; for another, marriage, unlike friendship is entered into on a particular date and subsequently celebrated. But the central difference seems to hinge on the presence or absence of sexual intimacy. Marriage, unlike friendship, therefore, is a conversation that involves an essential sexual component.

With this said, I hope it is clear that my agreement with Milton and Cavell in thinking of marriage as conversation does not commit any of us to the thought that sex has nothing essentially to do with marriage, that a real marriage is *only* a matter of achieving a meet and happy exchange of words. How could it be just this?

Or another way of putting this point is to say that even though marriage carries within itself an essential sexual component, that component itself—call it sexual intercourse—is qualified by its place, its being placed, within the larger conversation that the marriage constitutes, the larger sense in which marriage just is intercourse.

In marriage, private sexual intercourse is qualified (legitimated) by the public intercourse of the marriage rite. That is, the physical bond that sexual intercourse effects in private is qualified in marriage by a (higher?) bond effected by the public exchange of words, words of promise, of fidelity, of covenant, of law. This bond is public because it is effected before witnesses, because it is a matter of the public record, because it is a legal document, a social contract, and because its can be dissolved only by a public decree.

But I digress. Let us return to the issue before us.

If being alone is hell, or despair, or the sickness unto death, then being together, if not paradise, must be at least an essential element in the recovery from, or the prevention of, this sickness and suffering. The human condition, being what it is, that is, a condition, a speaking together, carries in itself the idea that being together is necessary for the achievement of human well-being, call this the achievement of human happiness. And this is so, I aver, despite what current pop psychology might tell us, that is, that we must find happiness within ourselves before we can find it with others.

But I do not say that the idea of individual happiness makes no sense. Rather, coming to my individual happiness (or as I have been putting it, following Kierkegaard, coming to exist in existential faith, that is, coming freely to embrace with gratitude my own existence as worth living, as good, that is, coming to be human) is not something that I come into, or can come into, alone. If it, as the term *happiness* suggests, befalls me, it does so in the midst of others, and necessarily so. My individual happiness is essentially tied up with my being present to and in the presence of others.

But let me put the point more paradoxically. I can be (an) I, find my individual happiness, only in relation to another I who I am not, that is, (a) you. Since coming to myself in this relation, that is, since coming to exist before some other in faith, since coming freely to embrace my self, the self I already am, since coming into my own individual happiness, is possible only in relation to an other, my own individual happiness depends on my capacity to, my willingness to, acknowledge and embrace the other and myself as separate, as individuals.

The paradox comes to this: our acknowledgment of our separateness from each other is the condition of the possibility of our uniquely human form of being together. Since our human happiness depends on our finding a way of avoiding being alone, we can find our individual happiness only insofar as we, as individuals, enter into some form of being together. Our uniquely human form of individual happiness, as a form of connection, as a form of being together, is predicated on our prior acknowledgment of our separateness from one another, on our acknowledgment that in some sense we are in fact not together. Adam was alone before he was with Eve.

Let me now qualify this logic of paradox in terms of choice. I will say that the hell of being alone is something that we human beings have the capacity to condemn ourselves to, or not. And strangely enough, we sometimes actually choose the hell of being alone, perhaps mistaking it for paradise. But my point is that having this capacity to choose to be alone, having the power to choose to block others out, to withdraw into oneself, and so forth, is an essential element of our humanness. It is essential insofar as having this capacity to choose to be alone is a prerequisite to being able to choose not to be alone, in being able to choose to embrace the other: I can only say "yes" to the other if I can say "no." On this logic of paradox, then, my capacity to choose to be alone is an indispensable element in my capacity for being together, and hence an indispensable element in my happiness.

To reiterate: my recognition of my capacity to choose to be alone acknowledges my separateness from you and you from me, that is, my separateness, and yours. Insofar then as I choose to enter into a connection with an other in marriage, in friendship, in political covenants, etc., I must refuse the real possibility open to me of living in separation, of being alone. I must say "no" to this possibility. Yet in existentially annulling this possibility, I acknowledge its reality, presuppose it, even testify to it. If human happiness is found in being together, it is also found, and necessarily and paradoxically so, in the shadow of the possibility of being alone. Heaven and hell, as well as being exclusive, are dialectically connected.

But what is unique about our human form of being together? Quite simply the answer to this is that we human beings form our uniquely human connections to one another in and through our speaking together.

I recognize, of course, that coming to be a speaker, an I, entails that I recognize my separateness from others, that I acknowledge that there is a wedge between me and you, between speaker and hearer. Hence, coming to be a speaker brings with it the possibility of aloneness, that possibility that threatens us so ultimately, so profoundly.

But even though becoming a speaker brings its own implicit threat, it also brings promise. The promise of speech, of our capacity to speak, is found in the resources it offers for establishing connections. Intrinsic to speaking are its syntactical and semantic powers, powers that can be used to establish connections between us, connections that bind us to one another in a uniquely human way. Words tie us together in agreements, agreements that form our basic human form of life. Agreeing in the words we use, we are able to establish further agreements, political covenants, personal promises, marriages, and so forth. For human beings, words are our life.

The promise of speech, therefore, is found in its power to bring us together, and hence in its power for preventing and curing aloneness. And if the finding of human happiness entails the finding of a way of preventing or curing our aloneness, that is, finding a way of being together, then the finding of human happiness seems inexorably tied to finding a way of participating in what we may call the ongoing human conversation.

And again there are various ways to participate. As I understand it, one can enter the human conversation, via politics and/or friendship, via teaching and learning, via cultural and religious exchanges, foreign and domestic relations, and even via commerce, public and private. It even makes sense to think of war and violence in terms of conversation, as something like the result of its breakdown.

Choosing to participate in the human conversation in this way or that is not therefore the most radical human choice. That is, if human existence is in its essence an ongoing conversation, the most profound human choice, the choice to be or not to be (a human being), is just the choice of whether to be or not to be a participant in this conversation—the choice of being alone or being together.

As I have been putting it, speaking together is essentially connected to being human insofar as being human is essentially a matter of being connected. If it is conversation that connects us to one another, then outside of it we are not completely human, we are alone—and it is not good than man should be alone.

Now clearly, Austin and Wittgenstein have shown us that there are different modes of speaking together (different modalities of human existence?). For example, we can speak felicitously or not, jokingly or seriously, ironically or in earnest. Such a personal backing to our speech-acts is an essential element in the fabric of making sense to one another, but not the only one. For example, what we say (and mean) depends on the circumstances, uptake, grammar, syntax, and so forth.

As Kierkegaard might put this point, there are various modes of saying, aesthetic, ethical, religious, and variations on each one of these. Yet for Kierkegaard, and I think also for Austin, Wittgenstein, and Cavell, and certainly for me, there exists a primary mode of discourse (call this our primary mode of making real connections with one another) on which other modes of speaking trade and depend for their meaning—a kind of ground, or at least bedrock in the Wittgensteinian stream.[7]

But this is a tricky point to make. I certainly do not mean to say that, for example, factual statements are more bedrock than mythological, or evaluative, or religious, statements; or even that statements are more basic than imperatives, or vice versa. What I have in mind here is something much different. So I shall just say it: for me, the ground of all of our speaking together, the ground of our mutual connection, is *ordinary language*. And I think this is also true for Cavell (and Wittgenstein and Austin) and this is what makes him (and each of them) a self-confessed ordinary language philosopher.[8]

By *ordinary language* I mean simply those forms of discourse that fill our daily lives, that are not specialized, as it were—forms of discourse open to anyone who can speak the language, forms of discourse that we both contribute to the making of and inherit. Ordinary language is a shifting yet amazingly stable set of shared, and thus public, linguistic conventions for doing all sorts of things—perhaps all of those things that are distinctively human. Via these conventions we sort out and refer to the kinds of things and activities there are in the world. But more importantly, by virtue of these shared lin-

---

7. Ludwig Wittgenstein, *On Certainty,* ed. G. E. M. Anscombe and G. H. Von Wright, trans. Denis Paul and G. E. M. Anscombe (Oxford: Basis Blackwell, 1969), par. 97.

8. As I see it, the appeal to ordinary language, to what we ordinarily say, is the appeal to criteria. And as Cavell puts it, interpreting Wittgenstein, "Criteria are 'criteria for something's being so,' not in the sense of its *being* so, but of its being *so*. Criteria do not determine the certainty of statements, but the application of the concepts in statements" (CR, 45). Criteria then are not mere conventions (in the sense of being arbitrary, or readily open to revision, or explicitly agreed to, as in "Let's agree to call these things human beings"), but they are convenient. The eliciting of criteria shows the astonishing degree of our prior agreement in the language we use, the degree of our attunement as to what kind of thing something is, as to what counts as something being this or that sort of thing.

guistic conventions we are able to engage in those activities that bind us together and make our lives human—worth living I would say. I mean activities such as making promises, forming covenants, dissolving them, getting married and divorced, having political discussions, talking about the weather, praying, complaining, praising, and so forth.

When I say that ordinary language is bedrock, I mean that it is necessary to our existence as human beings. The necessary connection between ordinary language and human being, or rather, being human, runs along these lines: all modes of being human are modes of being together, and all modes of being together are modes of speaking together; moreover, all modes of speaking together, regardless of how abstract, or specialized, are grounded, via our consent, in a bedrock framework of meaning which is our ordinary language. Or, going in the other direction, ordinary language is as bedrock to speaking as speaking is to being together and as bedrock as being together is to being human.

The term *ordinary,* in the phrase *ordinary language* is, of course, deeply ambiguous. In its richest, most lively existential meaning, the ordinary is not the same as the banal, at least insofar as the term *banal* carries with it a sense of the deadly routine of daily necessity. Following Kierkegaard's suggestion, I will use the term *ordinary* (the ordinary at its best lets say) as carrying within it a sense of the sublime (the sublime in the pedestrian, as Kierkegaard puts it) (FT, 52).

How does the sublime appear within the ordinary? Let's consider something ordinary, say hunger. Human beings know, at least ordinarily, as every animal does, what it is to be hungry, and what it is to seek food as a necessity for life, as every animal does. But we human beings, as speakers of a language, know what the word *hunger* means, that is, we know how to use the word. In learning how to use this word, we also may come to know what it is to be hungry in a higher more transcendent sense; and we may even come to learn that being hungry in this higher sense is an essential part of our humanness; and, moreover, that seeking to satisfy this higher hunger is as much a part of our ordinary existence as our daily bread—it is our daily bread.

Knowing what it is to be hungry in both senses, the sublime and the necessary, having the words to converse about it, being able to talk about food, about bread, about what we need and want, about what will satisfy us, is basic to our humanity, species-specific so to speak, regardless of the significant differences among us as to what our particular bread consists in.

Lofty conversations in theology, romance, politics, and so forth depend on this ground, and without devastating consequences, can never be completely uprooted from it. This connection of the lofty to the daily (to matters of daily bread) contributes to the common sense wisdom that ordinary human beings ordinarily do not deny: man shall not live by bread alone. And so the ordinary reaches into the sublime, that is, it is not merely daily bread, or daily bread is not merely bread. It is this picture of the ordinary, of its richness, I claim, that fits Kierkegaard's vision of the sublime as being manifest within the ordinary, the pedestrian. (The whole of Kierkegaard's philosophy in a nutshell!)

The idea of a human being who does not know the basics of ordinary human existence, what, for example, hunger is (or thirst, or love, or hate, or suffering, or joy, etc.), who has no words for these things, seems almost a grammatical impossibility. In fact, anyone who claimed such ignorance, who has at least the words for this claim, would seem to us somehow alien, even inhuman, but certainly not connected to us. How could we communicate with, connect to, such a being? How would conversation be possible? Would such a being be human?

But there are degrees of ignorance. We certainly can imagine someone who thinks that man does live by bread alone, that human life is confined to, or limited to, simply meeting the necessities of life. We might wonder of such a human being if he has become merely an animal. Certainly, in some conditions, a person has no choice in the matter, for the pursuit of bread is all that time and circumstance will allow—his existence has become a matter of survival. Yet such an existence from hand to mouth need not be banal, an existence in which the sublime has no place, for indeed, hungers can remain, perhaps even be intensified, even if unsatisfied. Banality takes over when the hunger for something more than bread has faded into cynicism or faded altogether.

The picture of the ordinary as stripped of its depths, of its sublimity, its adventure, its worthwhileness, the picture of everydayness as drudgery, necessity, boredom, emptiness, of human life as death, has certainly given the ordinary (the mediocre, the pedestrian, the average) a bad name. (I think here of the recent popular film *Joe Versus the Volcano* in which the lead character, played by Tom Hanks, is living a deadly life in the factory, living with a brain cloud killing him, a disease that only a romantic flight from it all will cure.) It is this idea of the ordinary that has inspired the myriad attempts, religious, romantic, rationalist, and so forth, to transcend it, to find a way of escaping the human, of escaping death, of finding immortality, of finding a better deathless life elsewhere, above it all, or below it.

When the ordinary has been so gutted, it is because conversation, the means of our connection, of our being together, of our happiness, has died. When this happens, the ordinary has become silence and despair. But what can breathe new life into this deadness? Some have thought our only hope for a cure for this death-in-life is to find a new life elsewhere—call this a resolve to celebrate disconnection, worldlessness, aloneness; or call it the quest for a romantic somewhere else, a somewhere beyond words, beyond the other, beyond the world, beyond time, beyond the ordinary.

But there is also another alternative, what Cavell calls the quest for the ordinary. This quest is founded in the hope for the resurrection of ordinary, worldly, human existence. This is the hope that it is possible to breathe new life into our words, into our conversation, into our human form of being together, into our humanness. This hope for the resurrection of our humanness, however, is essentially dialectical: one can come to hope for this only after the agony of having confronted its death, or the threat of its death. This confrontation is dialectically necessary if we are to see that our humanness is alive only insofar as we continually breathe life into it.

Now let's come back to the issue at hand, marriage as conversation, or more precisely, in light of the just made remarks on the ordinary, marriage as a bedrock form of ordinary conversation, or, if you prefer, the conversation of marriage as a basic form of embracing our humanness at its most bedrock level, that is, the level of our ordinary lives.

I want to defend the view, following the logic of paradox, that such an embrace of our humanness is possible only on the other side of the failure of this embrace, or at least the threat of such a failure. To see how this paradoxical logic is worked out in terms of marriage, we will turn to the genre of popular film about marriage that Cavell isolates and analyzes, namely, the Hollywood comedies of remarriage.

These films express this idea of marriage as the paradoxical embrace of the human, the ordinary, in all of its pedestrian sublimity. What they express is this paradox: the way that a marriage becomes legitimate is by its being chosen, but this can happen only if one acknowledges the dialectical possibility of divorce. The possibility that the bonds of marriage are ever subject to being broken tells us that their bonding effect is something we are called on to decide, and to decide continually. A legitimate marriage is a continuous remarriage, a continuous recommitment of ourselves to what is ours to refuse.

Here again, we meet the dialectic of paradox. Divorce, the breaking of a covenant, plays a similar role within a faithful marriage, a legitimate marriage, as despair plays within faith. Faith is, after all, a relation to the other, just as despair is the opposite of faith; that is, a broken relation. Yet relationships of faith make sense only in the consciousness of the possibility that they can be broken, that is, only in the consciousness of the possibility of despair. Faith, like marriage, then is a relation that we choose to enter. But this choice would fail to be a choice in its existential sense if it did not carry within it the ever-present dialectical possibility of choosing otherwise.

Faith refuses and so constitutes the fully realized possibility of despair, just as legitimate marriage refuses and so constitutes the fully realized possibility of divorce. But this refusal does not happen once and for all: faith and faithful marriage are perpetually and continuously called upon to annul their dialectical opposites, despair and divorce. As such, despair and divorce are inextricable and ever-present, as threats, to both faith and to a faithful marriage. It is these threats that faith and a legitimate marriage must work through in fear and trembling in the pursuits of our temporal and eternal happiness.

But let us turn to these films to see how this logic of paradox is presented.

The Walls of Jericho

The general philosophical issue addressed in Frank Capra's *It Happened One Night,* the earliest of the films that Cavell studies, is the issue that is central in all of the films in the genre, the pursuit of happiness. It expresses this high-minded pursuit in terms of the ordinary human experience of hunger.

The specific focus of the film is human separateness, or more precisely, the question of how human separateness figures into human forms of being together, into human happiness, especially that most specifically human form of happiness, marriage. This issue of separateness is addressed here in terms of the figure of the blanket-wall, an ordinary blanket that is transformed into what the male of the principle pair dubs the walls of Jericho.

As this film has it, human beings, real human beings, have a deep hunger for happiness, a hunger that can be satisfied only in being with another. But more concretely and more precisely, the film says that an individual can find his or her happiness only in being with some particular other. Moreover, this can happen only if both individuals desire each another, desire to be together, find being together satisfying.

Our film makes it clear, as if we need it to be, that there is an element of radical contingency in this matter of finding a satisfying form of being together, in meeting just the right person that will satisfy you and you her. We all have our romantic dreams; and even if they do not come true, we can delight in the happiness of others, and even go to the movies to delight in the happiness of unhappy stars playing out our dreams on the screen. But we all know all too well that we are lucky if we *happen* to find such a relationship—call this the happenstance of happiness, of a happy marriage. This film says this in its very title: *It*—the romantic dream coming true—*happened* (one night), after the pair happen to meet at a bus station.

But happiness, a happy marriage, is not completely out of our control—it does not merely happen. A happy marriage is one that both partners freely choose to enter and to remain in. Our film puts this idea forward indirectly, dialectically, we might say: it figures the bonds of marriage as escapable, it figures marriage in terms of divorce. The message seems to be that we are able to enter the bonds of marriage freely and to keep them from turning into a bondage only if we acknowledge our power to refuse, to escape. A bond that I can escape or refuse, but willingly and freely embrace, is a bond that does not enslave. This message is presented over and over in terms of the power to accept or refuse food: even though food is a necessity, I have the power to refuse it, thus transforming the necessity of eating into a matter of my own personal responsibility, a matter over which I have some say.

There is also another very important dialectical theme that is being worked out in this film, the theme of separation, or more precisely, its place in being together. The pursuit of a happy marriage in this film acknowledges the dread, the despair, of being alone in its dream of what a real form of being together would be like. In doing this, however, it therefore acknowledges our sense of our essential separateness from the other. It raises questions: What is it that separates us? Is our separateness a function of a metaphysical wall that is not of our own making? Or do we put up the walls? And are we free to take them down? Or do the walls between us—our separateness—make being together impossible? Or paradoxically, do they make being together possible?

To see how this works out, let me first present some basic elements of the plot. Ellie Andrews (Claudette Colbert) has just eloped with the playboy King Wesley, against her father's will. Now the father has locked his daughter away not in a tower, but on a yacht. Not only is he trying to get her to eat, to provide for her, he is also trying, as every good father does, to protect his daughter's virginity, an act made plausible by the fact that her "marriage" has not yet been consummated, or as the narrative has it, the "married" pair has not yet slept together under the same roof. While Ellie's father is trying to get the marriage annulled, she escapes, and in a bus terminal happens to meet a newspaper man, Peter Warne (Clark Gable). As the events unfold, she eventually not only pretends to be married to this new man in her life, she actually sleeps under the same roof with him, and enters into an ongoing conversation with him that is, for all practical purposes, the conversation of marriage.

In this film, the context of the pursuit of a happy marriage is escape and refusal, or as we might say, divorce. Ellie's first escape is from her father who is actively trying to arrange her divorce from King Wesley—call this Ellie's attempt to divorce her father. Ellie's second escape is from her remarriage to King Wesley—call this Ellie's attempt to remarry Peter. Or as Cavell puts it, this film (and all of the others of the genre) reflects on marriage in the context of divorce and hence in the context of the possibility of remarriage. As Cavell convincingly argues, and as I am attempting to reaffirm here, until marriage has confronted its dialectical other side, divorce, or at least, the threat of divorce, it cannot be legitimate. But on the other side of this confrontation, the legitimate marriage will of necessity be a remarriage—or better, a legitimate marriage will be an ongoing remarriage.

These basic elements of the genre—marriage, divorce, and remarriage—are present in this film, in a somewhat different way than all but one of the others. In *The Philadelphia Story, The Awful Truth,* and *His Girl Friday,* the marriage, divorce, and remarriage are straightforwardly presented: all of these films involve the same couple, who have divorced and are attempting to get back together. In *Adam's Rib,* the couple has to get back together even though they have never gotten a divorce in the legal sense, although the legality of marriage and hence divorce is at the center of the film. And in *Lady Eve,* the marriage, divorce, and remarriage involves "the same woman" with two different identities. By contrast, Ellie and Peter do not seem to be trying to get back together (except at the very end) nor do they seem, in any straightforward way at least, to be trying to get together. If anything, they are trying to extricate themselves from one another (a fact that makes this film of a piece with *Bringing Up Baby*) in the midst of her attempt to get back together with King Wesley. In what sense then is the eventual marriage of Ellie and Peter a remarriage? In what sense does it involve a divorce?

Cavell argues persuasively that the marriage between Ellie and Peter does involve a divorce and hence is a remarriage. How can this be so? On the surface, the film is about Ellie's divorce and remarriage from and to King Wesley. Moreover, she has never been married to Peter, so how could she be divorced from him, and hence, how could her eventual marriage to him count as a remarriage?

To see how the case can be made that Ellie and Peter do go through something like a marriage and divorce, and hence how their eventual marriage could count as a remarriage, we must return to the plot. The principal pair meet in a bus station and end up taking a bus ride, in the course of which they spend three nights together. She has not even spent one night with King Wesley. Moreover, the first night they spend together has all of the trappings of a wedding night, a night in a motel, the newness of the relation, its sexual excitement, its anxiety. In one exchange, as the two are lying next to each other in a motel, separated by a blanket-wall, she asks for his name. He gives it to her, as a man gives his name to a women in a traditional marriage, and says, "You are going to give it back to me in the morning." It seems that Frank Capra intended to present the scene in just this way, that is, to present this unmarried principal pair as married. Well, what is marriage anyway? Ellie's father has said to Ellie that she and her "husband" will never live under the same roof—that her marriage to King Wesley will never be consummated, that it is not real, and thus that it can be annulled. But, of course, if this is what marriage, real marriage is, or entails, that is, sleeping under the same roof, then Ellie and Peter are more married than Ellie and King Wesley. Hence, when this principal pair break up (toward the end of the film) before they are reunited (remarried, that is, married), this is more of a divorce than the annulment of her marriage to King Wesley, the annulment her father is seeking to obtain.

But this is not all. After the first night in the auto camp, the principal pair is having breakfast and the man is teaching this socialite how to be a real human being, instructing her on the proper way to dunk a donut. Their breakfast is interrupted by private detectives looking for Ellie. Peter and Ellie pretend to be a working class married couple, a pretension they had already made to the owner of the auto camp in order to get the room, and also on the bus to shut the loudmouth who was making advances towards Ellie. Moreover, beyond their pretended bickering, they really do bicker, constantly! That is, even when they are not pretending to be married, they carry on as if they were. As Cavell remarks, it is "as if a willingness for marriage entails a certain willingness for bickering" (PH, 86). This bickering is a spirited *conversation, a real* conversation, a real give and take predicated on a willingness to give it as well as take it.

And moreover, the conversation that Peter and Ellie establish, the form of being together that they embrace, the form of their embrace of each other, is, as I see it, the conversation of the ordinary, the daily. He is the ordinary in search of the sublime, she the sublime without any acquaintance with ordinary life. Together they find the ordinary at its best: they manage to find the sublime within the ordinary. Their conversation is about what every human being wants, about what they both want—it is about finding happiness, about finding someone to be happy with, but it is also the happiness itself.

The film casts the principal pair's pursuit of happiness, of each other, in terms of the ordinary human experience of hunger. In the very first scene of the film, on the yacht-prison, Ellie's father is discussing with the yacht captain Ellie's refusal of food. The conversation goes as follows:

FATHER: "On a hunger strike, eh? How long has this been going on?"
CAPTAIN: "She hasn't had anything yesterday or today."
FATHER: "Send her meals up to her regularly?"
CAPTAIN: "Yes sir."
FATHER: "Well, why don't you jam it down her throat?"

The very next scene finds Ellie and her father together in his cabin discussing her elopement with King Wesley and food. The porter appears carrying a tray of food, "Ah, the vitals," as Andrews puts it. This food is apparently for him, but no doubt it is also intended to be an enticement for Ellie to eat—Ellie has needs that are not being met. He sits down to eat and makes one more try to provide for her: he cuts a piece of steak and offers it to Ellie, saying, "You may work up an appetite; here have a piece of the this juicy steak, you don't have to eat it, just smell it, it's a poem." Steak as poetry—is Ellie's father trying to get Ellie to see the sublime in the ordinary? Perhaps so, but she does not accept his vision, or rather this vision *from him*. "I'm not going to eat a thing until you let me off this boat." Cavell reads this angry rejection of food from her father as Ellie's a refusal of love, of parental protection. Later she will also refuse food/love from Peter, and later accept it from him, in the form of a raw carrot. For now, she escapes, dives into the chaos of the water and ends up at the bus station when she begins an adventure and an education.

Whether she is really trying to get back to (or at) King Wesley is left vague in the film. But at the bus station we are left with no doubt that there is another King on the horizon of Ellie's life, and with the impression that she is not exactly closed to this idea. In the scene in which Peter Warne appears, he is talking on the phone to his boss at the newspaper where he works. He is surrounded by a group of rowdy guys, a little sauced up it appears. Although he is actually getting fired, he makes it appear that he is telling his boss off. His audience is delighted and hails him as "King!" The "king" then makes his way—or rather staggers, apparently from the effects of the booze he has been sharing with the others—through the throng. Eventually this "king" comes upon Ellie sitting in his seat on the bus, a seat that he has just cleared of the newspapers that would have told him of Ellie's identity. (Eventually he does recognize her from a newspaper photo and sees the possibility of a great story.)

His first words to her stake his claim; he says, with whatever double entendre your imagination will allow, "That upon which you sit is mine!" She tries to move, but falls into his lap, then moves. At their first stop someone steals her luggage, and he tries, unsuccessfully, to recover it. Fearing that her identity will be revealed, she prevents him from reporting the theft and says to him, "I want to be left alone." But she does not stay alone long. Eventually she ends up next to Peter and later awakes to find herself nestled against his shoulder.

And on this first night bus ride, food comes up again. Ellie wants to buy some chocolates—her appetite has also awakened. Peter forbids it, instructing her about economics. She has only $4 and the purchase of the chocolates would not be worth the price, as though chocolate would not be substantial enough to satisfy her hunger. And the theme of hunger arises on the second night's bus ride as a poor woman faints from hunger—the time frame of the film is after all the time of the great depression.

After spending their first night together in an auto camp, a night that we will come back to in a moment, Ellie arises to find Peter cooking breakfast for her. He instructs her about the economics of food—"not eggs" he says, "egg," just one is all that can be afforded; and he instructs her about the art (the poetry?) of eating, the proper way to dunk a donut.

On the second night together in an open field, she again says that she is hungry. He fetches raw carrots. The next morning he eats—Bugs Bunny style—a carrot and offers one to Ellie, who refuses, and instructs her on how to hitchhike. He fails, and she shows that the limb is mightier than the thumb in the famous scene in which she lifts her skirt bringing an oncoming car to a screeching halt. They are riding along with an obnoxious crooner who takes them to be a just-married couple. He stops for food. Peter refuses, against Ellie's will, for them both. The crooner bellows out the song, "Young people in love are never hungry"—recognizing that human beings, especially human beings in love, do not live by bread alone. After the man in the car leaves them and takes their luggage, and Peter runs after him, and somehow manages to bring the car back, minus the crooner, Peter and Ellie resume their trip. And huddled down next to Peter, she takes a carrot out of the pocket of his coat and eats it, accepting Peter as it were.

The other theme, the theme of separation, of its place within marriage, is treated in the famous blanket scenes in the auto camp. But before we come to this, or rather in the midst of the second blanket scene, we must consider briefly the most important scene about hunger, when it reaches its most sublime expression. This is the second night in an auto camp, just after the night spent in the out-of-doors under the stars.

With the blanket separating their two beds, Peter shares his dreams with Ellie. In response to her question, "Have you ever been in love, Peter?" he tells Ellie about his fantasy of going to an island in the Pacific and taking with him the girl of his dreams, the right sort of girl, somebody who is real, alive. He has even made plans: "That's where I'd like to take her. But she'd have to be the sort of girl that'd jump in the surf with me love it as much as I did. You know, those nights when you and the moon and the water all become one and you feel you are part of something big and marvelous. . . . Where the stars are so close over your head that you feel you could reach right up and stir them around. . . . Boy, if I could ever find a girl who's hungry for those things" (PH, 97).

Now clearly this fantasy of the sublime in the ordinary had already come true, it has already happened—it had happened the very night before. Peter had taken Ellie, over his shoulder, across a stream to a place (an island?) where they could stir the stars. Although he had not fully realized it yet, he had found the one he was looking for, someone real, someone alive, the sort of girl he was hungry for. She recognizes this first and comes from her side of the blanket to his to confess her love for him. He cannot come to grips with the reality of this and orders her back to her side. Later he does realize that his dream has come true in her and he leaves her asleep to make a pitch to sell her (their?) story to get the money to marry her. She awakes alone. In disappointment and resignation, she calls her father and goes off to remarry King Wesley.

Meanwhile the proprietors of the auto camp come into the room and take the blanket down. As Cavell notes, it is easy to take the blanket down if you don't know what it means. Well what does it mean? This takes us to the second dialectical theme of the movie, the issue of separation, the issue of its dialectical place within the happiness of being together.

The principal pair, not being married, but forced by circumstances into a situation of marriage, that is, into sharing a room for the night, must make the situation morally acceptable. The man has the idea of putting up a rope and suspending a blanket from it to make a curtain, or a wall between the two beds, a decent separation or separation of decency between the two. She says, "I suppose that makes everything all right." He then allegories the blanket:

"Behold the walls of Jericho. Maybe not as thick as the ones Joshua blew down with his trumpet, but a lot safer. You see, I have no trumpet." (Clearly here, we are prepared for the end of the film where the walls do in fact come tumbling down.)

Cavell raises these questions: What do the walls separate? and How do we get them to tumble? do we want to make them tumble? Or maybe, the real question is, what is holding them up? Is it our willingness not to transgress? (Obviously such a possibility readily exists.) And who has the trumpet here? He prepares to undress and tells her to join the Israelites, to get to her side of the blanket. But it is the Israelites that are the attackers; they have the trumpets. This leads us to conclude that what will cause the walls to tumble are the right sounds from her side of the bed.

What is it that the blanket-wall expresses? Something like this, I imagine: whether we live alone, or together, whether we are happy or not, is something we have a say in. Or as I might put this, human separation is something like the blanket insofar as it is something that we put up, that we keep up by our will to do so. That is, we remain separated from each other because either we will not to transgress the walls that separate us, or we are not willing to transgress them, or otherwise bring them down. In this sense, the possibility of transgression, or the possibility of bringing the walls of separation down, testifies to the fact that our happiness is something that we have a say in.

If happiness befalls me, if I am lucky enough to find a satisfying way of being with another, then I must make it happen. At the same time, since my happiness involves another, I do not have all of the say. As Cavell puts it, "to make things happen, you must let them happen" (PH, 109). Being together is a matter of mutual consent, of mutual decision: *we* have the say, as it were. And what reminds us of this, what reminds us that the walls between us have tumbled only because we allowed them to, is our recognition that we possess the power to put them back.

We can choose to be alone—isolation from others is a real life-possibility for human beings. And this possibility can be pursued either as a hypertrophication of will in a rebellious conscious decision to flee from what is taken as the entrapments of being together; or aloneness can be a matter of the failure of the will, a matter of default, or resignation, or a matter of not being able to choose.

And the fact that we remain alone if we do not choose, testifies to the peculiar nature of the human form of being together: *our separateness is the dialectical condition of our happiness and at the same time the source of our despair.* (And this puts Kierkegaard's emphasis on the individual in a light different from the usual tendency to think that he is the champion of the individual: being alone is not the solution to despair, it is despair! Being a separate individual is a condition for faith, just as despair is such a condition; but remaining a separate individual *is* despair. Again I quote Kierkegaard: "Had I had faith I should have remained with Regine.")[9]

In its most human sense, our being together is not our natural condition, say the natural relation between parents and child. The uniquely human form of being together presupposes our divorce from this, call this our growing up. Not until we come to be separate individuals, reach the age of accountability as we say, are we ready to enter into those forms of being together that are uniquely human. Being together, in its highest, most sublime, most human form, is thus not an inescapable necessity, in the way that being together in the animal world is, in the herd or the flock say, or even in the human extrauterine gestation period within the family, prior to reaching the age of accountability, prior to having grown up. But neither is it a matter of being lost in the crowd or of being in a suffocating bondage of responsibility to others. Rather the most sublime form of being together is something we are called to embrace, just as we are called to embrace our humanness. But I can embrace my humanness only if I have the power to refuse it. By a similar logic of paradox, I can choose to be together only if I can also choose to be alone, choose to flee from, or otherwise avoid the presence of others; I can choose to be together in a marriage only if I am free to divorce. And it is this logic of paradox that tells us that every legitimate marriage lies on the other side of the possibility or the actuality of divorce or separation and is thus a remarriage.

And here we arrive at the point of the last scene of the movie. The principal pair, now legitimately married, that is, remarried, return to the place of their first marriage, their first night together, their first wedding night, that is, the auto camp. And as we learn from the auto camp proprietors, they have a rope, a blanket, tokens of their first marriage, and a toy trumpet, the token of their remarriage, the token of the legitimacy of their marriage. And so the movie ends with the trumpet signaling to us what is outside of view, the walls of Jericho tumbling down. But unlike the biblical image, there is no conquest here, no violation; rather, we realize that the two have caused the walls that separated them to tumble—in a mutual consent. Knowing their full significance, they have taken them down together—they are together.

9. I wish he had put it at follows, "Had I had faith I would have returned to Regine."

Marriage as the Human Embrace (of the Human)

Marriage, from what traditionally we have called *the male perspective,* is thought of as bringing us down to earth. That is, marriage from this point of view is thought to be a descent—a descent prepared for by a preceding fall, a fall into love. As the traditional man is likely to see it, marriage forces us males to reckon with practical matters, maternal concerns, we might say. As such, marriage is thought to threaten our cherished, self-defining fantasy of freedom, call this our male proclivity to flight. Marriage is thus thought of as inevitably trapping the man—trapping him, he thinks, within the domain of domestic concerns: the household, food and roof, children. And without a doubt, it does force us males, traditional or not, to come face-to-face with the everyday. And this prospect almost always strikes terror, or at least reluctance.

But marriage is also thought of as an ascent, an ascent to heaven—call this the traditional female perspective. For the female, who is already on earth, who is the earth, who more naturally embodies maternal, domestic concerns, marriage is the sublime, the perfection of our human nature, our only comfort and security against the threats of contingency. It is marriage that makes life satisfying, fulfilling, worth living; it is marriage, a holy, a divine estate that brings perfection to our natural condition.

Marriage, that is, seems an equivocal good; it is charged with both threat and promise. Therefore, the holy estate of matrimony should not be entered into lightly, but deliberately, and soberly, and in the fear of God. Or as I would rather put it, marriage should not be entered into without due fear and trembling, without facing some hard questions. Does marriage drag us into the ordinary in such a way as to crush our freedom, smother us with responsibility, and thus ultimately kill our souls? Is marriage a trap? Or from the other side: Does marriage deliver on its promise to take us into the sublime? Or, more to the point, isn't the sober counsel of the disappointed true: marital bliss will not, cannot, last?

Or to put these questions more precisely in the idiom that Kierkegaard has given to us: Can marriage be a way of finding the sublime within the pedestrian? Can it be a mode of faithful existence? If so, how do we find a way of keeping our marital descent to earth, to the ordinary, the everyday, from taking us away from the sublime? And how do we find a way of keeping our marital ascent to the sublime from taking us away from the ordinary, the everyday?

I take questions of this sort as guides in the following reading I give to Cavell's treatment of the Hollywood comedies of remarriage. First, I want to look at two of these films, *The Philadelphia Story* and *Bringing Up Baby,* that I read as focused on the issue of coming down to earth, from a female and male perspective respectively—call this focus the problem of angelism, or to follow Kierkegaard, the despair of the infinite due to a lack of the finite. Secondly, I want to consider *Adam's Rib,* a film I read as focused on the opposite problem, a failure of transcendence, we might say, or in Kierkegaard's language, the despair of the finite due to a lack of the infinite. And finally, I want to turn to *The Awful Truth*—I mean the film—that I read as expressing just how the sublime can be embraced within the everyday.

I first take up George Cukor's *The Philadelphia Story* (1940), probably to try to diffuse the charge that I have too neatly sorted these matters out in terms of worn-out stereotypes of the male and the female. In this film, it is the woman, Tracy Lord (Kathern Hepburn)—an aptly lofty name—that is in need of coming down to earth; and it is the man who is trying to effect this descent.

Repeatedly in the film she is referred to as a goddess, worshipped not loved, aloof, unable "to tolerate human weakness, imperfection" (PH, 148). She had even changed the name of her sister from Diana to Dinah, the goddess of chastity ("Was this because she felt the name of the goddess of chastity belonged to *her?* Or that her sister was hers to name?" [PH, 15O]). It is Tracy the goddess that George Kittredge (John Howard), whom she is about to marry, has fallen in love with, or rather worships. He tells her that he wants to build her an ivory tower and worship her from a distance. And even her own father accuses her of being made of bronze and failing to have a loving heart.

On the first go around, Tracy's marriage to C. K. Dexter Haven (Cary Grant) had failed to crack what Tracy herself acknowledges as her tough exterior (hiding an inner vulnerability). On the occasion of her remarriage (to George Kittredge), Dexter reappears, with two reporters from *Spy* magazine—Mike Macauley Conner (Jimmy Stewart) and Liz Imbrie (Ruth Hussey)—presumably to get a story, but more probably to try one more time to bring Tracy down to earth and hence to herself, and perhaps even back to him. Tracy is not only divorced from Dexter, she is divorced from life; she is in despair.

Dexter is ambivalent towards his former wife; he calls her by a name no one else uses, his intimate nickname for her, "Red"; but he also addresses her as "your majesty." He is not sure that she can be brought to her senses, to herself, but encouraged in what he sees as a crack in her facade, he seems ready to try; or at least he is no longer afraid of trying. In one exchange, she gives him a stern disapproving look to which he replies, "Ah, the withering glance of the goddess! You're slipping Red. I used to be afraid of that look."

His most explicit attempt to get her to come down off of her pedestal, his attempt to get her to see the value and worthwhileness of an existence that embraces its own vulnerability, comes in the form of a lecture he gives to her in the bathhouse, where she and Mike are preparing to take a swim. He wants to tell her what true love is, and when his lecture is finished he presents her with a wedding gift, a model of the boat he practically built himself called *True Love*—the boat that carried them on their honeymoon.

It is made clear in the narrative of the film that the reason Tracy and Dexter had gotten a divorce was his drinking problem, what is referred to as his *gorgeous thirst*. The subject comes up when Dexter walks into the bathhouse and refuses to have a drink, telling Tracy that he no longer has that problem. As Cavell notes, this thirst of Dexter's is akin to the hunger of Peter Warne (Clark Gable) in *It Happened One Night*—both the hunger and the thirst are for true love.

Tracy tells him that his drinking was *his* problem, to which he responds, "Granted. But you took on that problem when you married me. You were no helpmeet there, Red. You were a scold." As Cavell notes, being a scold is a contrary to being a helpmeet, a contrary to entering "a meet and happy conversation." He says, "The conjunction of being a helpmeet with being willing to converse, a contrary to being a scold, comes up again in a late exchange between Tracy and Dexter as she refuses an offer of a drink from him, warns him never to sell the *True Love,* tells him that she'll never forget that he tried to put her back on her feet today, and then collapses on the remark, 'Oh Dext, I'm such an unholy mess of a girl,' to which he responds, 'Why that's no good, that's not even conversation' " (PH, 146). And further he says, "In adducing Milton's view of the matter of conducting a meet and happy conversation, I have emphasized that while Milton has in view an entire mode of association, a form of life, he does also mean a capacity, say a thirst, for talk" (PH, 146).

In the course of the lecture, he reminds her of that night when she got drunk and naked and stood on the roof screaming like a banshee, a night she had conveniently repressed. Her failure to remember, Dexter connects to her failure to acknowledge her own vulnerability and imperfection. He says to her, "You will never be a first-class [a term meant to contrast with the play of upper and lower classes in the film] person or a first-class woman until you" allow yourself to acknowledge your own human frailty and vulnerability.

Dexter sees that her failure to acknowledge her own humanness has turned her into a graven image of a human being, a stone goddess to be worshipped but not loved.

And just as he is leaving, as proof of his words, George shows up, noticing the *True Love* floating in the pool. She tells him of its being a wedding gift from Dexter, as she, like the boat, drifts off, she off into remembrance; she ruminates, "My she was yare." A working class person, no matter how high he has risen in society, would not know the language of yachting. He asks more than he knows with something like the following question, "What does it mean to say that [the] true love is yare?" This would be difficult to explain. And this was so not just because it was a matter of trying to explain a term of the upper class to a man who had only recently climbed out of the coal mines of his former working-class life, to a man who was now about to climb into bed with the Philadelphia elite. As it turns out, the real difficulty would be in trying to explain to him something about true love. Tracy's words did not penetrate: he seemed so awestruck by her and her world of wealth and privilege, the world he so wanted to be a part of, that he could not see or hear her.

Tracy tells him that she wants to be useful, loved not worshipped. Dexter's lecture was having its effect. George will not hear (of) this. In the midst of the stone statues around the pool, he insists that Tracy is like a statue. He intends to put her on a pedestal; she is a goddess to be worshipped. He tells her that he wants to build her an ivory tower, as if she needs one, as if she were not already living in one. But in these moments, she is beginning to realize this, to realize that what she most needs is to come down from her tower into the world, to be useful.

Tracy is primed for another divorce—call this a metaphysical divorce. This divorce takes place in the midst of another night of drunkenness and sexual inhibition. Mike Macauley, the poet/professor, will be her companion and her guide into this long and crazy night. He and Tracy will, the very night before her wedding, live out one of those downright poetic short stories that Mike was noted for writing—stories Dexter had earlier characterized as very "down to earth." Under the moonlight, beside the pool, high on romance and wine, Mike captains Tracy's descent back to earth, to her heart, to herself. Unwittingly, however, Mike will end up taking Tracy back to Dexter and himself back to his own lady in waiting, Liz Imbrie.

It is a wrenching night for both. And never was it more truly said than on this night, "*In vino veritas!*" The drunken conversation of these two ranges between silliness and seriousness, love and contempt, passionate desire and descent restraint. He lectures her, and she him. Her words to Mike repeat almost exactly the words that Dexter had just that afternoon directed to her, "You'll never be a first-class human being . . ."

On this passionate night, Tracy the goddess died and Tracy the human being was born. Dexter and George arrive to find Mike carrying Tracy, as a husband carries his new wife over the threshold, or as someone carries a person who has just been hurt, or is dead. Dexter asks, "Is she all right?" Tracy raises her head to say, "Not wounded sire, but dead." And as Cavell so aptly puts it, "We will hardly avoid seeing the carrying posture as symbolic of her death as goddess and rebirth as human" (PH, 141). It is also hard not to read this death and rebirth as metaphysically akin to the process of divorce and remarriage.

The next day, this rebirth is confirmed by Tracy's own words, but more profoundly in the fact that she agrees to remarry Dexter. To set the stage: the wedding to George is canceled, but the wedding party is assembled. Not wanting to waste the opportunity, Mike asks her to marry. She refuses. Dexter then asks for a second chance, a remarriage; she accepts. And just before she is to be reconciled with her true love, she is also reconciled with her father. As she is about to walk the aisle, her father tells her he loves her and that she looks the queen, the goddess, to which she replies, "I feel like a real human being."

Tracy's remarriage to Dexter betokens her embrace of her humanness and his. Only on this condition could she be a helpmeet and not a scold, only on this condition could she enter into a meet and happy conversation with Dexter. This is what his thirst was for, and ironically it was this thirst for alcohol—call this a thirst for the sublime—that brought them to their mutual divorce and to their mutual embrace.

In this remarriage, Tracy and Dexter found a way to legitimate their marriage, to satisfy their thirst for true love. But Cavell's point, and mine in following him, is that this marriage was made possible by divorce. But I shall take things a step further than Cavell.

Tracy's divorce is complicated. She had not only to divorce Dexter in order to marry him, she had to allow her divorce from him to awaken her to the fact that her life was a life of divorce—a life divorced from life, from the human. Tracy lived in an aesthetic flight from herself, from Dexter, from her humanity. She had found a way to escape the vulnerability that she knew was intrinsic to her humanity; she had, as Martha Nussbaum says of Socrates, become a stone: safe, self-sufficient, invulnerable. And this is just what George loved about her: George loved a fantasy, an image, not Tracy; he was an idolater.

To marry legitimately, she had to put this divorce away before she could put her divorce to Dexter away; she had to clear the metaphysical ground, as well as the legal. Tracy can renounce her divorce from Dexter, that is, re-marry him, that is, really marry him, only to the extent that she can renounce her own divorce from her humanness—she must refuse her refusal of life. In both cases, it is divorce that prepares the dialectical way for embrace. Her embrace of Dexter, of her own humanness, comes by way of a double nega-tion: she must divorce her aesthetic divorce from life; her final "yes" to Dexter's proposal for marriage comes by way of her renunciation of her re-nunciation of life.

As in *The Philadelphia Story*, it is Grant and Hepburn that play the roles of the principal pair in Howard Hawk's *Bringing Up Baby* (1938). In this film, however, their roles are reversed: it is the man who needs to be brought down to earth. The man in this case is an absent-minded professor known as David Huxley (Cary Grant). And the one who is to bring him down is a madcap woman known as Susan Vance (Kathern Hepburn).

The film opens in a natural history museum with a camera shot of Professor Huxley sitting high atop a scaffold built around a brontosaurus skeleton. He is sitting deliberately; and to indicate this, he is deliberately sit-ting in the position of Rodin's *Thinker*. We see this clearly, but it is confirmed in the opening lines of the dialogue. A fellow scientist/professor comes into the room carrying a telegram and greeting Huxley's assistant; she puts her hand up to the intruder like a librarian and says, "Shh! Dr. Huxley is thinking!" Here we have a perfect image of the intellectual male whose thought, or whose preoccupation with his work, has caused him to levitate above the world.

But from the beginning, we sense that David is not altogether happy with his life above the concerns of ordinary existence. As I would put it, he is ever as much in despair as Tracy Lord; both are metaphysically divorced from life. The trope for David's sense that something is missing in his life is a bone. We see this in this first scene when Miss Alice Swallow (Virginia Walker), his protective assistant, opens the telegram to learn that "the missing bone" has been found.

It is in the context of this announcement of good news that we find out that his assistant is also his fiancée, and that the two are getting married the very next day. As she is about to open the telegram, David mumbles to him-self, "I think this one," puzzling over a bone he is holding in his hand, "goes in the tail." Overhearing, Alice says, "Nonsense! You tried it in the tail yester-day and it didn't fit." He says, "Oh yes I did, didn't I?" (Cavell is right, I think, that the sexual dimension of the dialogue of this film—and it is consid-erable and pervasive—is best left implicit.)

Without benefit of a script, I will attempt to reconstruct the action and the next few exchanges in the dialogue of this scene. Alice, very excitedly says, "David, David, the telegram is from the expedition in Utah; they found it, the intercostal clavicle, the missing bone!" David is ecstatic and rushes down from his perch. In his childlike excitement he reads, "It is to arrive tomorrow! The missing bone." He kisses Miss Swallow—on the cheek. She is embarrassed (the other professor is still present) and pulling away from his embrace, says, "David, David, what will the Professor think? There is a time and place for everything." The other professor says, "Well, after all you are getting married tomorrow." But it is David who seems to need this reminder. He says, "Oh yes that's right, we're getting married tomorrow. How odd! [And indeed we will presently see just how odd.] Can you imagine two such important things happening on the same day?" (And what he doesn't realize is that something more odd and more important will arrive, call this his new life, or his new lease on life, and that it will be Susan Vance, not Alice Swallow, that will bring it to him.)

The Professor says that this calls for a celebration. In childlike abandon, David exclaims, "Oh don't worry Professor, we are going to celebrate, we are going to go away." Miss Swallow quickly douses this idea with cold water, bringing him back, so she thinks, to his responsibility, to his work. She wants him back up on the scaffold, free from the distractions of ordinary life. She is trying to help him along with his work, but what she does not realize, although perhaps he does, is that she is not being, nor does she promise to be, a helpmeet to *him*.

In Alice's following speech, we see just why David is unhappy with his life, and its future prospects with her. It runs roughly as follows: "Going away? Why what are you thinking of David? Why as soon as we are married we are coming directly back here and you're going on with your work. Now once and for all David, nothing is going to interfere with your work. Our marriage will entail no domestic entanglements of *any* kind." He mumbles, "You mean . . ." She confirms, "Of *any* kind!" Disappointedly, David again mumbles, "I was sort of hoping. . . . You mean children and all that sort of thing?" She says in no uncertain terms, "Exactly!" And pointing to the lifeless skeleton she says, "This will be our child!" And she adds, "Yes David, I see our marriage purely as a dedication to your work." David objects in a kind of boyhood lingo, "Well, gee whiz Alice, everybody has to have a honeymoon." Refocusing him on his work, she says, "We haven't time"; and later, "Remember who and what you are."

The film will end with this giant lifeless skeletal erection—what Alice has just called their baby—collapsing to the ground under the weight of another woman, Susan. This new woman is the one with whom he has become domestically entangled; she is the one with whom he has shared a childlike adventure of bringing up a baby (a leopard named Baby); she is the one whom he embraces in the final shot of the film.

As I see this, Susan is the one who awakens David from his metaphysical divorce from life, from its spontaneity, to the possibility of embracing it, of embracing her. And there is a philosophical lesson in this. It is not only existential faith that must reckon with its alternative possibilities, with the possibilities of resignation and refusal (Abraham's problematic). The nonknight of faith, the one in despair, the one who is outside of, or on the other side of the abyss from faith, also has to come to terms existentially, and in fear and trembling, with *its* alternative, that is, faith itself. If the refusal of the human in despair is to be refused, there must be some awakening to the possibility of existential faith, the possibility of the human embrace.

As faith must reckon with despair, so despair must reckon with faith: freedom realizes in fear and trembling that the abyss can be crossed from either direction. We might say that neither side of the abyss is safe from the temptations that come from the other side. As Abraham learned, this is certainly true of faith, it is not a safe haven immune from the temptation not to remain in faith.

David Huxley's problematic, like the predicament of most of us (certainly like Tracy Lord's), is different from Abraham's. His problem is coming to terms, from the standpoint of despair, from standpoint of a metaphysical divorce from the human, with the possibility of a meet and happy marriage, with the possibility that there is someone with whom it is possible for him to find what is now missing in his life. This someone, it turns out, is Susan Vance, whom we can see as a representation of faith's metaphysical lure, faith's call to embrace the human, faith's call to divorce ourselves from our refusal of to be human, what we might call faith's invitation to fall in love with our human condition.

How does Susan manage to bring this aloof scientist to his senses? How does she awaken him to her, to life? Strangely enough, by entangling him in a madcap adventure of one children's game after another. David meets Susan on the golf course where he is trying to convince Mr. Peabody to donate a million dollars to the museum. He is really not playing, he is working. When they meet, she *is* playing, and moreover playing *his* ball, the ball he had accidentally hit into the fairway where she is playing. She immediately turns the golf game into another game, follow the leader, whose got the ball, and so forth. And so the games begin: stealing and wrecking cars, pitching olives, more follow the leader, hide and seek, pretending to be a game hunter, fetch, looking for the bone, dress-up, playing house with baby, etc.

As I see it, these games that David is drawn into, seemingly against his will, are really welcomed by a deeper self within him, call this his forgotten childhood. David has become so lost in his work that the only thing that can divorce him from it is play, or rather being forced to play. When David became a man, he had put away childish things, and this had just about killed him. Susan is now teaching him that it is possible to recapture some of the adventure, excitement, and spontaneity of childhood on the far side of it. And in the midst of this madcap fun, it is clear that David, this thinker without spontaneity, is being re-created; he is coming alive again, he is being reborn, resurrected from his life among the dead, that is, his life in the museum of bones and bygone ages.[10]

A central figure in this adventure is the child, the baby. For Miss Swallow, the child is a lifeless relic of prehistory. It cannot be recaptured, only put back together like the shell of a hollow broken egg. But such a child, as Huxley knows, as we all know, is safe. To presume to recapture something of our childhood is dangerous as well as fun. This is why, I surmise, that there are two leopards in the film. The one leopard is tame, friendly, and fun; he purrs to the tune, "I Can't Give You Anything But Love Baby." The other is fierce, dangerous, and wild, an escaped killer. And we can certainly get these two leopards mixed up, as the film shows. But the fact is that we cannot recapture one without the other.

Now where does this all leave us? Does David divorce himself from his work for good? Does he divorce work in order to play? Does he divorce adulthood to reenter childhood? Perhaps so, but only as a prelude to a remarriage; I mean a remarriage to his work and to his adult life, a remarriage that betokens his rebirth, his new life, a life which refuses a previous life of aloofness from the world, from others, from himself.

What will David's new life be like? I get an answer to this from the last scene of the film. Susan has caused the lifeless relic of the past to collapse, call this David's former relation to his work and to his own childhood; call it his false erection. And for some wacky moments he had returned to his childhood, to an enchanted forest (Connecticut), to a hunt for wild game, and so forth. But, as the last scene shows, he did not stay there. Rather, what it does

---

10. It would be a mistake to think that Susan is not learning anything from David. As Cavell leads us to think, David is thought without spontaneity, she is spontaneity without thought. As she in fact confesses, "I just do whatever comes into my head" (PH, 125).

show is David again high on his scaffold, and Susan climbing up to him with the million dollar donation for the museum. The skeleton cannot support them together; she climbs the scaffold to him and causes the brontosaurus to fall. The scaffold remains standing, but Susan is in danger of falling with the collapsing bones of the brontosaurus. But David rescues her, and by the arm pulls her up to be with him. His work place thus remains intact, but it is different, transformed we might say by Susan's presence. He is not up there alone anymore.

His embrace of Susan in the final scene betokens, I take it, his remarriage to her—and it is a remarriage insofar as they had already played house and brought up a baby, and insofar as he had extricated himself from that domestic entanglement. But I also read his embrace as betokening his remarriage to his work, a work he had just divorced for play. And more generally, I read it as betokening his remarriage to the world, the ordinary, the everyday. As David embraces Susan, he mumbles the last lines of the film, "Oh my; oh dear; oh well." What he is saying, as Cavell interprets it, and as I agree, is this: "I am here, the relation is mine, what I make of it is now part of what I make of my life, I embrace it" (PH, 132). And my recurring angle on this is that David's embrace of Susan, of his work, of his life, was made possible only because it was an embrace on the dialectical far side of his refusal of it all.

George Cukor's 1949 film, *Adam's Rib,* reverses the theme of the previous two. In these films, the failure of self, the self's refusal of the human, was figured in terms of the human temptation to rise above the human, the temptation of angelism, we might say; likewise, the task of recovery was depicted as a matter of bringing someone down to earth.

In *Adam's Rib,* the failure of the self is pictured as the possibility of the self's sinking below the human, call this the human temptation to sink below the human into the barbaric, the uncivilized, the monstrous, the bestial. We human beings are not only tempted heavenward, that is, tempted to transcend our humanity by wishing to, and by trying to, live like angels, or gods, but we are also tempted downward or backwards, that is, tempted to transcend our humanity by wishing to, or trying to, live like brutes. This problem calls for a different sort of rescue, a different recipe for recovery. In this film, the task—the man's task in this case—is to bring the woman up, or at least back into civilization, back to herself, back to the realization that marriage is a connection of law, of contract, of covenant, not a connection of blood and revenge.

This does not mean that our sympathies are wholly on the side of the man in this film (Adam Bonner, Spencer Tracy). In fact, even the man's sympathies lie largely with the woman (Amanda Bonner, Kathern Hepburn). She is after all fighting a legitimate battle in the war of the sexes, the battle for equality before the law. She is fighting the idea that women are inherently subordinate to men, an idea grounded in the biblical myth that woman was made out of Adam's rib. But her brief reverses the usual point of that biblical story: just because she is flesh of his flesh, bone of his bone, she is equal to him. And on this point, Adam could not agree more with Amanda.

I think that the film is attempting to say, however, that Amanda takes the matter of the equality of the sexes in the wrong direction. I don't mean that it tries to show that she takes the equality issue too far, that she is not willing to acknowledge the differences between the sexes. Amanda readily acknowledges this, as does Adam. Although she is perhaps not as happy about these differences as Adam, the final scene of the film expresses, through the man, a common sentiment: "*Viva la difference!*"

So then, in what way does Amanda's "feminist" brief go awry? To see this, we must say just a word or two about the plot.

The story opens with a prologue in which a distraught woman, Doris Attinger, is stalking her husband. She follows him to his girlfriend's apartment, comes in on them as they are embraced, and with the handgun she has just purchased, she opens fire, shooting her husband in the middle of his big affair.

She is arrested and comes to trial. As it happens, it falls to the assistant D.A., Adam Bonner, to prosecute her case. Hearing about this, Amanda, his wife, who is also an attorney, but in private practice, decides to take on Doris's defense. This confrontation between husband and wife in court brings to trial not only the Attinger case but their own marriage.

Amanda's defense of Doris's illegal assault on her husband is built on the idea that her (Doris's) actions were justified because they were in defense of her home, her marriage, her children. But Amanda gives this defense a peculiar angle. Her assumption is that the laws of civilized society, laws against assault with a deadly weapon, for example, must on occasion give way to a deeper law, what she calls an unwritten law, what I would call the law of nature, the precivilized law of the jungle.

In her summation, Amanda says that we are all capable of attack, that assault lies dormant with all of us. True enough. But I read Amanda to be saying something more: that all human beings not only have a dark, brutish side, a violent, vengeful, uncivilized side, but that in certain circumstances—call these family squabbles or domestic matters—we are justified in letting these natural instincts guide our actions.

In the unwritten law of the jungle, the instinct for survival inevitably leads to violence: the male instinct is to fight to the death to protect his mate, or his rights to her; the female instinct is to protect her nest and young, even if it means having to kill or be killed. Amanda argues that on certain occasions, namely, when the issue is the survival of the home, the marriage, the family, it is this natural law that is operative, and rightly so, and not the laws of civilized society.

The argument finally leads to the point of her defense of Doris. Amanda claims that the natural right to protect the home is rightly accorded to men, but not to women. Men can resort to brutish violence in the protection of their homes with impunity. Women should be given an equal right to violence. This is what Doris was availing herself of, and she was justified in doing so, as justified as any man would have been.

This argument convinces the court but not Adam. And the reason Adam is not convinced is that he rightly does not accept the premise of Amanda's defense of Doris. The name he gives repeatedly to this premise is *contempt for the law.*

Adam operates with a different premise, a correct one, I believe: if there is anything that sets human beings apart from the brutish world of the jungle, that makes the human form of being together civilized, it is the fact that we are tied together by agreements, by covenants, by contracts, by laws. Moreover, these human forms of being together rest on reasoned consent.

Brutes do not live together on the basis of such social contracts. Or more pointedly, brutes do not marry, they mate, and this remains the case even if they mate for life. As Cavell puts this:,"[the bond of marriage] . . . requires a decision, and power to have it enforced . . . it is not natural, not, so to speak, a family matter" (PH, 216).

The basis of being together in the natural world is different from that in the civilized human world. And this is due almost exclusively to the fact that human beings can speak. It is the capacity for speaking to one another that generates the human basis of being together, that is, contracts, covenants, laws, and so forth.

For this reason, in nature there are no outlaws; in the jungle there are no criminals. But just as surely, in the precivilized natural world, there are no saints, no heroes, not even any upstanding ordinary good citizens. Brutes cannot fail to be brutes. And this is the difference between the brutes and us: human beings can fail to be human, we can be inhuman. It is this fact about us that makes our human form of being together, our way of being human, a matter of our consent, a matter, even, of our positive intention.

Amanda is right: humans carry a brutishness within them, just under the surface. And she is right that we are always subject to its pull downward into violence and revenge. As I see it, we would not be human without these possibilities, these temptations. But she is wrong to think that such actual regressions are simply signs of our humanness; or more to the point, that we sometimes yield to these archaic forces without yielding up our humanness. As I see it, to yield to such instincts of violence is to forfeit our humanness—again, something only human beings can do, and so in that sense, a sign of our humanness.

So we come back to the dialectic of paradox. If we could not forfeit our humanness, then we would not be human. I mean that our capacity for the monstrous and the inhuman is essential to our humanness, and yet it is precisely the mark of the human to exclude the monstrous, the inhuman, the brutal. The measure of our humanness, the mark of our civilization, is the extent to which we have succeeded in domesticating the animal within us all, that is, the extent to which we have managed to refuse our human temptation to refuse the civilized, our human temptation to embrace violence and brutality.

It does not make sense to say that human forms of being together are matters that require our consent if it makes no sense to acknowledge our capacity to withhold our consent. Or in other words, our consent to enter and to live with the social contracts of a democratic social order, to live under the law, and so forth implies a power to stand outside such structures of civilization. It is civilization that produces the possibility of the monstrous, and it is civilization that holds the monstrous at bay.

Marriage, for Adam, is a central token of human, civilized forms of being together. Like all such civilized forms of being together, marriage is a connection established by law, by agreement, by consent—Adam calls it a *contract.* (In the film one trope for the fact that marriage is a legal bond is Adam's and Amanda's mortgage on their Connecticut farm, a bond celebrated in the showing of the home movie "The Mortgage the Merrier." One of the things that makes divorce such a legal headache is the fact that marriage almost always involves property.) As Adam sees it, when the legal connection of marriage goes awry, there is legal, civilized recourse, that is, the legal procedure of divorce. No one has the right, natural or otherwise, to resort to violence. To do so is to sink below the human; it is to become uncivilized, brutish.

Surprisingly, what this amounts to saying is that the acceptance of the legitimacy of divorce within a society is a sign of its civilization. As we might say, granting legitimacy to marriage depends dialectically on granting a legitimacy to divorce. Without the legitimacy of divorce, the contract of marriage cannot be a matter of consent, that is, it cannot be embraced properly as one's own.

And here we are brought back to Cavell's reading of Milton's *Doctrine and Discipline of Divorce*. As Cavell sees it, and as I agree, "the covenant of marriage is a miniature of the covenant of the commonwealth"(PH, 151). In taking up Adam's claim to Amanda that marriage is a contract, a matter of the law, (and in this context I take *contract* and *covenant* as virtually equivalent) Cavell goes on to say, "The word 'contract,' at this climatic moment, to my ear names the social contract that was to express the consent that constitutes lawful society. . . . Here again the fate of the marriage bond in our genre is meant to epitomize the fate of the democratic social bond" (PH, 193).

Now if the bonds that form a democratic society are legitimated by our consent, then such a society must find a way to legitimate dissent. Consent without the power, the possibility of dissent, makes no sense. The parallel between marriage and society is striking: the moral and political acceptance of the legitimacy of dissent in a democratic society is as critical to the maintenance of its public, social bonds of consent in the commonwealth as is divorce in the maintenance of the covenant of marriage.

But let us return to the film at hand. Amanda's confusion—as I see it, her attempt to legitimize an uncivilized act of violence to settle a breakdown in the covenant of marriage—comes clear in the scene when she and Adam are giving each other rubdowns. As he is giving her a rubdown, Adam spanks her behind with a little more than the usual force of a masseur. She is offended by his brutish act; she cries; and her tears, "the juice" he calls it, brings him to apologize. At this point, she kicks him and says, "Let's all be manly."

This, in a nutshell is her brief for equality: women are as entitled to resort to violence as men. In this moment, it seems as though she has resolved: no longer will I be content just to cry, I want the right to hit and kick like any man. And so she kicks her own husband—almost completely out of her life. It will take his tears to bring her back.

But it is not just his tears that bring her back. Although Adam had lost in the courtroom, he will savor his own victory of bringing Amanda to see that she was wrong to defend violence simply in the name of sexual equality.

In a recasting of the prologue of the film, Adam purchases a handgun and breaks in on Amanda and Kip (the next door neighbor who has eyes for Amanda). Amanda and Kip, harmlessly and even playfully, embracing are startled by what they take to be Adam's mad resort to violence. He points the gun at her to take his revenge; she protests, "*You* have no right. . . . *Nobody* has a right . . ." At this moment Adam wins his case and Amanda back. He says to her, "No matter what you think you think, you think the same as I think, that I have no right, that nobody has the right to break the law." As Cavell remarks, "And this meeting of minds more earnestly constitutes, for both of them, his getting her back" (PH, 214–15).

Adam's resort to violence is not real but his revenge is sweet. We see this plainly when he turns the gun on himself, putting the barrel of the licorice gun in his mouth and eating it.

Amanda knows that he has won—perhaps she wanted to be won by him again. The threat of divorce, the bringing of the marriage to trial, to debate, forced the two to come to terms with what marriage is, with what makes it legitimate. Certainly we are not left with the sense that this is settled once and for all, how could it be?

Marriage is a conversation, perhaps even a debate; as such, it is ongoing. The film's way of saying this is in the closing scene's repartee in which we hear Adam's announcement that he is thinking about running for a judgeship on the Republican ticket. Following her agenda of equality, Amanda replies to his announcement with her own challenging question, "Who is running on the Democratic side?"

We would expect nothing less of a marriage that is a meet and happy conversation; we would expect that these two would continue to argue and to defend their independence. This willingness to bicker seems essential to their marriage, the source of its life, its vitality. But even so, the impression is strong in the last scene of this film that even though the debate, the competition, the bickering will continue, the terms of their conversation in this remarriage have significantly changed. Or better, the two have come to a new level of fundamental agreement, call this an agreement to be civilized; this new meeting of their minds will form the substratum for all of their future debates and disputes, but it is a new faithfulness that is found, that could only be found, on the other side of a wrenching quarrel, on the other side of the fear and trembling of existentially facing the loss of one another. Their return to civilization seems possible for this pair only on the other side of a walk through the jungle; as does their return to each other, to their mutual embrace of love seem possible only on the other side of a refusal of violence.

Leo McCary's 1937 film, *The Awful Truth*, reminds us again that the pursuit of human happiness can be satisfied only in finding a satisfying way of being with others: only this will allow us to avoid the despair of being alone. Its suggestion is that marriage is an emblem of such happiness, an emblematic form of human relatedness.

The specific issue the film brings into a clearly defined focus is what is also at stake in the other films of the genre, namely, the issue of marriage as an embrace of the everyday. Cavell puts this as follows, "I understand the point of the achievement [of this film] to be the tracking of the comedic to its roots in the everyday, to show the festival to which its events aspire to be a crossroads to which and from which a normal life, an unended diurnal cycle, may sensibly proceed" (PH, 237).

But if marriage is an embrace of the everyday, of dailiness, as Cavell names it, then it must also be a daily embrace, that is, a *repetition*—an idea, Cavell acknowledges he learned partly from Kierkegaard.[11] It is repetition that legitimates a marriage, that makes every legitimate marriage a remarriage, or better a continuous, a daily, remarrying. Again I quote Cavell, "Our genre emphasizes the mystery of marriage by finding that neither law nor sexuality (or, by implication, progeny) is sufficient to ensure true marriage and suggesting that what provides legitimacy is the mutual willingness for remarriage, for a sort of continuous reaffirmation" (PH, 142).

Since marriage is an ongoing daily form of being together, and since its day in, day out routines always run the risk of dullness, the achievement of happiness in marriage is possible only to the extent to which the marriage is comedic, that is, to the extent to which the marriage is able continually, daily, to find some laughs in the midst of the routines of ordinary married life.

How is this achieved? Cavell puts it in terms of developing a certain attitude towards the events of daily life. He calls this attitude comedic—as opposed to tragic—and says that developing it depends on something else that he learned from Kierkegaard, namely, it depends on "taking an interest in it" (PH, 238). As suggested by the title of one of Cavell's later books, this interest in the ordinary is something the finding of which requires a quest; we neither inhabit nor are interested in the ordinary merely by default.

---

11. Cavell plays as fast and lose with Kierkegaard's notion of repetition, as he also does with Nietzsche's idea of eternal recurrence. Kierkegaard develops a notion of repetition that has (at least) both an aesthetic and a religious form. Cavell seems to see only the religious form, call this the existentially positive sense of repetition. This is the sense of repetition that Cavell says he learned from Kierkegaard, the sense of it that he is trying to incorporate into his plea for the human embrace. This sense of repetition is, for Kierkegaard and Cavell (and me), an essential element of faith; for Kierkegaard, however, (and I think he is right about this) repetition can also be a technique of aesthetic transcendence of the particularity, the uniqueness and irreversibility of historical time and place. And as far as I can see, Nietzsche's idea of eternal recurrence does not have the positive existential meaning that Cavell thinks it has. If anything, Nietzsche's eternal recurrence is more like Kierkegaard's aesthetic notion of repetition, that is, has more to do with flight from existence than with the embrace of it. As I read Nietzsche, he, like archaic man, is terrified by history, and seeks to escape into his own version, colored I must say by a heavy dose of *resentiment,* of a peaceful eternity, call this his Hellenistic nostalgia.

And I would add something else, something I also learned from Kierkegaard: finding the comedic in the everyday, what we might call finding the sublime within the pedestrian, is not only a matter of what happens, it is also a matter in which our existential choice figures decisively. Happiness is not all happenstance; finding it depends on our being able not only to take an (infinite) interest in it, but on our being able to embrace it freely as our own.

But, to repeat, such an embrace of the ordinary in an existential choice of the daily is never made once and for all; the embrace of the ordinary is a repetition; it is a daily embrace of the daily, a continuous claiming of it, a continuous seeking and finding, a daily process of taking possession of the everyday.

Developing a comedic attitude towards the events of daily life requires that we acknowledge that we are dependent on the course of events, that happiness is connected to what *happens,* to fortune, luck, chance, contingency, to *happenstance*—the same forces that are the source of happiness may also produce unhappiness, suffering, the tragic. A key to the difference between the tragic and the comic, not to mention the external events themselves, or the seriousness of these events, is in the attitude we take toward what happens. But this is not just a matter of psychology, it is a difference in what we might call metaphysics. As I might put this, our attitude towards things is an element in the constitution of what there is.

Harkening back to Cavell's earlier work, we can say that taking up an attitude toward something is tied up with naming it. And clearly, what a thing is (called) has something important to do with what it is. Again, this is not just psychology.

And what's in a name? Well quite a lot. The name we give to something determines to some degree the kind of reality it is for us, its place in our world. Naming actualizes actuality; it calls the (our) world forth, so to speak. Calling an event an accident, a coincidence, fate, luck, the will of God, etc. makes all the difference in the world as to what the event is; the name I give it determines my attitude towards it; and this is an essential part of determining what it is.

As an example of this, Cavell considers the following line from the script of the movie *Breathless.* He says that when the hero of this film says, " 'There is no unhappy love,' he is not, as some may be, leaving the matter open to question, to evidence; for him it is knowledge a priori; you may say a definition" (PH, 238). Cavell's point is that the difference between taking a statement as true a posteriori as opposed to taking it as true a priori is something that may have all in the world to do with a difference in the attitude one takes to the statement.

The question arises, "What is my attitude toward the everyday?" That is, what is my attitude toward the ordinary, since the everyday just is the ordinary? Or what role do these words *everyday* and *ordinary* play in my narrative experience of the world? Is the everyday something to get through? Is everydayness hollow? dull? deadly? Is to live within the ordinary to live a life of quiet desperation? Is it to live a life of despondency and dejection? Is it to live a life of bedimmed averageness?

If this is the attitude I adopt toward the everyday, then it is no place for happiness. And surely it must be true, as the fairy tale declares, that happiness comes only at the conclusion of the story, when the events of daily existence have come to an end. Only then can we say, "And they lived happily ever after." This is to think of happiness as a kind of death, or at least, something achieved elsewhere, or on the other side of, or beyond, ordinary life.

Our film *"The Awful Truth"* tells us that the awful truth—the truth that strikes awe in us—is that happiness is found, if it is, within the ordinary, within our daily lives, within the routines of dailiness that marriage is one emblem of. It tells us that the awful truth is that there is no other world where happiness lies; that this life, its everydayness is sufficient. It tells us that life is not built around festivals, special days, but that, in Cavell's quotation of Luther's words, "All life should be baptism."

This film's take on this idea is something like this: "Everyday life should be festival." And more particularly, this understanding is expressed in terms of "some good laughs." This is what Lucy Warriner (Irene Dunne) says to her Aunt Patsy about her life with her now estranged husband Jerry (Cary Grant). As Cavell puts it, she did not mean that we had one laugh *at* life, this would be the laugh of cynicism. Rather, she means that the two had a run of laughs *within* their life together. Reading Lucy's mind, Cavell reads her remark about "some good laughs" as saying, "He is the one with whom that is possible for me, crazy as he is; that is the awful truth" (PH, 239).

This film asks us to think of happy marriage as a run of good laughs, it asks us to think of marriage as festive existence; it asks to seek, and thus to consider the possibility that we may find, the sublime within the pedestrian. And it gives us a hint as to how this way of thinking, of seeking and finding, is possible.

Seeking and finding the sublime within the pedestrian is not a matter of seeking or finding some new experience. It is, as Cavell says, "a matter of a new reception of your own experience"(PH, 240). I would call this a new way of embracing one's experience as one's own, a way of not only having experience but of owning it. Coming to own our ordinary experience is a matter of coming to accept it as worthwhile and valuable. It is a matter of being able to embrace "earth not heaven" (PH, 240), happiness now, not then, happiness within life and not in some future everafter. It is a matter of seeing that human happiness is found, if it is, "in a present continuity of before and after"; it is a matter of transforming "festival into festivity"; it is a matter not of correcting error but experience, or correcting our "perspective on experience" (PH, 240).

Happiness does not then depend on something that is yet to happen, but on something that is always happening, day by day. And putting this point in terms of marriage, we can say that a happy marriage entails a continuous reaffirmation—and hence the dialectical threat of divorce. It is in this sense that a legitimate marriage must be thought of as a remarriage, or as a daily re-marrying, and as carrying within itself the daily threat of divorce. Marriage is not simply a wedding festival that happens once and for all, it is a daily rejection of the threat of the dullness of repetition and a daily affirmation of repetition as festive existence: marriage is a ring of remarriage, a fact made clear by the ever-present possibility of divorce.

Another aspect of this paradox is that the recognition that happiness can be found within the dailiness of marriage, within the ordinariness of it, rests dialectically on our coming to terms with our capacity to seek happiness outside of the ordinary—call this the dream of a "home on the range" for Lucy, and the fantasy of living the playboy's life with the Vances for Jerry. The exploration of these possibilities, the threat of the temptation to find happiness elsewhere than where you are, provides both Lucy and Jerry the perspective they need to see the awful truth. Happiness for them is in their life together; it is something that is right before their eyes; it is theirs for the taking. All they are required to do is embrace it.

But this is not to suggest that what they are called on to embrace, or re-embrace, is the same life they had before the threat of divorce had had its wrenching existential effects. At the end of the film, when the divorce is about to be finalized, it is clear that the two come to see how the threat of divorce has radically transformed their perspective on their previous life together. They both know that if they re-embrace each other, their life together, it will be both the same and different. As the dialogue goes:

JERRY: In half an hour we'll no longer be Mr. and Mrs.—Funny, isn't it?
LUCY: Yes, it's funny that everything's the way it is on account of the way you feel.
JERRY: Huh?
LUCY: Well, I mean if you didn't feel the way you feel, things wouldn't be the way they are, would they?
JERRY: But things are the way you made them.

> LUCY: Oh no. They're the way you think I made them. I didn't make them that way at all. Things are just the same as they always were, only you're just the same, too, so I guess things will never be the same again. Ah-h. Good night . . .
>
> LUCY: You're all confused, aren't you?
>
> JERRY: Uh-huh. Aren't you?
>
> LUCY: No.
>
> JERRY: Well you should be, because you're wrong about things being different because they're not the same. Things are different, except in a different way. You're still the same, only I've been a fool. Well, I'm not now. So, as long as I'm different, don't you think things could be the same again? Only a little different?
>
> LUCY: You mean that Jerry? No more doubts?
>
> (Jerry locks them in the same room together. She lies back on the bed laughing!)

Marriage is a choice, but the existential, ontological impact of this choice does not dawn until the full force of the possibility of divorce is confronted. To say that a legitimate marriage is always and necessarily a remarriage is just to say that marriage, as a form of being together, and hence as a form of human happiness, must be a continuous re-embracing—of each partner by the other, of the continuity of the ordinary, of daily human finitude; and it is to say that this re-embracing always lies on the dialectical other side of the possibility (or actuality) of divorce—from each other, from the ordinary, from our own humanness.

On the logic of paradox, then, divorce is an indispensable dialectical component within a legitimate marriage, just as skepticism is such a component within knowledge. Only what can be repudiated can be embraced as our own. But what can be repudiated must be continuously re-embraced.

Three

NUSSBAUM

Techniques of Transcendence

Five

THE LOVE OF WISDOM

Martha Nussbaum's interest in ancient philosophy is by no means a merely theoretical interest. She is a practical philosopher first and foremost. Or as I might put this, she sees philosophy as more than an abstract aesthetic enterprise. For her, any philosophy worth its salt must have an existential dimension; it must have something to do with the concrete world, with human beings; it must address concrete human needs; it must be responsive to human perplexities, sufferings, joys; it must instruct us on how we as human beings ought to live if we are to live well, if we are to satisfy our innate desire for happiness *(eudaimonia)*. For Nussbaum, good philosophy is therapy for the human soul, the good philosopher its physician. This, Nussbaum tells us, is what the ancients thought, and this, she tells us, is what they have to teach us.[1]

Interestingly enough, she, like Kierkegaard and Cavell, approaches her existential interest in the human via an exploration of the human wish to transcend itself. Her exploration takes her to the Greeks, to Plato and Aristotle, and to the inheritors of this tradition, the Hellenistic Schools. It takes her as well to literature, where she sees these themes of transcendence being worked out in a way that complements and completes the work of philosophy—or better, in a way that humanizes philosophy; in a way that gives philosophy more existential import.

1. The two works where this is most emphasized are *The Fragility of Goodness: Luck and Ethics in Greek Tragedy and Philosophy* (New York: Cambridge University Press, 1986) (hereafter FG); and *The Therapy of Desire: Theory and Practice in Hellenistic Ethics* (Princeton: Princeton University Press, 1990) (hereafter TD).

By way of introduction to Nussbaum's thought, I will say a brief word about what I take to be a key distinction in her understanding of human existence. This distinction cuts human events into two mutually exclusive and opposing kinds: happenings that are uncontrolled *(tuche)* and those that are controlled *(techne)*. This opposition is the hermeneutical key to Nussbaum's understanding of the philosophical enterprise of the ancient Greeks and Romans. But not only does this distinction form the framework for her interpretation of ancient philosophy, I believe that it is also key to her interpretation of contemporary texts of literature and contemporary philosophy and the need of the one for the other. And I might even go a step further: I would not be surprised to learn that the opposition between *tuche* and *techne* organizes not only her intellectual life, but more practically and concretely, her life.

So then what do the words mean? We must be more precise than to say merely that *tuche* names the uncontrolled and *techne* names the controlled. The Greek word *tuche* is usually translated simply as luck or chance (good or bad, fortunate or unfortunate). But more precisely, it names events that merely *happen* to human beings either by chance (luck) or by necessity (fate). For Nussbaum, being exposed to the forces of *tuche* is a, if not the, defining mark of the human condition. As she sees it, the human is, if anything, fragile, and fragile to its core; and it is this exposure to *tuche* that makes it so.

Nussbaum's claim that our exposure to *tuche* is definitive of our human condition, that it is bedrock in our humanness, tells us something important about our human world. It tells us that we human beings live in a world that is, at least partially, independent of our wills. Moreover, it tells us that we are beings whose definitive mode of existence is *anxiety*. This existential anxiety over the consciousness of uncontrolled happenings disturbs our souls; it is a major source of our sense of fragility. And it is no wonder, for while *tuche* sometimes brings us good fortune, it also, and perhaps far too often, brings us misfortune. But whatever it brings, it befalls us independently of our wills.

And it is not just that our human exposure to contingency, to possibility, can and often does bring with it actual misfortune or fortune, the real source of the anxiety and the sense of fragility is in the consciousness of the uncertainty and the unpredictability of it all. It is this element of being conscious of unknown possibilities that makes our lives seem so exciting and so very vulnerable. But it is the dread of the possibility of misfortune that disturbs us most deeply. Somehow it has seemed to us that knowing that some particular misfortune is definitely and inevitably on the way makes it easier to take, easier to prepare for, easier to endure. Or as we might say, the threat of, the possibility of, misfortune is more disturbing than its actuality; and even the dream of good fortune sometimes seems more exciting than its realization.

Our English usage of the word *anxiety* reflects the essential duality of *tuche*. When we are anxious, it may be because we are excited and happy as we anticipate some good that we *hope* is about to happen. (I emphasize *hope* here to capture an all too familiar experience—call this disappointment.) And just as well, it may be that we are anxious because we are dreading something bad happening. While we may anxiously await great things happening to us, the sun shining on us, as it were, and though we may welcome the open field of possibilities in natural contingency with youthful excitement and enthusiasm, we, like fools, may not have reckoned with the dark side of the idea that we live in a world in which "anything is possible." In fact, if we manage to face just how wide open this *anything* is, we are usually struck with terror. And instead of running headlong into an unequivocal embrace of *tuche*, we may find ourselves paralyzed with a different sort of anxiousness.

It is not surprising then that *tuche*, however basic it is to our human condition, has most often not been welcomed. Just how much of it can we live with and still have a good life? Many have concluded that the slings and arrows of contingency are simply too outrageous, too overwhelming, to tolerate at all. Convinced that the good life must be secure from the forces of uncontrolled happenings, many have wished for and searched for a way of living in which *tuche* is completely banished.

The wish for, the search for, a way to live in which *tuche* is banished is a wish and a search for what Nussbaum calls a *techne*. She defines this term as follows: "*Techne*, then, is a deliberate application of human intelligence to some part of the world, yielding some control over *tuche;* it is concerned with the management of need and with prediction and control concerning future contingencies"(FG, 95). And further, she says that to employ a *techne* is just to attempt "to eliminate luck from human life . . . [and] to put that life . . . under the control of the agent"(FG, 3–4). For Nussbaum, *techne* stands in opposition to *tuche*: the former is a form of control or management, and the latter is defined as that which is uncontrolled. They form what Nussbaum calls an antithesis (FG, 89, 94). *Techne* always aims at supplanting *tuche;* it is the human power of control.

For Nussbaum, the human urge to formulate techniques of control *(technes),* however human the urge might be, represents a strange human wish to transcend itself. It is certainly not strange to want to flee from the outrages of fortune and misfortune, but if our exposure to *tuche* is indeed definitive of the human, then it follows that the formulation of *technes,* designed to subdue or eliminate this exposure, can only be seen as expressing a desire to transcend this condition. Against this urge to find a technique for transcending the human, Nussbaum suggests that there is wisdom in the embrace of the human. Such an embrace requires that we embrace our exposure to *tuche,* and that we embrace our fragility as our essential human condition.

One way to resist the temptation to formulate and to follow such techniques of transcending the human is the vigilant and critical examination of the various philosophical voices of our culture that seek to tell us what it is to live well as a human being. Sometimes these voices tell us that the best human life is one that seeks to transcend *tuche,* and sometimes the voices counsel us (or seem to) to embrace it. In any case, submitting these voices to critical examination, Nussbaum thinks, is therapy for the soul.

Certainly Socrates, Plato, and the Hellenistic Schools thought that progress toward the good human life is made when we develop a *techne* that will take us in the direction of eliminating ungoverned natural contingencies. Only when we devise a way to be safe from the ravages of *tuche* can we find a life worth living. This is what Socrates (and Plato and the Schools) thought philosophy can do for us: philosophy can provide us with a technique for the elimination of such contingencies from our lives.

What philosophy teaches, Plato tells us, is the love of wisdom, for this is our only protection, our only safety, our only path to self-sufficiency and invulnerability. To be wise is to know what is good, what is real; and if we are wise then we know that nothing unreal can harm us (LK, 17). And what is not real? Plato's startling answer is everything in the natural world of appearances. But, if we know this, we know that nothing in this shadowy illusion of reality can harm us. Practical wisdom is thus a *techne* of detachment from the natural world, a detachment that enables us to be free from anxiety, free from disturbance, free from natural contingency; it is a *techne* that enables us to master contingency and secure our fragile human lives. As such, practical wisdom is a *techne* that can save us; it is the sure path to human happiness.

There is certainly an irony in all of this. If we are seeking the best human life, and if we think that exposure to *tuche,* to its temporal ravages of unpredictability, of aging and ultimately of death, is definitive of our humanness, and if we accept the Socratic/Platonic/Hellenistic prescription for the good life, that is, if we develop a *techne* that will enable us to transcend *tuche,* then we are left with the conclusion that the best human life is a life that seeks to transcend its own humanness. For these philosophers, the best human life is one that gets as far as is possible away from living as a human being.

Now, as I read her, Nussbaum is, as I am, trying to get us to see that the human flight from *tuche* via a philosophical *techne* is ultimately a flight from our humanness, an attempt to transcend it, and ultimately a form of despair, or even madness. Against this flight, she argues in favor of something like what I have been calling a full-bodied, robust embrace of the human. And brilliantly, she seeks to expose the many pretensions to embrace the human, especially in the Hellenistic Schools, for what they are, namely, disguised variations on this flight.

But when it comes to Nussbaum's own version of the human embrace, nagging questions remain, at least for me. The main problem, as I see it, is the way that she construes the distinction between *tuche* and *techne*. Even though the distinction has proven enormously productive for me as an interpretive framework, it has also proven problematic. Let me comment briefly on this.

What are the forces of *tuche?* What are the forces the exposure to which Nussbaum thinks defines the human, that defines it as essentially fragile? It does not help to say simply that these are the forces of contingency, for contingency can be of at least two kinds. I mean the word *contingency* can mean *natural contingency* or it can mean *moral contingency*. Moreover, I think there is a good bit of ambivalence and even vagueness on Nussbaum's part as to whether she takes the term *tuche* to capture one or both of these kinds of contingency. This is partially so because she does not draw this distinction explicitly.

But even so, the weight of Nussbaum's (theoretical) analysis seems to be on the side of taking *tuche* as capturing natural contingency. I say this because I see in Nussbaum a decided tendency to favor organic metaphors for human existence. She, like her mentor Aristotle, is drawn to think of human beings as plants, or at least like plants insofar as both are rooted in the ground and dependent on, and exposed to, external conditions for survival and fruition. That is, I take Nussbaum to take *tuche* as referring primarily to the (blind?) forces of nature.

Although Nussbaum does not explicitly draw a (theoretical) distinction between organic and moral contingency, she does explicitly draw a distinction *within* the organic, a distinction between two different forces of nature. *Tuche* may refer to either an external or an internal natural contingency. The former is what *happens* to a human being from the outside, from the natural world; the latter is what *happens* to a human being from the inside, from the vegetative soul as it were. The former consists of forces like storms that blow our ships to treasure or to disaster; the latter of forces like appetites and drives that keep us alive and give us pleasure but also threaten to drag us into ruin.

Both sorts of contingent natural happenings simply befall us; neither is brought about by our agency. As Nussbaum puts it, "What happens to a person by luck [*tuche*] will be just what does not happen through his or her own agency, what just *happens* to him, as *opposed* to what he does or makes" (FG, 3, italics added). Although both external and internal natural contingencies are events that may or may not happen, neither of them is brought on, either directly or indirectly, by human agency.

Having said this, we must note that our agency, especially our moral agency, does, of necessity, generate its own contingencies; things often happen to us as a consequence of our own agency. In particular, our moral actions set into motion the moral actions of others, actions that are beyond our control. Entering the realm of moral action then exposes us to contingency and to fragility, as much so as our exposure to natural forces. This is what I would call moral contingency and moral fragility; it is the contingency and fragility that we bring upon ourselves (directly or indirectly) through our agency. Moral action always carries suffering within itself.

Yet, as Nussbaum explicitly defines *tuche,* it seems to stand in opposition to human doing, moral agency included. That is, for her, it names only those cases in which what may or may not happen is independent of what we do; it names only those happenings that we suffer but which we do not bring on ourselves. It is in this sense that, for her, *tuche* is *opposed* to our doing, to agency.

As I see it, this is too narrow a view of contingency, of *tuche,* and leads to too narrow a definition of human agency, and to too narrow a view of the human. Of course, human beings are subject to suffering what just happens to us from nature without our asking. We find ourselves in a condition of being born in a particular place and time, with these particular abilities or disabilities, subject to the uncertainly and unpredictability of time, the restraints of embodiment, neediness, dependency, mortality. Moreover, these natural conditions fix the kind of beings that we humans are, namely, fragile to the core. Yet human beings are also called on to suffer a different kind of contingency, a different sort of fragility. Human beings may enter into a realm of moral agency that is as much a realm of time and its inherent unpredictability and uncertainty as is the realm of nature. To enter this realm is to enter into a realm of contingency that is presupposed by our moral agency and that is intensified as a result of it—call this the contingency of moral freedom. As I reckon, we humans are exposed to *both* moral and natural contingency. Indeed, for me, it is the latter contingency (moral *tuche)* that is distinctive to human being, or more precisely, distinctive to being human. At the same time, it is both kinds of contingency that render us humans fragile to the core; human suffering is caused by both moral and natural contingency.

At times, Nussbaum seems to agree. She says, "I am an agent, but also a plant. . . . [I am] . . . able to deliberate and choose, to make a plan . . . [and at the same time I am] . . . rooted in the dirt and [stand] helplessly in the rain (FG, 2, 5). In fact, despite her (theoretical) preference for natural metaphors (plants, flourishing, etc.) for the human, her analyses of tragedy and modern literature, especially her treatment of love, focuses on the human sufferings that are produced by moral agency (betrayal, rage, etc.). She is ambivalent. But even though she is ambivalent between moral and organic metaphors for the human, and even though she seems to me to lean (theoretically) toward the organic, one thing is clear, and I think correct: for her, the human is *essentially* fragile.

So then, what is the source of this fragility? Is it solely in the fact that I am a plant standing helplessly in the rain? Or is it also in the fact that I am an agent? Again, we are confronted with Nussbaum's interpretation of *tuche* as *opposed* to *techne*. My haunting question is this, Is moral action simply another form of *techne?* I don't think that she wants to say this, indeed the contrary, but this implication is at least plausible on the basis of the way she draws the *tuche/techne* distinction. If moral action is itself simply another *techne* for controlling *tuche,* then it would seem that it would not generate fragility, but would be designed to secure us from it. Is moral action a source of fragility or a bulwark against it? Is it both? These are very complicated questions.

As it is becoming clear, my view is that it a mistake to take the source of human fragility as being exclusively in the fact that human beings are patients, that is, subject to things happening to us. For me, the fact that we are agents is also a, if not the, distinctively human source of our fragility. I am not suggesting that Nussbaum does not know that we are both agents and patients, she does. As I quoted above, she surely agrees that we are *both* plants, dependent on the rain, *and* agents, possessing the power to change things (or keep them the same), the capacity to make things better (or worse). Yet, for her, the power of agency seems (theoretically) not to be a source of our fragility but a source of our attempt to control it, or subdue it.

What Nussbaum needs, I suggest, is to make more (theoretical) distinctions within her basic distinction, so as to exclude moral action as simply another *techne.* She might do this by distinguishing, as for example, Hannah Arendt does, among different kinds of doings. Arendt is famous for distinguishing three human activities, labor, work, and action. For her, both work and action, unlike labor, are distinctive to the human, but are themselves very different kinds of doing. Work is making, building; it is world-making, world-building; moral action is something that takes place within that world, between human beings, and, for her, is the most definitive human activity. As Aristotle might put it, it is the activity of moral action that is available neither to the beasts nor to the gods; it is the human activity that both Aristotle and Arendt call political.

Given the way that Nussbaum defines *techne,* wouldn't she be forced to say that work and action are both technes? But surely there is a difference. Both forms of doing are not simply techniques of control. While it is the case that making a world (work) is a project of human agency that aims to control natural contingency *(tuche),* it does not follow that every form of human agency has a similar aim. Certainly work is a *techne* in this sense, but moral action is not. If anything, moral action generates contingency and fragility. Moral action secures us in some sense, but it does so in the midst of contingency, not by attempting to eliminate it. Or better, moral action secures us *within,* rather than *from,* contingency.

If moral action is included, as Nussbaum seems to do, as a technique of control, then it becomes paradoxically at war with human fragility, at war with the human itself. This position is puzzling, and disturbing, since it militates against Nussbaum's self-declared aim to embrace the human. As it stands, Nussbaum's position seems to lead to the conclusion that moral action is just another *techne* for escaping from *tuche,* just another attempt to escape from the human. What she needs to say, and what I want to say, is that moral action is indeed constitutive of the human. But, as I see it, moral action is not a technique of control; rather it is a source, perhaps the most profound source, of human fragility.

In summary, I will say that, for me, as it might well be for Nussbaum in fact, human actions, especially moral actions, and the fragility these actions generate, are not intrinsically forms of *techne* (as she suggests), but are nevertheless intrinsic to, and definitive of, the human, as much so as exposure to *tuche.* But this theoretical disagreement aside, Nussbaum's practical concern, and mine, is that we be alert to this fact: when human agency is transposed completely into technes for eliminating every contingency from our lives, as it often is, such a wholesale transposition of human agency into technique can only be bred of a desire to transcend human fragility, and ultimately, a desire to transcend the human. We both agree, this is madness.

In this chapter, I will return, from time to time, to my theoretical worry that the logic of Nussbaum's position runs the risk of seeing moral action as a technique of control. However, my main focus will be on the persistent temptation of the human to transcend itself, something Martha Nussbaum and I completely agree on. We will begin by setting out in more detail Nussbaum's philosophic problematic. What seems to be at the center of her philosophic agenda is what she calls "the ancient debate." Let us turn then to see what the issues of this debate are, and how they have shaped her philosophic project.

The Ancient Debate

Plato started it. He launched an attack on the poets and the artists that they are still reeling from. He set the agenda for the debate between the sciences and the arts/humanities that continues to this day. And by and large, he has won the day. Or, at least, compared to the arts and the humanities, the sciences and technology have won a more respected place, indeed the central place, in the intellectual and popular imagination.

I will not pursue Plato's beef with the visual artists, except to say this. It is arguable that Plato's objection to their craft stands in ironic contradiction to Plato's own theory of forms. As he understood it, visual artists go astray in dealing only with copies and shadows and not with real things—the eternal forms. But as thinkers like Kierkegaard have pointed out, it is perhaps the visual arts that have discovered the perfect form for expressing pure Platonic form. As Kierkegaard might well say, the aesthetic plastic arts are the forms of expression perfectly and uniquely suited to capturing the absolute stasis, the unchanging eternity, of the *eidos*. Perhaps Plato dismissed the visual arts too hastily.

My focus here, however, is on Plato's attack on the poets, especially the tragic poets. Tragic drama, like the other media within the arts, is essentially an aesthetic form; yet its use of the existential medium of language makes it closer to life, less abstract, than most of the other arts. But beyond its use of the existential medium of language as its form, tragic drama is also more concrete than most of the other arts—especially the visual arts—in its content.

Tragic drama is intensely focused on life in the world—what Kierkegaard has called the realm of the existential. In fact we might say that tragic drama mimics or imitates life. To be sure, actors in a tragic drama do not act in the existential sense of this term—they are only play acting. Yet what they do on stage is clearly meant to have a bearing on existential actuality, on real life action in the world.

For Plato, this is just the problem: this interest in life in the world is just what he held against the poets and their poetry. That is, for Plato, the poets go astray in not having a proper subject matter: they mistakenly have their focus on existence, on life in the world, and hence divert our attention from reality, the eternal forms.

To Plato's credit, he saw something very important in the very nature of dramatic tragic poetry. That is, he saw in just what way the dramatic action of the tragedies, while only an aesthetic representation of existential action, was addressed to the concrete situation of human beings in the world. What he saw was that the tragic drama's main concern was with worldly attachments, and hence with the possibility and actuality of loss and reversal.

For the tragedians, this world is the setting of our search for happiness. It is therefore important that we understand what this world is and how it works. First, the world is defined as a fabric of attachments, a network of connections, familial, political, erotic, etc. Second, how does the world work? Well there are certainly forces at play in it that are beyond our control—the forces of *tuche*, both natural and moral. Hence, because the world is a fabric of attachments and because these attachments are exposed to the forces of *tuche*, our worldly attachments are subject to being broken. We are therefore constantly confronted with the possibility of loss. Life in the world is fundamentally fragile—perhaps fundamentally tragic.

This logic led the poets to conclude that our exposure to *tuche*—the double-sided risk of exposure to chance and necessity—must be confronted. The burden of their dramas was to express their tragic view of life and to bring their audiences into a cathartic confrontation with the hazards of exposure to *tuche*. Nussbaum puts the basic elements of the tragic view of life as follows: "The elements of this view include at least the following: that happenings beyond the agent's control are of real importance not only for his or her feelings of happiness or contentment, but also for whether he or she manages to live a fully good life, a life inclusive of various forms of laudable action. That, therefore, what happens to people by chance [*tuche*] can be of enormous importance to the ethical quality of their lives; that, therefore, good people are right to care about such chance events" (LK, 17). (As it turned out, the side of *tuche* that most urgently preoccupied the tragic poets was the problem of exposure to necessity, what they called fate.)

It was to this general tragic view of life, which accorded importance to these matters of worldly attachment and loss, that Plato so vehemently objected. His particular focus however was to the tragedians' idea that the human exposure to *tuche* is an important consideration in the search for the good life. The tragedians wanted to show how we are exposed to *tuche;* Plato ✓ wanted to show us how we can avoid this exposure. The only way to avoid it, Plato reasoned, was to banish *tuche,* not just by banishing the poets from the republic, but by banishing it via metaphysical argument. He set out therefore to show that *tuche* was unreal. If unreal, and we know it, then *tuche* cannot ll harm us.

For Plato, the only way for human beings to save ourselves from tragic disaster is to make our souls immune to the threat of *tuche.* And the way to do this is to find a *techne* that will subdue it and ultimately eliminate it. Do we have such a *techne?* Plato says that we do. He offers philosophy as the most viable candidate. For him, philosophy can save us from tragedy, not to mention the tragedians; for him, philosophy can save our lives: "The need of human beings for philosophy is, for him, deeply connected with their exposure to luck; the elimination of this exposure is the primary task of the philosophical art as he conceives it" (FG, 90). *cf. Nietzsche*

What does philosophy as *techne* have to teach us about the good life? It tells us that to live well is to live aloof from exposure to *tuche.* How do we do this? And why should we? Plato argues that we must turn our souls to what is real and away from the concerns of what is not—mere appearances. And what is not real, or fully real? The short answer for Plato is this world of becoming. For him, it is a waste of effort and a manifestation of our ignorance to focus our care and concern on the affairs of this temporal world, or on bodily needs, or worldly attachments of any kind—attachments that by their very nature do not last. Philosophy offers us a technique that will enable us to live above these concerns, to live absolutely without external need, without dependency on anything in the external world of fleeting shadows and mere appearances. The lover of wisdom is the one who has learned to live an absolutely self-sufficient life; and ultimately such a lover is the one who has learned that he or she must live this life absolutely alone.

But is there a slight of hand in all of this? Is there some hidden implication in Plato's contention that *tuche* is not real and in his offer of philosophy as a *techne* for escaping from it? Doesn't the Platonic plan to save human beings from the ravages of *tuche* turn out to be a plan to save human beings from themselves? Is philosophy for Plato a technique for transcending the human?

Well Plato had nothing to hide. He would readily accept this characterization of his proposed philosophical technique. He knows full well that the aim of philosophy is to transcend the human. Nevertheless, he recommends it as the only way to find a life worth living.

Well what exactly does he recommend? What exactly is Plato proposing in his efforts to save us from our mortal human condition via the *techne* of
philosophy? What kind of life does the philosopher live? How is the philosopher's life the model of the best life for a human being? The answer is as simple as it is startling: the lover of wisdom, the philosopher, must learn to live
as an immortal god, for only the gods know true *eudaimonia*.

What we usually hear from Plato (Socrates) is that philosophy is preparation for death. But if I am reading Nussbaum's interpretation of Plato correctly, the practice of philosophy turns out to be the practice of dying to the
world in order to be safe from death. That is, what the practice of philosophy
turns out to be is preparation for *immortality*.

The philosopher overcomes exposure to *tuche* by dying every day to the
attachments of everyday worldly existence; but this death is in the service of
the aim of living as an immortal god, completely self-sufficient, completely
invulnerable. To live in this way, to turn our cares from things outside of ourselves and hence outside of our control, is to free ourselves from their effects.
The prize of living in worldly detachment is invulnerability to loss. This is,
for Plato, absolutely necessary for happiness. To be happy is to live beyond
the threat of loss, and to live beyond this threat is to live like the gods; such a
person will not suffer, and like the gods, will not die.

The philosopher who practices such a technique of godlike detachment
must carefully extirpate the emotions from his soul, for the emotions are the
traps the world sets for us. This is particularly true of love. This emotion at-
taches us to our friends, our family, our lovers, in just the way that will cloud
our reason and inevitably bring us suffering and loss. If we love finite things
and persons, we love what does not last; hence we love what we can lose. For
Plato, wisdom tells us that we must love only the eternal; hence the lover of
wisdom loves nothing in this world.

The good life requires that even purely sexual attachments be transcended. Sex is a passing pleasure, meditation on the forms is eternal. The
true philosopher, as Socrates knew, must become as cold and as impenetrable
as a stone:

> It is not without reason that Alcibiades compares Socratic virtues to
> statues of the gods. For, as we have seen, Socrates, in his ascent towards
> form, has become himself, very like a form, hard, indivisible, unchang-
> ing. . . . It is not only Socrates' dissociation from his body. It is not only
> that he sleeps all night with the naked Alcibiades without arousal. There
> is, along with this remoteness, a deeper impenetrability of spirit. Words

launched 'like bolts' have no effect. . . . Socrates refuses to be affected. He is stone; and he also turns others to stone. (FG, 195)

It is no wonder that Alcibiades committed his famous sacrilege. One night he went for a walk, drunk on the divine madness of eros and frustrated by the impenetrability of Socrates-the-stone, and in a rage of madness mutilated the statues of the gods, smashing their faces and genitals. Here we see a human being rejecting Socrates' cold and inhuman definition of the best human life; here we see a human being raging against the lure of the inhuman. To live as a stone, as a god, frees us from the conflicts of passion, from the vulnerability to loss, from dependence, from neediness, from the effects of *tuche,* but at what price? For Alcibiades that price is too dear.

Plato's attack on the poets then can ultimately be traced to his attack on *tuche.* He attacked the poets not because they saw *tuche* as definitive of the human condition; he agreed with this. He attacked them because they thought that we were stuck with this condition and hence that we must seek the good life within the limits of our exposure to *tuche.* The tragic poets tried to tell us, however indirectly, that if we find a good life we must do so within this exposure.

Plato thought this was impossible, and perhaps the tragic poets, in the final analysis, did also. But the difference was that Plato thought that we can, through the practice of the right *techne,* that is, philosophy, transcend the human condition of exposure to *tuche;* the tragic poets thought this wish for transcendence was impossible, perhaps unintelligible. While Plato thought that we can find a life worth living only when we learn to live as gods and thus above the effects of *tuche,* the tragic poets thought our only option was to live within it; their task was to inspire the courage to confront *tuche,* or at least the wisdom of resignation in the face of it.

There were dissenters in the philosophical community in this ancient debate. Aristotle was the most notable one. If the poets were to have a champion, it was in Plato's star pupil. Contra Plato, Aristotle defended not only the poets but something broader, something more like the common sense of Greek culture. Central to this common sense was a deep ambivalence felt towards the gods, towards a godlike immortal existence.

As Nussbaum puts it, one way to understand the gods would be to think that they are unequivocally *better* than humans, superior. This is Plato. Their existence is better because the gods lack what we call human limitations: they are immortal, omnipotent, omniscient, or almost so.

On the other hand, the gods may be conceived more equivocally. They may be thought of as simply and strangely *different;* as different as an alien might be, and so as suspicious; as different as some superhuman from some other planet, and so as frightening; as different as another species perhaps, as an ape say, and so, as intriguing. This is Aristotle.

Aristotle himself is certainly equivocal on this issue. Sometimes he leads us to think that the aspiration to live among such beings, to live as such an alien being, to live as a god, would entail forfeiting a core goodness in our human existence. At other times he seems to identify such a godlike existence as the best kind of life. So then, for Aristotle, does the good life entail that we live other than a human existence? And would we want to, even if we could?

Nussbaum seems more impressed with Aristotle when he speaks from the anti-Platonic side of his ambivalence, when he argues that a godlike existence would not be the only kind of life worth living. She nicely illustrates the Aristotelian alternative to Plato, and her admiration of it, with a story from Homer.

Nussbaum puts this question of whether we would want to live as gods if we could in terms of an offer made to Odysseus by Calypso to stay with her and become a god, immortal and ageless. The offer would require that Odysseus turn away from his quest to return home, that he resign from the concerns of human finitude. He refuses the offer, though he has already stayed with Calypso for some time, and even though he stays one more year. The reasons he offers are as follows:

> Goddess and queen, do not make this a cause of anger with me. I know the truth of everything that you say. I know that my wise Penelope, when a man looks at her, is far beneath you in form and stature; she is a mortal, you are immortal and ongoing. Yet, notwithstanding, my desire and longing day by day is still to reach my own home and to see the day of my return. And if this or that divinity should shatter my craft on the wine-dark ocean, I will bear it and keep a bold heart within me. Often enough before this time have war and wave oppressed and plagued me; let new tribulations join the old. (LK, 365)[2]

2. It is interesting to note here that Calypso's offer to Odysseus to remain with her is an offer not to transcend the natural order, but precisely the opposite. She is tempting Odysseus to refuse to stand out from nature. It is true that the temptation she offers is a temptation to depart from human existence, but this departure is not in the direction of an aloof god. Rather, her temptation draws Odysseus in the opposite direction, the direction of the Earth Mother, we might say (Calypso is portrayed by Homer as a nymph not a goddess). Odysseus resists the temptation to be engulfed by the immanent, to re-enter the womb, her cave, to live wholly within the natural order, even if such an existence would be as deathless as nature.

I owe this insight to my colleague R. Taylor Scott. In fairness to Professor Nussbaum, how-

So Odysseus chooses his own life, his own human existence with all of its vulnerability to change, to aging, to death; he chooses a real aging and mortal woman over an ageless, deathless, beautiful nymph. For Nussbaum, and for the Aristotle that she most respects, Odysseus's choice seems not only intelligible, but virtuous.

The issue in this ancient story is really the subject of the recent popular film *Cocoon*. Here the question is simply put: we, aging and dying human beings, have a chance to leave St. Petersburg, the nursing home, to have our health and youthful vigor, including sexual potency and desire, restored, and to live forever; all we have to do is to go somewhere else, all we have to do is to leave the earth; do we want this?

In the film, most who are invited to leave reckon that they would be crazy not to. But there is one holdout; one character who refuses, who takes this rocket flight to be a metaphysical flight from humanness; one character who chooses to stay, to die (he is, I might point out, a Jew). In the sequel, one couple changes their mind and decides to return to the earth, to their grandchildren, their children, even if this means that they must die. And somehow this seems the noble, the human choice, a kind of argument, we might say, that Aristotle and the poets are right.

What, from the Aristotelian point of view, would we miss if we could actually become gods? Nussbaum considers some interesting examples.

(1) First, athletics. Wouldn't the value of, the glory of, achieving excellence in athletics vanish if we were unlimited? Is it not the case that it is the structure of the human body and the conditions of space and time, etc. that provide the necessary conditions for making sense of athletic excellence? Athletic excellence is species-specific; we don't think of it in terms of races or contests with other animals, or aliens, or robots. We frown on that which is outside of, that which is unnatural to, the human species; we do not admire something that would give an unfair advantage—drugs or bionics, say. What makes athletic excellence excellent is determined by the natural possibilities of the human species as such—by the kind of beings that we are. The offer of Calypso then appears not an offer of a better human life but a radically different *kind* of existence, a nonhuman one.

---

ever, I must note that she does think of the lure of transcending the human as a lure in two directions, upwards to the gods or downwards to the beasts. She says, "[T]he human being is also the being that can most easily cease to be itself—either by moving (Platonically) upwards towards the self-sufficiency of the divine, or by slipping downward towards the self-sufficiency of doggishness . . . both involve the closing-off of important human things" (FG, 417). In fairness though to Professor Scott, she does make it seem that Odysseus is tempted in the Platonic direction, which on her own terms, may not be the case, or at least, it certainly need not be.

(2) Consider political associations. One thing, a point Aristotle force-fully makes, that marks human beings off from both the beast and the gods is that we are political beings. What is the glory of this? Nussbaum says, "Politics is about using human intelligence to support human neediness; so to be truly human you have to have both elements. Beasts fail on the one count, gods on the other" (LK, 372). Aristotle does not allow the idea of a com-pletely self-sufficient life—a life that would not depend on the presence of others, a solitary life—to count as a fully human life; for him, the relation-ships of care and dependency that bind citizens together in the state, that bind families and friends together, are intrinsic to the good human life. A complete human existence must include them, even though such an inclusion will gen-erate risks, vulnerabilities, disappointments, pain, as an essential part of the good life, as an intrinsic part of happiness.

And (3) what about the virtues that Aristotle thinks are ingredient to the good life? Courage, for example? Nussbaum remarks, "Homeric gods usually cannot and do not have it, since there is nothing grave for them to risk. On the other hand, courageous action seems to be a fine *human* achievement" (LK, 374). And of moderation, she says, "Moderation will go out too, since for a being who cannot get ill or become overweight or alcoholic, there is not only little motivation to moderate intake, but also little intelligibility to the entire concept. On the other hand, moderation is a challenge and a fine thing in human life: there are so many ways to go wrong here, so few ways of finding what is truly appropriate" (LK, 374). And what about justice? She says, "Aristotle seems right that the whole notion of the gods making contracts and returning deposits is ludicrous, makes no sense at all. . . . Human beings are in a sense worse off than the gods because they suffer; but they also know how to deal with suffering, and their morality is a response to the fact of suf-fering. The gods are better because they *can* simply overlook, look over, the sufferings of human beings, without involvement or response" (LK, 375). If justice requires us to recognize the needs of others, to have compassion for them, to want to put a stop to suffering where we can, then human beings are better off than the gods in terms of their capacity to understand, to pursue and to achieve justice.

Not only do the gods seem worse off in important ways in comparison to human beings, they also seem to know this, that is, to envy human exis-tence. The Greek gods do fall in love, not with each other though, but with mortals. It seems that "they long . . . for that which displays effort and long-ing, need and striving, achievement against odds. . . . So the transcendent ones long, it seems for a certain sort of transcendence: for transcendence of their own limit, which is to lack limit and therefore to be incapable of virtue" (LK, 377).

So where does this leave us? It seems here: for Aristotle, the good life does not necessarily mean living as a god. He sees the possibility of there being something like a *human eudaimonia*. This human happiness he envisions is achieved not by finding a *techne* for transcending the human; this human happiness is not found by trying to eliminate the so-called human "limitations," most notably our exposure to *tuche*. Rather, it begins in the acknowledgment that human "limits" not only don't keep us from something, most notably happiness, but make happiness possible. For Aristotle, this is the beginning of practical wisdom.

As Aristotle reckons, practical wisdom teaches us that the good life for human beings is the virtuous life. But virtue needs a context—call this the human context. But simply because human virtue requires a human context does not mean that the virtuous life is somehow restricted, or confined, or limited *by* this context. Perhaps it only means that it is limited *to* this context.

Does the context of human limits then keep us from something, from being gods say? Well, on the one hand, of course; but not more or less so than any species-specific set of limitations. Just as clearly, the gods, by the limits that define the kind of beings they are, are kept from being human. On the other hand, such species-specific limitations also create possibilities not open to different kinds of beings.

Consider the virtue of courage. It seems clear that outside of a context of contingency, a context of risk and danger, the exhibition of the virtue of courage is unintelligible and *a fortiori* not admirable. Since the gods are not exposed to *tuche,* courage is not something they know or could know in themselves, although they might well admire it in human beings.

All Aristotle needs to make his claim for a human happiness is to think of virtue as *limited to* the human kind, as defined by the kind of beings humans are. And again, part of this context certainly has to be our exposure to the hazards of *tuche*. This exposure, rather than keeping us from something, makes it possible for us to live virtuously. If we were to eliminate *tuche,* therefore, we would also eliminate virtue.

Insofar as Aristotle realized that living virtuously is unintelligible outside of a context of exposure to *tuche,* he also realized that practical wisdom must not be permitted to become a *techne*. This is so because the aim of a *techne* is to subdue *tuche*. Mastering contingency, which every *techne* seeks, would make the virtuous life impossible. As Nussbaum puts it, "The decision that practical wisdom is not a *techne* or *episteme* and that the best judge is one who does not use a *techne* both supports and is supported by the view that the best life is more vulnerable to ungoverned *tuche,* more open and less ambitious for control, than Plato said it was" (FG, 290–91).

And this is just where Plato and Aristotle part company. Plato thinks that we can make philosophy, or at least practical wisdom, into a science, a *techne* and Aristotle thinks that we cannot.

Well why would we want make practical wisdom into a *techne?* Why did Plato want to? Again, Plato's argument runs something like this. Our exposure to uncontrolled happenings often leads to human suffering, to pain and to loss. This makes human existence essentially fragile. Since the human exposure to *tuche* makes us vulnerable to loss, the way to reduce the harmful effects of loss is to transcend it.

How do we transcend loss? How can we be safe from it? Plato recommends detachment. The logic is familiar. The problem is this: attachment to things and people in the world implies that they matter to us and this is exactly why we feel pain if luck or fate causes us to lose them. Plato's solution: do not be a lover of the world, be a lover of the eternal; do not let the things and people of the world matter to you; this will allow you to detach yourself from them and free yourself from the threat of their loss. Dying to worldly attachments keeps us safe from loss.

The centerpiece in Plato's strategy of detachment is his doctrine of the commensurability of all values. According to this doctrine, all values are reducible to one value, for example pleasure or "the fine" *(kalon).* Differences among valuable things, on this doctrine, turn out to be differences in quantity not differences in quality. Let us consider how this works with *kalon.*

In Plato's *Symposium,* the subject is erotic love. Here, it is acknowledged that our passionate attachments to particular people and things in this world can lead us to disaster; that is, to loss, to death, to departure, to betrayal, etc. Such a lover will be so anxious over these possibilities that happiness will not be possible for him. Can we avoid this anxiety?

Of course, Plato says, if we adopt a *techne* of commensurability; that is, if we reconfigure our sense of value. Imprisoned within the shadowy cave of the world, ordinary lovers mistakenly identify what they love with the object of their passionate attachment. Philosophical reflection tells us something different: it tells us that when a lover loves some particular body, what he really loves is not the body itself but the *fineness,* the *beauty,* the *kalon,* in that body. Further reflection tells him that other bodies can also manifest the same quality. And finally, the lover, who is becoming a lover of wisdom, comes to see that *kalon* is "a vast ocean, whose components are, like droplets, qualitatively indistinguishable" (LK, 115).

In the full light of the sun, the philosopher comes to see that the droplets of *kalon* that temporarily dance over the sea of *kalon* differ only in quantity, in size, in amount, not quality. *Kalon* is ultimately one thing, one homogeneous sea. As far as manifesting this quality goes then, one droplet is just as good as another. Although we might well find *more* of it in some particular droplets, say the bigger ones, than in others, the quality itself is not essentially connected to the particular object that manifests it.

What the lover of wisdom comes to see is that to love an object that manifests *kalon* is to love wrongly. Such a misguided love will surely lead to disaster, since these particular objects can be, and inevitably will be, lost. Wisdom comes to conclude that a proper love is always directed to the eternal quality an object manifests, not the object itself. If we loved only this quality, we would love what cannot be lost.

Nussbaum thinks that this *techne* of commensurability has staggering consequences. I agree. She asks us to try to take Plato's vision seriously. What would it be like to think:

the body of this wonderful beloved person is *exactly* the same in quality as that person's mind and inner life. Both, in turn, the same in quality as the value of Athenian democracy; of Pythagorean geometry; of Eudoxan astronomy. What would it be like to look at a body and to see in it exactly the same shade and tone of goodness and beauty as in a mathematical proof—exactly the same, differing only in amount and in location, so that the choice between making love with that person and contemplating that proof presented itself as a choice between n measures of water and $n + 100$? (LK, 116)

Clearly this radical revisioning of our ordinary ways of seeing things would release us from suffering the tragedy of loss and reversal, for it would release us from attachments to particular things and persons. And it is these that can be lost. But the price of this release is the devaluation of the particular. But this is not all. With this devaluation, particular persons and things become exchangeable. In such a flattened world, everything is replaceable. If I lose my wife, or my friend, no matter, I can find what I found in them in many other things: I am therefore immune to loss.

For Aristotle, however, it is just these attachments to particular persons and things, to family, to friends, to fellow citizens, to property, and the like, that make life worth living; it is just these attachments that make happiness possible. As Nussbaum remarks, Aristotle "rejects the suggestion that a life without political ties and ties of personal love and friendship could count as *eudaimonia.* . . . He reminds his interlocutor . . . that we are beings who think of these ties as not just necessary but as fine; not just a resource but also an intrinsic good. A life without them is not even worth living—far less a candidate for *eudaimonia"* (LK, 374).

Because passionate attachments to particular persons and things matters as much to Aristotle as they did to the tragic poets, he resists the Platonic plan to reduce practical wisdom to a *techne* and sides with the poets against Plato's attack. Aristotle, like the tragic poets he defends, is convinced that real practical wisdom comes in acknowledging that human values are plural, that there are real differences in quality, differences that will not yield to the quantitative reduction implied in the search for a *techne.* As far as Aristotle is concerned, to turn practical wisdom into a science is to rob life of its worth-whileness.

Yet there is an understandable rationale to Plato's desire to make practical wisdom a matter of *techne.* If values are plural and irreducible to quantitative measuring, then conflicts are sure to arise. It is this conflict among valuable things that makes important decisions so agonizing. If we had an ethical *techne,* this would make our choices easier. They would become something like mechanical procedures, what economists call cost-benefit analyses. Here *techne* would subdue moral *tuche,* it would eliminate the need for, and the danger in, moral action.

To turn practical wisdom into a technique of measurement then would ironically take human beings out of the loop in the great and difficult moral decisions that face us. Would this be a good thing or not? Well, certainly devising a moral *techne* would take the struggle out of difficult decisions, but it would do so at the price of taking the decision out of "wise decisions?" I mean, within a moral *techne,* wouldn't human responsiveness to the nuances of particular cases be irrelevant in practical wisdom? Wouldn't it leave human judgment out of the human picture altogether? Wouldn't it think that the fine discernment of human perception in concrete cases was not important in coming to wise decisions and wise actions? Wouldn't it ignore the value of the human capacity to improvise in unique and unprecedented cases? As far as Aristotle, and Nussbaum, and myself, are concerned, the answer to all of these questions is a disturbing "yes!" Which leads to a further question, Isn't the price of reducing practical wisdom to a moral *techne* simply too dear?

Or maybe our question should be different. Perhaps we should ask, Can we have it both Plato's and Aristotle's way? Can human happiness require both the embrace of our exposure to *tuche* (Aristotle) and the embrace of a *techne* for transcending this exposure (Plato)?

Aristotle himself seems to want both. He is notoriously ambivalent on the matter.[3] Where does he finally come down on this issue of the highest human happiness? It is certainly arguable that he finally turns away from the position that I have just been describing and sides with Plato: the best life is the life of a god.

Aristotle's *Nicomachean Ethics* ends on Plato's side of the ancient debate. Aristotle says there that only the gods are truly *eudaimon*. Consequently, the best life for human beings is to live as they do, to live a life of contemplation not action. As J. O. Urmson puts it, "[Aristotle] tells us that the life of contemplation is most like the life of god and that god is the supremely *eudaimon* being. He says that we should not heed those who say that, being men, we should think of human things; 'so far as possible one should act as an immortal and strive to live according to the highest in oneself' " (JOU, 120–21).

But even if he finally concluded that the *vita comtemplativa* is higher than the *vita activa,* certainly Aristotle does not want to exclude the latter as a candidate for a life worth living. Unlike his teacher, he insists that a virtuous human life of moral action—call this the practical, the political life—is a worthy path to happiness.

It is Aristotle's second highest kind of human life that Nussbaum wants to praise and to hold up as a viable alternative to Plato. The choice between the alternatives is a choice, for Nussbaum, of whether human happiness is found in the embrace of the human condition or in the transcendence of it. Clearly Nussbaum wants to press the case in favor of the Aristotelian alternative. I could not agree more.

While I believe that Nussbaum is right in preferring the Aristotelian embrace of the human over the Platonic desire to transcend it, questions remain as to what this entails. In contrast to Plato, for whom *tuche* seems the unequivocal enemy of the good life and *techne* its unequivocal friend, does the embrace of the human entail a full embrace of *tuche* and a complete rejection of *techne?*

This appears to be a reasonable way to look at the alternatives given Nussbaum's contention that *tuche* and *techne* form an antithesis. That is, the way Nussbaum puts the alternatives, it looks as if we are forced to embrace one or the other but not both. And certainly there is some plausibility to this: it seems that the Platonic alternative is simply to embrace *techne* and reject

3. See J. O. Urmson's discussion of this ambivalence in *Aristotle's Ethics* (Oxford: Basil Blackwell, 1988), especially 118ff. (hereafter JOU).

tuche, and the Aristotelian alternative is simply to embrace *tuche* and reject *techne.*

The matter, however, is not so simple. Nussbaum seems not to want either of these alternatives. Rather, she seems to think that the good life is found in finding a balance between *tuche* and *techne.* Moreover, she seems to suggest that this is really what Aristotle was himself recommending. Or expressed differently, she seems to think that the Aristotelian path to happiness requires some control of *tuche* (some *techne*) but not too much. This alternative would make both *techne* and *tuche,* when balanced, friends of the good life, and both, when one is in excess over the other, its enemies.

But there is a complication in Nussbaum's position. Her analysis seems to divide the world up into two kinds of events that are exhaustive and mutually exclusive. Events are either controlled (by human agency) or uncontrolled (by nature). *Techne* seems to capture the first kind of events and *tuche* the second. My question has been whether this exhaustive bifurcation of events is plausible.

This is an especially urgent question when we try to fit moral action into either the category of the controlled or the uncontrolled. The fact is, it simply does not fit either. Yet certainly moral action is definitive of the human condition and important in figuring the path to human happiness. Certainly Aristotle thought so, and certainly Nussbaum wants to agree.

I want to suggest that if we enrich Nussbaum's framework by adding action as a third category of worldly occurrence, and consider its relation to both *tuche* and to *techne,* we will make strides in making sense of how we might accept their opposition and yet embrace both. This enriching will make for new dialectical oppositions however. The most notable will be the dialectical opposition between *techne* and moral action. This dialectical relation will turn out to be one in which the two are opposed but also require each other.

These are matters that I will turn to in the concluding section of this chapter. Before I get to this, however, I want briefly to introduce Nussbaum's treatment of the inheritors of the Platonic prescription for human happiness, the Hellenistic Schools.

Doctors of the Soul

In her book *The Therapy of Desire: Theory and Practice in Hellenistic Ethics,* Nussbaum shows how and why the Hellenistic Schools, the Epicureans, the Stoics, the Skeptics, carrying on the Greek philosophic tradition they inherited, formulated their theories to serve the practical needs of real human beings. She undertakes her study of the Hellenistic Schools with her own practical aim: assuming that contemporary philosophy, at least of the analytic variety, has become a sterile and convoluted enterprise, she uses these ✓ ancients to show us how we might go about rehumanizing philosophy. She clearly thinks that the study of these Schools can instruct us on how philosophy can again become compassionate and responsive to the needs of ordinary human beings, and why it should be.

She focuses on the Hellenistic idea that philosophy is most properly conceived on a medical analogy. According to this model, the task of the philosopher, like that of the physician, is to restore the ill patient to health. Just as physicians use medicine to heal the body, the philosopher is concerned about a different sort of sickness—a sickness in the soul.[4] The therapy that is prescribed by the Hellenistic doctors of the soul is logical argument and critical reasoning. It is thinking, reasoning, desiring, and believing aright that will bring the soul to health.

And it is health that is the primary concern of these doctors, health that they are primarily concerned to restore. This primacy of health marks a difference between the interests of these premodern physicians of the soul and our modern physicians of the body; it marks a difference in conception of the relation of health to disease.

In modern medicine, the focus of interest is disease. What accounts for this difference of focus? We might say that health is much too much a normative concept to be of interest to science. In the interest of scientific description, modern medicine has defined health negatively and in terms of disease. For moderns, health is simply the absence of disease—to be healthy is to have nothing wrong with you. This is perhaps understandable since disease can be readily understood descriptively in terms of physics and chemistry and treated accordingly. We can know (measure quantitatively) what disease is, but health is a different matter, a matter of quality we might say. Health is hence thought (by moderns) to be mysterious, and hence difficult to define.[5] Indeed, until the recent interest in preventative medicine, the idea of modern

4. This is very close to Kierkegaard insofar as he conceived of the most dangerous human sickness—the real sickness unto death—as a sickness of the soul. But Kierkegaard's cure could not be further from that suggested by the Hellenistic philosophers. For Kierkegaard, the cure for the sickness of the soul is not philosophy, or at least philosophy as the Hellenistic Schools conceived it—the cure for the sickness unto death is faith.

5. This may be particularly true in the field of modern psychiatry, in which drug therapy is the most common prescription for the mind (soul?).

physicians being in the business of promoting good health and in preventing (rather than curing) disease, was unheard of.

So then this modern notion of health and disease is a reversal of the Hellenistic conception. Given their primary interest was in health, it was necessary for the Hellenistic physicians of the soul to formulate a clear and well thought out idea of health. The conceit of these Schools was their pretension to have done this, to have firmly in hand a normative definition of what living well consists in. Moreover, the drive of their philosophical mission was to help the troubled and the perplexed by imparting to them their prescription for the good life.

Insofar as the Hellenistic Schools were unashamedly normative in their diagnosis of human misery and in their prescription for health, they carried on the earlier Greek—especially the Aristotelian—notion that human beings are constituted teleologically. According to Aristotelian tradition, the human being has a normative structure—there is a way that human beings ought to live, if they are to be healthy, if they are to live well.

Following this ontological and axiological assumption (that there is a way that human beings ought to live, if they are to live well, if they are to reach the human telos of *eudaimonia*) the Hellenistic philosophers concluded that the disease of the soul, the misery and pain this disease brings, can be traced to a failure properly to understand the nature of the human telos. As these philosophers saw it, disease (unhappiness) is the result of having false beliefs about what health (happiness) is. And the cause of our having false beliefs can be traced to a failure to think clearly and reasonably. The Schools offer to teach us how to reverse this failure.

Not surprisingly, such an insistence on clear and reasonable thinking did not lead to agreement as to what the true beliefs are. In fact, the different Schools came to very different conclusions about what the good life is. Not only did different pictures of the healthy human soul, and accordingly, different prescriptions as to how to live well, emerge among the different Schools, differences also surfaced within the Schools themselves.

While Nussbaum thinks that it is important carefully to consider the content of these various pictures of health, which she does, and important to consider the issue of which, if any, is the best (the true?) one, when there are so many differences among them, and within them, she thinks that there is another issue that needs to be brought to our attention as important. We can call this the recognition of the importance of the *common project* of the Hellenistic Schools. In fact, we can reject all of their competing pictures of human flourishing and still appreciate the importance of what they were up to:

the importance of confronting the issue of what it means to be human, or more precisely, what it means to be fully human and what it means to fail to be.

I celebrate with Nussbaum this positive contribution of the these early thinkers. And there is much to celebrate, much to recommend their approach to philosophy, especially when that approach is compared to the highly theoretical approach of much of Anglo-American analytic philosophy.

The Hellenistic philosophers can serve as a much needed corrective here. The fact is that most of the work of modern analytic philosophy is conducted within the narrow confines of the academic ivory tower. Most of this work is conducted within technical, specialized journals with narrow circulations and in professional presentations to highly specialized audiences. And there is good reason that these philosophers talk only to fellow philosophers: much of their jargon-filled exchanges is simply unintelligible to the untrained philosopher.

But it is not just professional philosophers that are plagued with philosophical questions, not just professional philosophers who have a need to answer them. Indeed, it is hard to imagine that any person who is conscious and moderately alert could long escape the most basic such questions.

But where do ordinary human beings turn to find out if their beliefs are sound? These days where do ordinary folks get the answers to their deepest philosophical perplexities? Given the current state of philosophy, it is not surprising that they do not turn to professional philosophy. Rather, they most often seek help from popular psychology and/or religion.

Shouldn't philosophy serve the concrete human needs of human beings by seeking to provide answers or at least helpful ways of thinking about our most basic philosophical questions? If so, it must be more than just good theory, and certainly more than just academic jargon available to an inner circle of professionals. As I read Nussbaum, this is exactly the lesson that the Hellenistic philosophers have to teach modern philosophers about what philosophy ought to be. What I take her to be saying is something like this: attention to the Hellenistic Schools and to their focus on practice can serve to awaken us (that is, Anglo-American philosophers) from our esoteric trance and bring us to recognize the need to rehumanize philosophy.

And what would such a humanized philosophy be like? For one thing, it would certainly not be just directed to scholars. It would be directed to ordinary life, to everyday people; it would be addressed to every concrete human being who shares a common human desire to answer the most practical and the most urgent human question, "How should I live?" The Hellenistic philosophers practiced such a humanized philosophy; for them philosophy always had a practical goal: to provide prescriptions for ordinary human beings that promise to make their lives better.

But we must be careful here: recommending and celebrating an approach to philosophy, or better, an approach of philosophy to life, is one thing, but accepting the substantive conclusions of any particular approach is quite another. And so we must ask, Do these Hellenistic philosophers have anything to teach us substantively? Do they give us good answers to the good questions they pose?

Nussbaum herself is equivocal about the conclusions of the Schools. Clearly she loves these thinkers, and clearly she has learned from them; they are her mentors and she reads them as if for life. Yet, it is safe to say that she does not accept their general conclusions. Although she has obviously learned from them, Nussbaum is no Epicurean, no Stoic, no Skeptic. She is an Aristotelian through and through. Or more precisely, Nussbaum is what we might call a modified Aristotelian, and in large measure, much of this modification has come via her study of the Hellenistic Schools.

While I agree with Nussbaum that there is much to learn methodologically from the Hellenistic philosophers, I look at the matter of their substantive contribution to philosophy a bit more dialectically than she does. That is, when it comes to matters of substance, my interest is not focused on the positive elements of their prescriptions; I am not primarily interested in picking out the positive elements of their prescriptions that we can legitimately appropriate in our quest for a good life and in simply discarding the rest.

As I say, my interest is more dialectical: I think we learn most from these doctors of the soul when we see how their prescriptions for the good human life actually work against their patient's quest for the good life. Or as I like to put it, even though the Hellenistic philosophers intended to offer a plan for a good life, what they actually offered was a plan of refusing the human condition. Yet, strangely, we can learn a great deal from this. The formulation of their plan of refusing the human had the unintended and ironic result of deepening our substantive understanding of just what it means to embrace the human.[6]

The common practical argument of the Schools runs something like this. The most urgent human problems are rooted in our false beliefs: as they reckon, many, if not most, of the beliefs that we hold are demonstrably false; or, if the Skeptic is right, they all may be. Moreover, holding such false be-

6. This is close to Kierkegaard's interest in the alternatives to existential faith as points of entry into an authentic embrace of the existential: his interest say in despair as the opening to faith.

liefs, being guided in life by them, is the cause of our human misery, our sick-ness unto death. But all agree on this: the most destructive false belief is the one that tells us that the pursuit of the satisfaction of the passions will bring happiness; holding this belief is perhaps the root cause of human misery. Only a life devoted to reason, a life with the passions (especially eros) con-trolled, or kept at bay, if not extirpated, can be truly happy. Like Plato before them, these doctors of the soul conclude that the best human life is the life whose soul is completely undisturbed by the passions; and the model of this happiness is the life of a god. To live well as a human being is to live as a god.

Where do our beliefs go wrong? Where in particular does the belief that the pursuit of the satisfaction of our passions can bring happiness go wrong? At the most obvious level, it is simply false, in the way that children's beliefs often are. We can believe that the acquisition of this or that toy, for example, will bring us just what we need to make us happy. And of course adults can be as misguided as children: we can believe, for example, that having money or power will do the trick. But reason will tell us that these things do not sat-isfy, that they ultimately disappoint. And this is painfully true of the most per-nicious false belief, namely, the belief that the satisfying of our passions will make us happy. For these doctors, the medicine of practical wisdom comes in realizing what things are worth our desiring and having. We can, and often do, desire the wrong things because we falsely believe that they will bring happiness. In response to this common malady of wanting what is not good for us, the Hellenistic doctors offer us a therapy of desire, a prescription that tells us which desires do and which do not advance our quest for happiness.

But this therapy of desire has a deeper dimension. The Schools seem to agree that most human beings go wrong at a more basic level of belief. Human beings seem naturally to assume that we are stuck with our human condition, that we must make the best of it as we find it (the position of the tragedians). The Schools question this basic belief and suggest that it is possi-ble to transcend our condition of being stuck in our humanity. In fact, their entire program, which is supposed to move in the direction of formulating and providing us with a prescription for living a good human life, ends up being driven by the desire to transform and overcome our humanness.

The irony here is palpable. What the Hellenistic philosophers tell us is that the most pressing human problem is the humanness of our existence, and that the only solution to this malady is in transcending that humanness. In formulating the problem and the solution to the problem in this way, the Hellenistic philosophers end up in a deeper irony: insofar as they propose to tell us about how to overcome our humanness in order to live a good human life, the net result of their analyses of the problems of being human is that they shed an enormously important light on the nature of the human. As we might put it: to overcome the enemy, we must study him carefully and know him intimately; in making the human their enemy, the Hellenistic Schools tell us much about the human condition.

The main thing that these philosophers tell us about the human condition is that it is essentially fragile. That is, to be human is to be fragile and there is no getting around fragility without getting around our humanness. Why is fragility a problem? Here we meet a deep assumption of the Schools: human happiness is a state of peace, of rest, of freedom from disturbance, from suffering, and so from contingency, and from the anxiety contingency inevitably generates. As they reasoned, to live in a condition of fragility is to live in the dynamic flux of constant anxiety—and this is the core of our unhappiness, our misery.

But if human existence is essentially fragile at its core, if human existence is threatened at every turn—threatened by external conditions, uncontrolled events *(tuche),* and so forth, then how can human beings ever be happy? Are we not destined to misery by our very condition of fragility? It certainly looks this way when we meet with daily suffering, pain, loss, misery, misfortune, and death.

Here is where the Hellenistic Schools proclaim their gospel. Their good news to the troubled and perplexed is that human fragility can in fact be overcome. A life devoted to reason is the path we must take if we are to overcome our fragility. If the human condition of fragility can in fact be overcome, if our humanness can in fact be overcome, then our misery and unhappiness can find relief. In the next chapter, I will look in more detail at some of their prescriptions.

In their efforts to find a way to show that human beings can transcend the condition of fragility, the Hellenistic philosophers have much to show us about its nature. And insofar as they do this, they tell us much about what it means to be human. Ironically then, the Hellenistic prescriptions for the good life, which turn out to be plans of escape from the human condition of fragility, end up as substantive explorations of human fragility and as such, substantive explorations of what it means to be human.

In making it clear in just what ways human existence is essentially fragile, and hence in telling us much about what it means to be human, the Hellenistic Schools help us to clarify the question of, and advance the quest for, the good life. What I mean is this: insofar as the Schools tell us that the search for the good life must begin in the acknowledgment of the fragility of the human condition, they provide us with a clear question that can serve as a good starting point for our quest: if fragility is our basic human condition, then finding the good life or not will turn on what we do with this basic fact. This clarifies our options; as well, it makes it clear that there really are paths open to human beings that are paths of refusing the human, of transcending it.

The great contribution of the Hellenistic philosophers is found in the fact that they brilliantly work out these paths of refusal and transcendence; in addition, they existentially live them; but more disturbingly, they tempt us to follow them. Well then, do we follow? Do we try to escape or deny our human fragility, the source of our sickness and misery, as they would have it, and take the medicine of transcendence that they prescribe? Does happiness come, as they tell us, only when we have found a way to become invulnerable? Is transcendence the only path to human happiness?

In wrestling with these questions, irony again surfaces. Listening to the voices of these Hellenistic doctors of the soul, just may lead us to ask this question, Are there any side effects of this medicine of transcendence? If so, what are they? But more importantly, are these effects worth the promised cure? Is the medicine of transcendence they prescribe the kind that cures the disease but kills the patient? Do we want this? Indeed, the supreme irony in this is that reflection on these questions may indeed constitute the opening, the backdoor perhaps, to wondering about the wisdom of the human embrace, the wisdom of refusing their path of refusal. Surely, such reflection makes it clear that whether we embrace our humanness or not is something that is open to us to decide, open to us to enact. When we are existentially confronted with this deepest human choice, to embrace or to refuse our humanness, and when the side effects of the prescription for transcendence are existentially faced, perhaps the wisdom of the human embrace will dawn. Perhaps this is the only path, as both I and Nussbaum think it is, to a healthy soul. One thing such a reflection will make clear: we *can* embrace our humanity, and we have the power to refuse it. Upon realizing this, the next step, the most profound question arises, *Which path will we choose?*

The Truth of Transcendence

Although Nussbaum spends a lot of time discussing human action in tragedy and in the novel, when she turns to her philosophical analysis, her tendency is to define the human almost exclusively in terms of its *natural condition* of exposure to *tuche*. That is, it seems that for her, our humanness is more centrally connected to the fact that things happen to us than to the fact that we do things, that we act. And certainly she is right in seeing that our exposure to uncontrolled events is a definitive element in the human. The question I have, however, is whether this element is the most central, or somehow more central, than moral action.

Nevertheless, it is clear that we are creatures of nature and that as such we bear a connection to it that figures in the kind of beings that we are. This natural condition of human beings is a condition that exposes human beings to the contingency of *tuche*. It is obvious that it is dangerous to exist in a state of nature, exposed to the elements, as it were. This exposure generates anxiety and contributes significantly to the fragility of human existence.

Human beings need protection. The aim of *techne* is to provide this. That is, the aim of *techne* is to control natural happenings, to transcend our natural condition so that we can shore up our fragile existence.

To exploit a previously mentioned distinction that Hannah Arendt makes in *The Human Condition,* I can agree that work is a *techne,* but not action. For Arendt, work builds a world out of nature and provides an appropriate space for moral action—call this a city, a polis. In controlling *tuche,* work allows human beings the leisure to turn their attention to activities other than merely trying to survive—call these activities political. Appropriately used, *techne*-as-work serves the human enterprise by making a world, a polis. This artificial world, made with our hands out of nature, controls nature and protects us from the outrageous slings and arrows of *tuche;* without this control, we would lack the freedom to engage in political action; that is, *techne* (work) allows us to engage in that form of activity that is, as Aristotle puts it, available neither to the beasts nor the gods.

Protection from natural forces is indeed necessary if the human species is to realize its uniqueness, if human beings are to rise to a quality of life that is not known in the natural order, if human beings are to become fully human. This being so, *techne* (as work) is one of the definitive marks of the human. Neither beasts nor the gods work—although beasts certainly know the pain of labor—the activity that Arendt says is essentially connected with creating, maintaining, and sustaining life itself. Thanks to the techniques of work, human beings have managed to leave the jungle where all activities are devoted to survival—where even play is practice for this end. *Techne*-as-work forges out of nature a uniquely human habitat, a world that is essentially unnatural, that is essentially human. The human enterprise in this world aims at more than survival.

But this departure from nature, this protection from it, this transcendence of it, can go too far. *Techne* can aim to control the natural condition altogether—to eliminate natural *tuche* completely. If Nussbaum is correct, and I think that she is, that our exposure to natural *tuche* is a definitive element in our humanness, then to transcend it completely would be to transcend our humanness. To transcend nature completely would be to become something other than a human being. Insofar as we want to keep our humanness intact, natural *tuche* must be kept at bay, but not eliminated. If not unrestrained, therefore, *techne* can also become the enemy of the human. We must be suspicious of *techne* if it dreams of uprooting us completely from nature and thus of transforming our existence into something other than human—the dream of the mad scientist, the bureaucrat, the romantic.

Natural *tuche* and *techne*-as-work, then, are both friends of our humanness and both are its potential enemies. The way to keep them from being the enemies of the human, the way to embrace our humanness, is to keep them in an appropriate tension, that is, in a tension appropriate for a human existence.

But what counts as an appropriate tension? Where do we draw the line here? To draw this line, we must decide what counts as the core of human existence. With Aristotle, and with Arendt, I suggest that we look at political/moral action as the core of our humanness. That is, I want to say that the definitive center of human beings is our *political/moral condition,* the condition of being capable of free and responsible action. Here is where we draw the line.

This political/moral condition, like its corresponding natural condition, is also a condition of contingency. It is as dangerous, perhaps more so, to act as it is to live exposed to the forces of nature. As Arendt points out, our actions and their consequences and the actions of others are essentially unpredictable and irreversible. Living among others exposes us to an extranatural contingency that puts our lives at risk. Indeed, what we do, and what others do, can bring us to ruin as much so as the natural events that befall us.

(This may just be the difference between Greek and Shakespearean tragedy. Oedipus did not bring disaster on himself; it was fate that determined his downfall. Hamlet is very different: he brings his ruin on himself, by his actions, which are the reactions to the acts of others.)

Our exposure to political/moral contingency generates anxiety and makes human existence fragile. But again, the fragility here is not a matter of being exposed to impersonal forces that simply befall us, forces that lie outside of the orbit of our decisions (what I have been calling our natural fragility); rather it is a fragility of being exposed to the unpredictability of moral action and of its consequences (what I would call the fragility of human affairs).

As I see it, *techne* has no central place, perhaps no place at all, in this world of human affairs, since control, even a little, is the enemy of moral action. Moral action is neither determined by necessity or fate nor is it a matter of blind luck. Moral actions are grounded in free and responsible human decisions; the idea of a controlled moral action makes no sense. Because *techne* is an activity of control, it is the enemy of moral action. Its dream is to eliminate the fear and trembling of moral decision; its wish is to replace human decision with mechanical procedures, or with natural or social forces (e.g., the market). This replacement would relieve the agony of moral decision, but at the price of removing the human altogether. Moral action cannot be a *techne* without self-destruction.

Even though moral action excludes *techne* on this model, even though it does not have a proper place *within* the human political/moral condition, it does have its proper human place. This is, on one level, the truth of *techne,* the truth of transcendence. That is, even though the human enterprise of moral action excludes *techne,* being human also must include it, since being human would be impossible without it. Making a world is different from acting in a world; making is not acting. Yet *techne*-as-work is necessary if human beings are to have a world within which to act. And certainly, living in a world, as opposed to living in nature, is necessary for moral action. If moral action defines humanness, then clearly *techne* is an essential component of the human and at the same time excluded from it.

In general, this is where we draw the lines of inclusion/exclusion in trying to strike an appropriate tension between *techne* and *tuche*: an appropriate tension is defined in terms of service to moral action—service to the human. If *techne* serves action, it is a friend to the human, otherwise it is its foe. It serves moral action insofar as it contributes to making a world that is suitable for it. It is the enemy of the human insofar as it builds a world that is not suitable for moral action, or that obstructs it, or insofar as it tries to transform moral action into *techne.*

We must draw a line that excludes the transformation of moral action into *techne.* If we allow *techne* to cross this line, then it becomes the enemy of the human. If *techne* intrudes into the world of human affairs and tries to replace moral action with techniques of measurement, with mechanical decision procedures, cost-benefit analyses, and the like, it will destroy moral action and, along with it, the human. The temptation to turn moral action into *techne* is a temptation to eliminate the anxiety of moral *tuche;* it is a constant threat in the world of human affairs. As I contend, however, moral *tuche* is intrinsic to moral action. Therefore, the temptation to control it must be continually refused if moral action is to maintain its integrity as such.

Nevertheless, as the logic of paradox dictates, this temptation to find a way of controlling moral contingency can work positively as a constant reminder to us that moral action is something that is ours to refuse and hence ours to embrace. This recognition that the embrace of moral action is ours to refuse or to embrace is especially urgent in our own modern society which harbors the dream of finding technological solutions to all of its problems. If I am right, however, this dream of control may well turn into a dehumanizing nightmare; if the human is to survive this assault on itself, we humans must find the resources that will enable us to refuse this temptation.

The human temptation to transcend contingency, however, is not easy to refuse. Who among us has not harbored the wish to find a form of existence that is other than our own? Who among us has not at one time or another fantasized about being a god, about being omniscient or omnipotent, or at least immortal? Who among us has not dreamed of being ageless, griefless, painless, and so forth? Who has not dreamed of being relieved of the fear and trembling of moral decision? Wouldn't we have to be inhuman, or perverse, or insane, not to want to live so transcendently and so invulnerably? Doesn't this wish seem perfectly intelligible?

But is it? Is this wish coherent? Is it perverse? Doesn't the wish have devastating side effects? And if so, isn't it perfectly intelligible that human beings would refuse or reject an other-than-human existence were it ever actually offered to us as more than a dream, more than a fantasy? Would we really want to have what we sometimes think that we want to have? Would we really resign from our own finitude, our own humanity? Would we really want to be gods if this were more than an idle fantasy? Think again of Odysseus's choice of his own human finitude, a choice he makes at the price of his own mortality.

Nussbaum certainly takes Odysseus's choice of his human life as a model for the intelligibility of the refusal of transcendence, as a model for the existential embrace of the human, just as much as I take Abraham to be such a model. Insofar as we both hold to these models of the human embrace as our models for human happiness, is there any way that we can also grant any truth to the wish for, or to the dream of, transcendence?

It seems at times that for Nussbaum the human wish to find a *techne* of transcendence is simply and unequivocally false. It seems at times that for her the lure of godlike transcendence simply has no proper human place. It seems that she would always advise that we resist the lure of transcendence for the sake of our humanity. At other times, she seems to say that the wish to transcend our humanity is a wish constitutive of, intrinsic to, our humanness. She says that only human beings can (have the capacity to) wish to be something other than they are. Hence she implies that the complete repression of this longing to, or at least of this temptation to long to, transcend our humanity would be itself a repression of our humanness, a kind of transcendence of our wish for transcendence. As such, this repression or rejection of the lure of transcendence would be as much a wish to transcend the human as the wish it seeks to repress.

So we are brought to this question: How do we reckon with the human lure to divinity, with the human temptation to want to transcend itself, without destroying the human, without destroying ourselves? Nussbaum recognizes this as a problem and tries to sort through it by introducing two conceptions of transcendence, what she calls—I think unfortunately—external and internal forms of transcendence.[7]

Nussbaum makes this distinction in response to a question that Charles Taylor asks her in his review of her book, *The Fragility of Goodness*. His question is simply this: Where does she stand on the issue between Plato and Aristotle on the point of whether the Platonic aspiration to transcend the human must be excluded from an Aristotelian *eudaimonia?* Taylor presents two positions and asks which Nussbaum thinks is correct: (1) the inclusive view that the good life, Aristotle's *eudaimonia* (happiness), includes, even though it is in tension with, the Platonic aspiration for transcendence; (2) the exclusive view that the good life (Aristotelian *eudaimonia*) is only—that is, purely—human, with no place for extrahuman transcendence.[8]

---

7. I take this to be unfortunate because the idea of internal transcendence may be construed as a retreat into oneself. This sort of transcendence is as much a wish to depart from our humanness as is the transcendence of the external sort. Indeed, the risk of interpreting internal transcendence in this way is particularly acute in our own time where everything is subject to being psychologized. What Nussbaum wants to say, I think correctly, is that transcendence, in some form, is intrinsic to our humanness: this is human transcendence. What she doesn't seem to resolve is the place of extrahuman transcendence within the human. Is this also intrinsic to human existence?

8. Nussbaum says that she will not pursue a point that Taylor raises about her placing the issue of transcendence exclusively in the context of Greek polytheism. Taylor wants to know why she does not consider transcendence in the Judaeo-Christian context. This, I think, is an important point. Søren Kierkegaard argues that it was Christianity that introduced radical transcendence into the world: he called this concept of transcendence spirit, a concept that Greek consciousness lacked: the Greek understanding of spirit was as psyche, not pneuma. See "The Immediate Erotic Stages" (EO I, 47ff). Nussbaum may be guilty of reading a Judaeo-Christian concept of transcendence into Greek polytheism and Greek philosophy. If Kierkegaard is correct, the Greeks had a notion of transcendence, but it was finite—a kind of higher form of finitude; this is transcendence as psyche. For Greek consciousness, the idea of a radically other-than-the-finite was not available, or what is the same

Now Taylor asks, Which view does she support? "The view that our proper human goal is activity according to complete human excellence plus some form of transcending? Or the view that, in order to pursue appropriately the whole human good, we must leave aside our desire for transcendence" (LK, 378)? Refusing to identify herself with either of these views, Nussbaum answers Taylor as follows: "It may appear that I am in fact supporting, as Taylor suspected, the second view. But I believe that matters are more complex" (LK, 378).

In what way are these matters more complex? This is where the distinction between the two forms of transcendence, internal and external, becomes relevant. The internal form of transcendence does not aim at some otherworldly, extrahuman existence, nor does it hover above this world in a kind of abstract philosophical detachment from it. Internal transcendence enlivens the ordinary, the everyday, by introducing into it a sense of spirit, a sense of spontaneity, surprise, novelty, improvisation, freedom, and so forth that keeps the human life from becoming banal. As she puts it, such a transcendence takes us "above the dullness and obtuseness of the everyday" (LK, 379). But it is more than this: internal transcendence has a moral and political dimension. Internal transcendence is more than an aesthetic rising above; it is a rising above in moral and political excellence; it is the transcendence of practical wisdom. This sort of transcendence does not aim at transcending our humanity. Quite to the contrary, it aims to deepen our sense of humanness, it makes us more aware of the riches of our human existence. This is the sense of transcendence that we must cultivate for a life of complete virtue.

The second form of transcendence she calls external. In its every manifestation, the lure of external transcendence is the wish to depart human life altogether. It is this form of transcendence that Nussbaum is particularly concerned to reject as incoherent. She says, "[W]hat my argument urges us to reject as incoherent is the aspiration to leave behind altogether the constitutive conditions of our humanity and to seek for a life that is really the life of another sort of being—as if it were a higher and better life for us" (LK, 379).

Nussbaum cautions, however, that it is not always easy to draw the line between these two forms of transcendence: "The puzzle then is, when does

---

thing, the Greeks lacked the idea of spirit, of the infinite. One reason that the Greeks lacked the conception of spirit is that they lacked the biblical conception of the universe as a creation; it simply was inconceivable to the Greek imagination that the cosmos had come into being, and a fortiori that it came into being as the result of a free, contingent act. As such, the Greek mind could not imagine the radical transcendence of such a creator vis-à-vis the creation; such a transcendence imagines the creator as radically other than the creation.

the aspiration to internal transcendence become the aspiration to depart from human life altogether?" (LK, 380).

At one point, she seems to me to be very Aristotelian in her suggestion that what we need to do is to moderate the lure of external transcendence, to keep it from going too far, to keep it in check, as it were. She invokes here the Greek idea of pride *(hubris):* "There is a kind of striving that is appropriate to a human life; and there is a kind of striving that consists in trying to depart from that life to another life. This is what *hubris* is—the failure to comprehend what sort of life one has actually got, the failure to live within its limits (which are also possibilities), the failure, being mortal, to think mortal thoughts. Correctly understood, the injunction to avoid *hubris* is not a penance or denial—it is an instruction as to where the valuable things *for us* are to be found" (LK, 381).

But then she takes a different tact; more dialectical, I would say; now the terms she uses are the terms of tension, even contradiction. She asks, "Does this mean that one should actually not want the people one loves to live forever?" Her response, "Yes and no." She even admits that this tension is close to being a contradiction, but asserts that it "seems to be a part of the best human life" (LK, 381). In summary, "the best human life in my own conception contains more tension and conflict around the issue of transcendence than Aristotle's best life, in which the fear of death plays a very small role. Not enough, perhaps, to make it Taylor's 'inclusive view.' But more than his 'narrow view,' insofar as he identifies that with Aristotle's" (LK, 381).

So, does she or doesn't she? Does she or doesn't she reject altogether the place of external transcendence within a fully human life, and specifically the Platonic version of this transcendence, the aspiration to divinity? Does she reject this lure to divinity as figuring in the good human life as Aristotle seemed to? Granting that transcendence of the internal sort is necessary for a good human existence, what, if any, role does the lure of external transcendence, or at least, the wish for immortality, play in the good life? On the one hand, she seems to want to reject it altogether as incoherent; and on the other, she seems to want to say that it is a constitutive element in the good human life. Is it coherent to want to live forever? "Yes and no," she says. Can she have it both ways? What would it mean to have it both ways?

At the time she wrote *Fragility,* it was quite clear that she did want to have it both ways. By the time of the writing of "Transcending Humanity," she seems to have abandoned altogether the thought that such a transcendence has any coherent role to play in a fully human life. I think that her original position and her current one betoken what I would call Nussbaum's failure to be dialectical enough, or better her failure to allow her incipient dialectical imagination its head. It is precisely at this point that she could learn from Kierkegaard.

In *Fragility,* it is clear that Nussbaum thinks that if we were unequivocally to reject the Platonic aspiration for immortality, we would flatten our existence. She calls on Nietzsche, an anti-Platonist, to support this positive dimension of the Platonic aspiration to divinity. Nietzsche's description of the "last man" *(Zarathustra)* envisions the extinction of humanity as the result of "the extinction of the Platonic longing for self-transcendence" (FG, 163). That is, we had better be careful when we reject the Platonic aspiration for divinity that we do not throw out with it something that is essentially human, something that, if missing, would result in the extinction of our humanness. For Plato, the longing for immortality is part of the nobleness of our humanness. He saw clearly "the humanness of denial and dissatisfaction, the depth of our human longing for something better than what we are. Plato would say that to cease to see and feel these things would be to cease, in some way to be human" (FG, 163).[9]

At this point in Nussbaum's evolution therefore, she thinks that the Platonic aspiration for the extrahuman is not all bad. Her way of thinking about the positive function of such a transcendence is, however, not dialectical enough. As she thinks about it at this point, it is as though contemplation or transcendence of the Platonic sort were a nice capstone to a fully human life, at least, if not taken too far; as though a fully human life needs a little of the salt of transcendence, though too much will make it unsavory.

Again, by the time of the writing of "Transcending Humanity," Nussbaum completely rejects any positive place for Platonic transcendence within the fully human life. This categorical rejection, however, is hardly categorical. Again she is unsettled.

You might think that this absolute rejection of Platonic transcendence would lead her unequivocally into the arms of Aristotle. Not quite so. Aristotle, she thinks, doesn't have a healthy fear of death, and so does not feel the drive to press the limits of human mortality. We need to press in just this direction. But isn't this to press for immortality? And are we not right back into the Platonic longing for divinity? Nussbaum thinks that her position

9. Strangely enough, the remarks that Nussbaum makes about the positive contribution of Plato's aspiration to divinity, a kind of striving to make things better, a striving to live a noble life devoted to truth, goodness, and beauty, make it seem that what she really admires in Plato is what could well fit into her notion of *internal transcendence,* that human form of transcendence that deepens our humanity, and keeps our ordinary lives from degenerating into banality.

comes close to being a contradiction, yet she embraces it and refuses to identify her position with Aristotle's simpliciter.

So, are we left with the earlier position wherein the good life must strive to establish some sort of equilibrium between giving in completely to the Platonic aspiration to immortality and simply and categorically rejecting such an aspiration? Or, are we left with the later position which finds no place at all for extrahuman transcendence within the fully human life?

My question in all of this simply is, Why must we settle for these as the exclusive options? Why must our choice be either (1) the good, fully human life needs a little, but not too much, Platonic transcendence, or (2) the good life has no place at all for, indeed, cannot coherently wish for, such a Platonic aspiration? That is, why must we settle with Nussbaum for the idea that internal transcendence—now understood as a modification, almost a Platonic modification, of Aristotle's conception of the virtuous life—is sufficient for the fully human life?

What Nussbaum flirts with, but does not consider seriously enough, I contend, is the plausibility of a third dialectical approach to the issue: isn't it possible coherently to say that the Platonic aspiration to divinity must be rejected completely and absolutely in a fully human existence and at the same time say that it must also figure positively as a constitutive element in the good human life?

I suggest that the Platonic aspiration to extrahuman transcendence figures essentially but dialectically within human existence. To be fully human, it is necessary that we be able to wish for, that we be able to think about, that we be able to want, that we be able to conceive of, something other than our human existence. To be fully human, it is necessary to be able to detach ourselves from everything that is human, to be able to refuse human existence. Why is this necessary? This is complicated and tricky.

It is possible to be a fully human being only if it is possible not to be; but one can actually be fully human, however, only if one is already a human being. Being human then requires a certain transcendence, a level of self-consciousness in terms of which being human has become problematic for a human being. In order for a human being to become a problem to himself, he must have a capacity for distance from himself; he must have a capacity to think that he can be divorced, or otherwise separated from himself.

This is why beasts are not problems to themselves: they are not called on to decide to be or not to be beasts, the way a human beings must decide to be or not to be human; humans can become human and may even become beasts; but beasts do not choose to become beasts, and however human they may sometimes seem, they cannot choose to become human.

There is a dialectical other side of the fact that human beings exist within the possibility of self-alienation. The wedge that self-consciousness brings, the wedge that threatens to separate me from myself, provides the space, the conditions as it were, that enable me to come to myself, to embrace my existence as my own.

Perhaps we can see this if we return to the story of Odysseus and compare it to a favorite story of Kierkegaard, the story of Abraham's call to sacrifice Isaac.

Both Abraham and Odysseus are called to resign from their human existence, to give up what is valuable to them, and to do this for some higher calling. Abraham is called by God to sacrifice, or at least be willing to sacrifice his own and only son; and along with this, his hopes to be the father of a great nation—that hope which first uprooted him from his ancestral home, that had made of him a nomad, a wanderer in history, the Father of faith.

The lesson here seems to be something like this: faith requires an uprooting from nature, it requires that the faithful find his or her absolute center of gravity outside of his or her natural home in the finite world; that the faithful find his or her place in history, before God, and hence, in its primary orientation, outside of the relative, in the Absolute, the absolutely other, in the divine. Faith requires, in summary, transcendence. Transcendence implies a break with finitude; infinite resignation provides this break.

But this is not all: faith also entails receiving the finite back, every inch. What is given back to the faithful self (the finite, Isaac) is the same as what was given up, but the relationship is radically transformed; transformed from what we might call a natural relation to a personal one. This latter relation to finitude is personal insofar as it is qualified by radical contingency and choice, by an existentially felt vulnerability to loss, by a consciousness of the finite as relative. No longer is finitude thought to be ours by default, by natural right, as it were. Rather, finitude can now belong to us of our own free and responsible choice; now we can embrace it as our own, as a gift from the hands of the Eternal. It is just this difference that allowed Isaac to belong to Abraham in a more deeply personal way than before the knife had been raised to him.

Resignation drives us toward transcendence; drives us from the world; faith drives us, as spirit, back into the world. But we do not come back from Mt. Moriah the same. The movement of resignation, when it is really made, irreversibly transforms our relation to finitude. The paradoxical result of resignation is that finitude becomes exponentially higher in value. It is ever so much more precious because on the other side of resignation it becomes ever so much our own, just as Isaac came to belong to Abraham so much more intensely after he had been willing to give him up.

Odysseus, on the other hand, refuses the offer to resign from his humanity, to give up his adventure, his wife, his home. Unlike Abraham, therefore, he does not, is not willing to, make the first movement of faith, the movement of resignation. Indeed, it seems that under no conditions would he make such a sacrifice. He is ethical through and through. It seems that he could not seriously entertain the possibility of doing what Abraham did, lifting the knife to his son, to his wife. Odysseus has, we might say, no distance on his humanness.

Yes, Odysseus is a human being. But does he choose his humanness, as Nussbaum thinks he does? Only in a qualified sense, a less than radical, less than personal, sense. It is almost as if Odysseus were being given two options one of which was inconceivable for him actually to take. In this context, the choice of the other option seems to lack the force of a real choice; and despite the meaning of Odysseus's name, his choice seems not to reflect any real struggle, any real suffering. It is almost as though there were no *real* possibility for him to annul, to refuse. Yes, the temptation to Odysseus is there, to become a god (or, perhaps to retreat into Calypso's cave), but he never goes so far as to let that possibility become more than a dreaming fantasy; more than one more obstacle to his return home. He was not able to allow it to take on the existential actuality Abraham's temptation had in the biblical story. But precisely because Odysseus could not conceive of giving up Penelope, he was in no position to relate to her as one would relate to someone who has been dialectically given up and miraculously restored.

Nussbaum thinks that Odysseus has chosen life, decided that the human is better than the life of a god. But if I am right, he never allowed the possibility of transcendence to have its existential power and force. As such, his reunion with, his embrace of, Penelope does not have the passion, the existential fear and trembling, that it seems to have in the case of Abraham and Isaac.

My speculation is that this is what Nussbaum actually wants to say, but lacks the dialectical resources to pull off: she tries to capture a very deeply un-Greek dialectic within Greek categories. She rightly recognizes that the issue is transcendence: that the issue is choosing what is ours, ultimately choosing our world, our finite mortal home, our humanness. She thinks that this is exactly what Odysseus did. What she fails to see, however, is the more dialectical point that such a radical choice is inextricably tied not just to the abstract possibility of loss, the abstract possibility of resignation, but to the concrete existential confrontation with that possibility. Indeed what faith does is to embrace what we can lose, but only after that possibility has been faced in fear and trembling. And it is this concrete historical realization of human fragility that faith constantly carries inside itself.

To reject the urge to transcend our humanity is an easy move, if the urge to transcendence is not played out as a real possibility in one's life, if the knife is, as it were, never really lifted, if the will to resignation is only a pious self-deception. In this case, what is ours cannot be chosen as ours in any radical sense, and so remains less than ours in any deeply personal sense.

Six

THE WISDOM OF LOVE

Is the passion of love an uncontrolled happening? Is it merely a matter of chance or luck? Is love an emotion we merely fall into? Or is it merely a matter of being subject to fate? Is love an emotion that we cannot resist or refuse? And will this fall into, or this assault by, love inevitably harm or help us? Some have thought that love is the definitive human emotion, that without it we would not be human. And yet others see clearly that the passion of love can, and almost always does, bring as much misery as it brings joy. No other passion seems to have the power of love, yet no other seems so fragile.

The passion of love raises so many difficult questions. Can a human life be happy without it? Or is the real question this, Can a human life be happy with it? Does human happiness require that we find a way to control, or even extirpate this most volatile of human emotions? Do we need a *techne* to keep love at bay or to control its potential excesses? Or does human happiness require the existential embrace of love? And there are further, perhaps more profound, questions: If love is an uncontrolled happening, do we then not have a say in it? Or is our only say a matter of developing a *techne* for defending ourselves from its ravishes? Is there a vaccination we can take to avoid the sickness of love? Perhaps if we infect ourselves with a mild case that we can easily get over, we can make ourselves immune to being hurt by the real thing. Or maybe we need a potion if our aim is to become infected by the real thing. Is there any wisdom in love?

These are our questions; they are Nussbaum's questions; they are the questions much modern literature wrestles with; they are the questions to which the Hellenistic Schools propose answers.

Nussbaum's essay "Love's Knowledge" begins with a discussion of Marcel Proust's *Remembrance of Things Past* (LK, 261–85). Her opening remarks depict the power and danger of love as a jolt to the heart. (As we all know, jolts to the heart can kill us, or save our lives.) As she puts it, it is the force of the words that announce Albertine's departure that, for the first time, strike Marcel's heart with a jolt that makes him realize for the first time that he loves her. This knowledge of love that comes from the heart shatters his intellectual pretension to know himself, a pretension that just moments before had convinced him that he did not love her. What happened?

This opening scenario recalls a familiar experience, something captured in the expression "You don't know what you got till it's gone." We have all seen this theme repeated in popular film, in plays, in philosophy. But mostly, I think we all have lived it. One of my favorite versions of the story is told by T. S. Eliot in "The Cocktail Party." In the denouement of that play, Lavinia Chamberlayne, suddenly and unexpectedly leaves Edward, her husband. This departure shatters Edward and brings him to see his wife for the first time, as though it took the shock of her absence for her to be present. "Before," Edward ruminates, "we had taken each other for granted. Why speak of love? We were so used to each other." Why was her presence only apparent to him in her absence? Why was his love for her awakened only after she had left him?

Proust's Marcel had first thought of love as something discernible intellectually and as something within his absolute intellectual control. If you want to know if you love someone, or if you should, then just do a little introspection of the heart with the mind's eye and decide it for yourself. He thought of himself as the absolute master of love, not the reverse. As Nussbaum puts it, Marcel's first view is that love's knowledge "can best be attained by a detached, unemotional, exact intellectual scrutiny of one's condition, conducted in the way a scientist would conduct a piece of research" (LK, 262). Marcel was secure in thinking that he had a *techne* for controlling love's uncertainties. In fact, Marcel had just completed such an introspective research project and concluded that he was tired of Albertine, that he did not love her, and that he desired other women. Yet, just at that moment, when he is certain that he does not love Albertine, the word comes that she has left. Strangely, this departure leaves Marcel more certain than ever that he does love her, and that he is not in fact in control of his own passions.

In puzzling over these matters, it certainly seems appropriate to ask, What *happened* to (in?) Marcel when he learned of Albertine's departure? I mean to emphasize *happen* here, for romantic love is something that happens to us, that befalls us, or at least, partially so. This is why we speak of love as something we fall into. But if this is so, then is there a place in it for our choice, for our moral responsibility? Do we have a say in when, or if, it happens? Do we have a say in whom we want to fall in love with? Can we be faulted or praised for falling? Is love hopelessly foolish? Again, can there be any wisdom in love?

Marcel's negative certainty, based on his intellectual theory of love, of how one knows love, is shattered by Albertine's leaving. But does this shattering of his pretension to control his passions result in his embrace of love's essential uncertainty? its essential fragility? Or does he simply exchange one form of certainty for another? Well, what is his new theory of love?

Marcel's jolt to the heart has convinced him that love is not a matter of the head, as he had thought, but indeed a matter of the heart, a matter of feeling, not thinking. His characterization of this new theory of love is in terms of chemistry, as though love were simply a matter of a "cataleptic impression."

On this new theory, love, reconceived as a "cataleptic impression," is thought of as a physical impact on the heart. On this view, love is seen as a kind of heart attack, or at least as a kind of smoke that gets in our eyes clouding our judgment, or a kind of moon that hits us right between the eyes like a big pizza pie, knocking us off our feet. But this is no new conception of love. The idea that love is a matter of chemistry is as old as the ancient tales of, and wishes for, a love potion. As well, it is a very contemporary romantic image of love, an image that praises *love at first sight,* as if the chemistry of love is magically and mysteriously set into its irreversible motion in a first physical meeting, in a touch, or perhaps simply in the meeting of hungry eyes across a crowded room.

Marcel has been struck by such a cataleptic impression. His impression, however, is not a reaction to someone's presence; rather, it is a reaction to Albertine's absence. But, more importantly, it is something that happens *in* him, not something that happens *between* him and Albertine. For Marcel, love is a chemical reaction inside himself, one that causes pain, suffering, anguish, nausea. Marcel learns that love can make us sick.

Why is it that Proust takes absence to be a requirement to make an impression on Marcel? As Nussbaum explains, the fact is that Marcel is too used to Albertine. As she says, "Marcel has been able to conclude that he is not in love with Albertine, in part because he is used to her" (LK, 264). Proust's way of thinking about this is in terms of habit: being with Albertine had become a habit. And for Proust, the workings of habit threaten to rob us of surprise, of spontaneity, of particularity; habit blinds us to what is right before our eyes. Strangely then, Albertine was absent when she was present, because her presence was swallowed in habit. It took her departure to cause the scales of the blindness of habit to fall from Marcel's eyes; Albertine became present to him only in her absence.

What then are we to make of Marcel's "new" conception of love, his "new" conception of love's knowledge? Before, Marcel had thought that love was an emotion that he had absolute control of. Now, he seems to be realizing that it is something over which he has absolutely no control, absolutely no say in. Do these alternatives exhaust the field?

Does Marcel's reversal of his previous theory of love's knowledge bring him to an embrace of love's essential uncertainty? Does it bring him to an embrace of love's essential fragility? Does Marcel now see that love always carries in itself an unsettling, anxiety producing question, the question of love's knowledge: "Can we ever really know if we love someone—really love them, we might say—and can we ever really know if the other really loves us?" Does Marcel now existentially face this issue of certainty, or more precisely, this issue of uncertainty?

The short answer is "no." Marcel (Proust) is a Cartesian: love's knowledge for him is a matter of achieving indubitability, a matter of overcoming, not embracing, its uncertainties, its fragility. As he reasons, I am certain that I love you and that you love me if and only if I have no doubt about the matter. Appearances to the contrary, he is not shaken from this Cartesian picture of knowledge when he receives the blow that Albertine has departed. Of course he is shaken from the view that certainty is a matter of intellectual scrutiny and absolute control, at least in matters of the heart, but he remains faithful to the idea that knowledge is a matter of indubitability: if love is to be certain, it must root out every trace of doubt within it.

Seeking a new and more secure certainty, Marcel turns from the certainty of thought to the certainty of passion, to the certainty of cataleptic impressions. But this does not mean that he turned from his Cartesianism. Lest we forget, Descartes, who grounded certainty in thinking, also wrote *The Passions of the Soul*. In this work, the passions are conceived mechanically, as though they were part of a hydraulic transmission system in the machine of the body. What happens in this system is, we might say, causally certain, and in principle predictable. That is, the certainty here is of this sort: when I am hit on the head, it is difficult if not logically impossible to doubt that I have been struck; or if you will, putting this in the more familiar philosophical context: love is like pain, we cannot coherently doubt that we feel it, that we are suffering it, anymore than we can doubt that we have a headache. Marcel is in pain; he has found his certainty in suffering. In short, Marcel has found another *techne* for transcending love's essential uncertainty, its essential fragility.

Nussbaum points out that this idea of love as a cataleptic impression is not that far from the early position which sees love as a matter of intellectual scrutiny. She says:

> We said that the attempt to grasp love intellectually was a way of avoid-ing loving. We said that in the cataleptic impression there is acknowl-edgment of one's own vulnerability and incompleteness, an end to our flight from ourselves. But isn't the whole idea of basing love and its knowledge on cataleptic impressions itself a form of flight—from open-ness to the other, from all those things in love for which there is in fact no certain criterion? Isn't this whole enterprise just a new and more sub-tle expression of the rage for control, the need for possession and cer-tainty, the denial of incompleteness and neediness that characterized the intellectual project? Isn't he still hungry for a science of life? (LK, 270)

In the end, Proust acknowledges that love cannot be only a matter of chemistry, of something over which we have absolutely no say. His final posi-tion, Nussbaum points out, is one in which cataleptic impressions are ordered by reflection and interpretation. On this final position, there is room for cor-rection, for interpretation. But she also points out that this is a move that does not amount to much. Proust remains a kind of Baconian scientist: the role of the scientist is to interpret the data, but the data themselves are given and are therefore not in any sense chosen by the knower. We cannot go wrong about the data, the impressions of love say, but we may go wrong in our interpreta-tions of them. We cannot deny our intense feeling about someone, but the feeling may not be love; it may be, for example, hate, or envy, or whatever. And just so, we may be mistaken in interpreting our feeling toward someone as hate when it is actually love. Nevertheless, Proust does not abandon his view that love's knowledge is indubitable. Resting on this bedrock of cer-tainty, he is relieved from the anxiety of, the fear and trembling of, the exis-tential choice of, love. He does not come to see that love is ours to refuse, ours to embrace, ours to risk. Love is like pain: we don't choose it anymore than we can refuse it; and although we can publicly deny it, we cannot make it go away, anymore than we can bring it on; and nothing is more certain.

Unsatisfied with Proust's final position with regard to love, Nussbaum proposes her own. To make her substantive as well as methodological point, she presents her alternative through a story, "Learning to Fall," by Ann Beattie. The story tells us, among other things, just how central time is to love's knowledge.

The unnamed narrator of the story, let us call her N, is, like Marcel at first, an intellectualist, a skeptic, convinced that love must be measured, impersonally assessed, and diligently scrutinized in terms of costs and benefits. The symbol for her intellectualist drive to measure and to control is a digital watch, a Christmas present given to her by her husband (Arthur) to whom she is unhappily married. The denouement of the story comes when she realizes that her watch is wrong: she has missed her train back to Connecticut and to her husband, and so now has time to call Ray, her former lover—the lover that she has recently broken up with because he had too much power over her and because he confused her.

What she came to realize in her failure to depart was similar and yet profoundly different from what Marcel came to realize in the shock of Albertine's departure. Both came to realize that the time of love is not the time of a measuring *techne;* both came to realize that the time of the human heart must break with the rhythms of mechanical measurement and control.

At first, both Marcel and N wanted to transcend the human condition of vulnerability, of uncertainty, of doubt, of fear. As Nussbaum has put it in the quotation just cited: at first both of these characters are in flight from themselves. They both seek a *techne* of control to keep their emotions manageable and in hand, to keep their fears at bay. They seek to transcend the anxiety of human time by taking safe refuge in the measured time of machines; they abstract themselves from the lived time of human existence in which human relations are formed and develop; they seek to escape from the human. And they do this at first for good reason, for they are convinced that the time they seek to escape is the time which subjects human beings to *tuche,* to fortune, to loss, to suffering. And so they deny their own feelings; they conclude that they do not love: Marcel does not love Albertine; N does not love Ray.

The existential fact, however, is that they do love. Marcel wakes up to this, to the fact that he loves Albertine, in the moment he receives the news of her departure. N finds out that she loves Ray when she forgets her watch time and takes the human time to be with Ray. Marcel's love awakens in an absence; N's in a presence; Marcel's in an instant; N's in a slowly developing sequence of time.

Both want to recant their futile attempt to transcend the human; indeed, both want to find a way to embrace the human emotion of love. Marcel, however, fails. He ends by substituting one escape for another; call this the exchange of an escape *from* time for an escape *into* time, into the moment; call it an escape from the other into himself.

Marcel substitutes the certainty of thought with the certainty of the cataleptic impression, with the certainty of feeling. This would seem to be enough to move him in the direction of a more human life. We might think that his cool, almost godlike intellectual detachment, rocked by the in-break of an instantaneous moment of eternity that hits him in a blazing, blinding flash, would give away to an acknowledgment of his vulnerability and fragility, to a more human picture of himself. We might think that in the wake of the crisis of Albertine's departure, when he becomes disoriented, paralyzed, shattered by love, that at least he would have gotten closer to being in touch with his human emotions. And in this condition, he does, no doubt, come somehow closer to an embrace of his own humanness, only then to turn away.

He comes to realize that he cannot any longer deny or doubt his feelings. But he does not abandon his search for certainty. He simply exchanges the certainty of the mind for the certainty of the heart. Even though matters of the heart, unlike matters of the head, cannot be controlled or intellectually measured, they also cannot be denied. In fact, he realizes that the cataleptic impression is even more certain than even the most certain intellectual determination. He has, after all, just found out that intellectual certainty is not as certain as he thought it was. When love strikes, the heart knows it, and it knows it with absolutely indubitable certainty; like smoke that gets in our eyes, love leaves us with something inside that cannot be denied.

But not only is the cataleptic impression of love more certain, the dynamic moment of its in-break is more powerful, more exciting, more involving, even if more uncontrollable, than the static, godlike moment of intellectual, detached scrutiny—the eternal moment of *sub specie eternitatis.* The moment of the impression is sudden, surprising, mysterious, magical. And even though it is instantaneous, it seems to have its own kind of eternity and even finality to it. The moment of the impression appears to us like a moment frozen, like a moment that will last forever, or at least like a moment that will never be surpassed. Joan Baez's "Diamonds and Rust" expresses perfectly this frozen moment of finality, "Speaking strictly for me we both could have died then and there."

To say that the cataleptic impression takes place in an instant and that it has the character of the indubitability of a feeling is just to say that it is not a relation, and *a fortiori,* that it does not involve a mutual choosing that takes place over time. Because the impression of love that strikes Marcel is something that he feels inside himself, it strangely does not involve Albertine; the love he feels is not something they discover together; it is not something between them, call this a mutual and continuing choice of the one by the other. And it couldn't be, for if love were such a relation of mutuality, it would necessarily take place over time, not in the instant. Because Marcel thinks of love as a chemical reaction, he cannot think of it as such a relation. As Nussbaum puts it, "It is because it [the cataleptic impression] is not a relation at all—it has really nothing to do with the other, it is a chemical reaction in oneself—that it can have this instantaneous character" (LK, 277).

While the young woman in Beattie's story (N) also turns from the time of intellectual scrutiny, as does Marcel, she does not turn, as does Marcel, to a suspended moment within her own isolated consciousness. Both Marcel and N want to turn from the abstract time of the measured moments of clocks and digital watches to try to find a more human time, a time in which the other can appear. Yet, Marcel does not succeed in finding this more human time; a time in which Albertine can appear. Even after his conversion, he is still alone.

It is N, Nussbaum says, that makes the more human turn, N that learns to give herself existentially to the human embrace. N is more successful than Marcel at finding a way to be embraced by love, by Ray. As Nussbaum says, she, echoing the title of Beattie's story, learns how to fall.

N learns not only that love is something that one falls into, after being struck by it; she learns also, and more importantly, that *love is something that one must allow oneself to fall into.* (This is something that Marcel did not learn; on his view, we are simply struck by love, and as such, are in no position to resist it, or to allow it to move us.)

On her trip to town she has taken Andrew, the slightly brain-damaged third grader son of her best friend Ruth. She has done this, perhaps unconsciously, as a way of avoiding Ray, even though all the day long she thinks of him. At the breakfast table at Ruth's house just prior to Andrew and N's departure for the City, Ruth had said to him, "I love you." She follows this with, "Did you guess that I loved you?" To this he responds, a bit embarrassed and annoyed with his mother, "I know it."

Later, after the return train is missed and Ray is called and has joined them for coffee, Andrew will teach N more about love, about love's knowledge. Andrew begins to tell them that his mother is learning to fall. He explains that this is what she is doing in her dance class. Ray asks, "Does she just go plop?" "Not really," Andrew replies, "its kind of slow." What N learns from Andrew, from Ruth, is that when something is about to happen, when we are headed for a fall, then we must let it happen, we must "aim for grace." Nussbaum comments on this narrative:

> She [N] knows what Ruth knew all along: what will happen can't be stopped. But what this means is that she lets herself not stop it, she decides to stop stopping it. She discovers what will happen by letting it happen. Like Ruth, slowly falling in the class exercise that teaches and manifests trust, she learns to fall. As Andrew says, she doesn't just go plop (as Marcel did, abruptly plunging); she gently, slowly yields to her own folding, to the folding of his arm around her. She lets that touch not startle her. Like Ruth's bodily fall . . . *it's something done yet, once you do it, fundamentally uncontrolled; no accident, yet a yielding; an aiming, but for grace. You can't aim for grace really. It has so little connection, if any, with your efforts and actions.* (LK, 278, italics added)

Clearly Nussbaum herself is unsettled in or by all of this. What can it mean to say that falling is something done, but has little, if any, connection to your efforts and actions? But, before I try to answer this, let me say a word about Nussbaum's idea of the certainty of love.

One thing surely that she wants to say and rightly is this: love brings with it its own certainty, call this the certainty of faith. The certainty of faith, like the certainty of love, does not exist outside the context of the possibility of doubt, the possibility of uncertainty. Or as I have put this matter earlier, faith includes doubt as an ever-present, annulled possibility. As Nussbaum says, "Faith is never beyond doubt" (LK, 279). For me, this means that the certainty of faith, or love, is never beyond doubt and uncertainty only insofar as what it is possible to doubt is in fact (and as a matter of mutual consent) not doubted. As I understand it, what puts love's knowledge (certainty) beyond doubt is the absence of the demand for proof (LK, 279). Or as I would rather put it, what puts love's knowledge beyond doubt is the fact that we mutually consent not to doubt what could be doubted. This ongoing act of mutual consent is both the source of love's fragility and its insurmountable strength.

But this does not settle what seems yet unsettled in Nussbaum. In this matter of falling in love, what say do we have? Unlike Marcel, who goes from thinking that we have an absolute say, to thinking that we have absolutely no say at all, she thinks, or at least suggests, that our say is only negative: in matters of love, we can only decide to stop stopping it from happening to us. If this is so, then the embrace of love is not something we are called on to choose in any positive sense of the term. Rather, our embrace of it is more in the order of a yielding, a resignation we might say, to our luck or fate. Our choice is at play in love only insofar as we can, at least for a while, or even always, yield or refuse to yield to it.

Although Nussbaum has presented us with a great advance over Proust's interpretation of love, I do not find her account fully satisfying. Or to put the point in terms of the more general theme that I am pursuing here, what I do not find satisfying in her attempt to offer an alternative to the human wish to transcend the human is her account of that alternative. I agree that the alternative to the wish for transcendence of our humanness is the existential embrace of it. My problem with her view, however, is that *her picture of this human embrace of the human focuses too much on yielding (or refusing to yield) rather than on acting (or refusing to act); too much on being embraced, rather than on the act of embracing.*[1] A fully satisfying account of love's knowledge must include both. Let me elaborate.

Put the idea of falling along side another idea, the Kierkegaardian idea of a leap. Certainly there is a difference. Suppose that I am learning how to be a free-falling parachutist. Finally the day comes for me to take my first jump. Suppose that day I fall out of the plane, that I cannot stop myself from falling. I might be able to recover and at least control my free-fall and land safely. But surely we would not say that I jumped, that I made my first jump. Or suppose, secondly, and more like the story of learning to fall, that I can't bring myself to jump, but, due to a strange set of circumstances, I do not let myself stop myself from falling out of the plane. Again, this is not the same as taking the leap out of the door. Still I cannot claim to have made my first jump. By the same token, when I do finally decide to jump and in fact jump, I also and of necessity must fall. Leaping involves falling in a way that falling does not involve leaping.

Certainly love involves a fall. But doesn't it also involve a leap? Doesn't it involve a decision, say a decision to want to want to be with this particular other? And isn't this so because love, of necessity, involves the

---

1. In thinking about this, I cannot help but wonder if Nussbaum is worried about falling prey to an old masculine sexist prejudice, namely, the idea that it is the man's role to embrace, the woman's to be embraced, the man's role to lead in the dance the woman's to follow, the man's role to initiate, the woman's to yield. She does seem to want, and I think rightly, to keep to a kind of feminist agenda that recognizes that love requires a willingness on the part of the man to be embraced, to yield, to follow. But surely such an agenda would also want to recognize the role of the woman to embrace, to lead, to initiate. Or perhaps, she is simply worried that the idea of embracing is inextricably bound up with some sort of attempt to immobilize, or to dominate. But surely, on her own account, Ray does not embrace N in this way; N's willingness to be embraced in not a willingness to be dominated or immobilized.

bridging of an abyss? Doesn't love call us, both of us, to cross this gulf? And don't we think that we have a positive say—a mutual positive say—in the making of such a mutual crossing? If not, then we seem hardly justified in thinking of the mutual claims that love entails as our own. The idea that we fall across the abyss, or even that we do not stop ourselves from falling across, does not allow full weight to the idea that the relation of love is ours to enter, ours to refuse, ours to dissolve; or what is the same thing, that the relation of love is ours.

If the idea of a leap makes more sense of the idea that love is our own, then Nussbaum will have to reconsider whether she wants to continue to think that the aim for it, like the aim for grace, has little connection, if any, to our efforts and actions. If I am right, love must not only learn to yield to the embrace of the other, it must learn to embrace. Again, how else can we think of love as a relation of mutual trust and care that is our own to have and to hold?

Love as a bond mutually chosen and continually rechosen over time, unlike the cataleptic impression, necessarily involves a mutual presence of two individuals. Love exists, we might say, between two separate and separated individuals by establishing a bond that reaches across the gulf that separates them; love holds them together through time in an embrace that is only as good as the mutual consent of the two to continue to hold each other. As such, this bond of trust and care that love establishes, this mysterious hyphen that holds the I and the Thou together, is not something that we can simply fall into, or simply allow ourselves to fall into. There must be a mutual leaping across the abyss, as well as a mutual yielding, if we are to claim the relation as our own.

But, leaping, as much so as falling, is a risky business. It is no wonder that we human beings are as reluctant to leap as we are to fall.

Love and Madness

If we have a say in the leap of love, it follows that we can refuse it. But why should we? Or, what is just as relevant to ask, why shouldn't we?

Isn't love the most wonderful thing in all of the world? Wouldn't a life without it be impoverished, perhaps not fully human? Who can live without it?

At the same time, isn't love inevitably tied up with anger and violence, with pain, hurt, and ultimately with the deepest unhappiness. Who needs it?

Nussbaum tracks one of the most famous attempts to deal with this double orientation of love, the poetry of Lucretius. A first century (B.C.E.) Roman and follower of Epicurus, Lucretius worked out an intricate and complex argument designed finally to justify his master's dictum, "a wise man will not fall in love." He concluded that because the dark side of the doubleness of love is so overwhelming, so consuming, the leap into love most likely will turn out to be a leap into madness. Happiness requires that we either refuse to leap, or at least that we leap wisely.

Nussbaum teases out Lucretius's arguments from his six-book poem "On the Way Things Are" in her essay "Beyond Obsession and Disgust: Lucretius on the Therapy of Love."[2] In this section, I will tease out of Nussbaum's essay the salient and relevant issues that bear on our primary concern here: How does the human emotion of love figure in the human quest to find a technique for transcending the human?

Lucretius is particularly relevant for our own time, Nussbaum points out, because he clearly saw that the love of love is a kind of secular religion. In the wake of the modern eclipse of the gods, love has become for many the last available point of entry into transcendence. As Professor Nussbaum puts it, "[I]n our time, when religious sources of individual salvation are widely mistrusted, personal erotic love . . . has come . . . to bear the weight of many people's longings for transcendence" (TD, 142).

Contemporary true believers in love stand ready to resist Lucretius's critique and final rejection of erotic love. They think it is insane to agree with Lucretius's final conclusion that true happiness comes only when erotic love is avoided and rejected. To such true believers, the thought of a life without the passion of erotic love is the most dreadful thought, it is no life at all. Consequently, the voice of Lucretius that condemns this passion as madness sounds itself like the voice of madness.

But, on the other hand, in moments of honesty some stand ready to heed Lucretius's attack on romantic, erotic love as the voice of wisdom. We know that the love fantasies that fascinate us, and the love stories that we live, weave their plots around the deadly themes of obsession, escape, madness, violence, suicide. And in moments of despair, we wonder with Lucretius whether eros is good for us after all, whether it is only a source of madness and misery. And so we wonder also if we would not be wiser to live without it, if we would not be happier without it. "Who needs a heart when a heart can be broken?"

---

2. "Beyond Obsession and Disgust: Lucretius on the Therapy of Love," (TD, 140–91). In the following discussion I will present Lucretius's view of love as Nussbaum interprets it.

Let us turn then to the details of Lucretius's critique of erotic love to see where it comes out. But more importantly, let us proceed to see if we can agree with the Epicurean dictum that a wise man will not fall in love.

First, a word about Epicurus, the master. Nussbaum tells us that he taught that there are three classes of desires: (1) empty desires, that is, desires that are socially taught but desires that are based on false beliefs; empty desires cause our unhappiness, our misery (the desire for wealth, for example); (2) natural/necessary desires, the primary such desire being the desire for pleasure, something we share with the rest of the animal kingdom; these desires are not socially taught, yet they are desires that we cannot refuse without jeopardizing our happiness (as we note here, for Epicurus, the natural is the healthy, the socially taught, the disease); and (3) natural/non-necessary desires, that is, desires that do not originate in social teaching, but can be refused without jeopardizing happiness. Indeed, these desires must be refused, if we are to be happy, for such desires, like empty desires, are based on false beliefs. Love, the desire for sexual intercourse, falls into this third class.

Epicurus is less ambiguous about love than is Lucretius. He thought unequivocally that, as Nussbaum quotes him, "it is not prudent to have intercourse . . . because of the frequently adversarial relationship between sexual individuals and the orderly conduct of the rest of life" (TD, 132). He also thought that children were a bad thing for the wise man—they cause too many distractions from the things that are really necessary for happiness (TD, 153).

Why is romantic love a bad thing for Epicurus? Except for the fact that it is a natural desire and not socially taught, such love is like an empty desire insofar as it is based on a false belief. Even though erotic desire is natural, we are free either to pursue it or not. The one who pursues it does so because he or she thinks it will bring happiness. In point of fact, however, it actually brings pain, or at least the pain it brings always and inevitably outweighs its momentary pleasures. Since pain is unhappiness and pleasure is happiness, and since a proper understanding of erotic love shows clearly that it brings more pain than pleasure, then it must be avoided, or at least replaced. For Epicurus then, the erotic desire for sexual intercourse must be replaced with a different sort of love, a love of wisdom, that is, the pursuit of philosophy. "The cure for bad desires comes through a love of arguments that dispels illusion and leaves us with truth" (TD, 134).

Lucretius, in the end more ambivalent about the doubleness of the erotic than his master, attempts nevertheless to substantiate Epicurus's essential rejection of erotic love's place in the good (happy) life. His argument begins with a circuitous story of the evolution of eros, a story that traces its emergence from the animal to the early human and beyond to the late human where it turns into a divine madness and then back again to its professed re-embrace as a controlled human emotion.

Before I tell this story of the evolution of love, let me admit that I have intentionally blurred the distinctions among the terms *romantic, erotic,* and *sexual,* as well as the distinction between these forms of love and other forms of it. I do this first because it is not clear where to draw this line; and secondly, because drawing the line is part of the story of love that Lucretius attempts to tell.

The love story begins with the natural world of animal life, or at least Lucretius's Epicurean vision of it. Once upon a time the natural world of animals resembled what we might call a Disney-like forest, the forest of Bambi or Snow White. Everything was peaceful and Venus, Lucretius's trope for the power of love, permeated it all. Her power was "felt in the sea, in the mountains, in swelling brooks, in the leafy homes of birds, in green fields" (TD, 159). This is a joyful world, a world of peace and harmony in which everything is beautiful in its own way. Here "[t]he animals who respond to the pull of Venus are full of a strong vital energy that is exuberant, playful, and nonconflicted" (TD, 159).

Clearly such a romantic idealized natural order ignores some important facts of animal life. The animal world is not all light and joy; there is a darkness in the jungle. Animals are brutes; they are violent; they abandon and eat their own and other's young; they are aloof to the pain of others; they struggle with each other for survival; they compete, often to the death; and in some sense they are viciously and violently jealous and possessive.

Nevertheless, this idealized vision of Lucretius is not far from many a modern-day romantic for whom the vision of a precivilized natural harmony and peace is the only viable alternative to the madness of a society that has become itself a brutal, dark jungle.

Love as sexual desire is of course present in the peaceful animal world that Lucretius envisions, but, as he is quick to point out, animals are not in love. Hence, in this setting, the power of sexual love is benign; it generates no anxiety, no pain, no jealousy, no obsession, no violence, no murder, no war. As Nussbaum puts it, in Lucretius's picture of the animal world, there is "no madness . . . no cruelty either to self or to the other" (TD, 160).

The first human beings, Lucretius tells us, were like these animals, living together in harmony and accord. Love was present in them, that is, the power of Venus permeated them, but as a natural innocuous sexual instinct.

As Nussbaum remarks, "The first human beings, tough and hardy, had no set-tled dwelling places, no love for their offspring, no ability to think of the common good, no morals or laws. They lived by instinct, on whatever came their way. . . . [I]n one sense [theirs was] a far better life than ours . . . [for these early humans] lacked the ills caused by *eros*" (TD, 161, 162).

Then came the establishment of households and families, and the be-ginnings of the institution of marriage. This change was a softening of the toughness of the earlier life in the wild. "Parents formerly hard now felt ten-derness for their children; and we may assume that this same tenderness and friendliness now also characterized the relationship between husband and wife" (TD, 162). In this new world, Venus is still present, but she changes es-sentially, "She becomes civilized" (TD, 162).

This evolution of Venus was perhaps inevitable given the differences between animals and humans. The fact is that human beings are intrinsically socio-political creatures. We humans are drawn to be together, not as birds in a flock, but through the mediation of our words. As speakers we require the presence of others who respond to our words and who issue words for our re-sponse. We human beings cannot live by instinct alone, nor can we live alone. We live in and by agreements, covenants, and laws; we have an interest in, and converse about, matters that go beyond our own individual welfare; as in-trinsically socio-political animals we have an interest in the welfare of others; first we are interested in the welfare of those close to us, but beyond that we may even develop an interest in what we may call the common good.

Language opens human beings to various forms of being together that are distinctively human. Because of the capacity for speech, human beings can form relationships of friendship, political alliance, moral responsibility, and so forth. Most importantly, however, language opens human beings to what we might call the conversation of love. In this conversation of love, in which mutual declarations of commitment are exchanged, and mutual claims are made, a new and perhaps the most distinctively human form of being to-gether emerges.

It is just these bonds of love that our conversations establish that tie human beings together in a way that separates the human from the animal world. Venus is civilized when she speaks. And with this civilizing of love, this humanizing of it via language, a human world comes forth. And with this world comes socio-political institutions; and most likely one of its first such institutions was marriage. While some animals mate for life, no animal gets married.

The evolution of natural sexual desire into civilized love, and the acceptance of this love as the distinctively human form of being together brings with it a double-edged awareness. At once human beings began to see just how removed they were from the natural animal world. Some came to see their capacity for civilized love as a mark of divinity, or as a divine gift that offered liberation from the jungle. Surely all saw that the human capacity for love was, if nothing else, the human capacity for transcendence.

At the same time, this recognition of the divinity of love brought an ill that before was unthinkable. Lucretius depicted this ill as a drive, an urge, or a longing, to become divine. That is, the very love that separated human beings from the natural world, if left unchecked, may turn into a desire that separates the human from itself. Just at the moment that love brings the human into its own as distinctively human, it threatens to seduce the human into thinking that the human must be transformed into the divine. Unchecked, love may well seduce human beings into wanting to transcend their own humanity. Lucretius sees very clearly just how easily the divinely qualified human capacity for love can turn into a divine inhuman madness.

How does this happen? How does love become madness?

As an Epicurean, Lucretius is concerned to find a way of life that leads to happiness. This means avoiding all those courses of action that lead to pain. But this avoidance is possible only if we are clear about what courses of action in fact lead to pain. Sometimes, of course, we believe that a certain course of action will lead to pleasure when in fact it will lead to pain. Accordingly the first step toward happiness is the elimination of false beliefs.

With regard to love, Lucretius's therapy was to show that the common belief that the path of eros is, without qualification, a sure and certain path to pleasure is false. As he points out, more often than not, eros is a sickness, a disease that leads only to pain and unhappiness. To show that it is a false belief to think that erotic desire brings only pleasure, Lucretius attempts to show how it most often entails pain.

But first this qualification: for Lucretius, there is nothing wrong with love, if the lover loves aright, if he or she loves in accord with civilized love. Such a sane love aims at pleasure, indeed at the mutual pleasure of the lovers. And for the Epicurean, of course, pleasure is the ultimate aim of the good life.

But this proper love can and most often does become corrupt. The desire for the other can quickly turn into a desire for union with the other; the passion for closeness can quickly turn into a passion for fusion. When this happens, love has gone mad.

It is simply a false belief to think that the aim of love is fusion and false to believe that fusion with the other can bring us pleasure. It is false for an obvious reason: two cannot be one. The aim of fusion cannot in principle be satisfied. If this is what love aims at, it is destined to be frustrated, incomplete, unsatisfied. As Nussbaum says, "The separateness of the other . . . is not delight to these lovers, but a painful frustration of their dearest wish, which is to eat the other sexually, feeding on that other mind and body and having it completely" (TD, 174).

But why should a lover want to devour the other? From Lucretius's perspective, that is, from a male perspective, the answer is tied up with the man's perception of the woman as a goddess. As the man sees it, his woman is perfect, absolutely divine. So why devour her? The male thinks that by devouring the woman he can himself ascend to divinity. In fact, his passion makes him mad with a desire to transcend his own humanity, to become a god.

A consequence of this mad passion to transcend the human is the destruction of a civilized sane love—that form of love that aims at the mutual pleasure of the lovers. Oddly enough, the apotheosis of the woman, coupled with the man's desire to devour her, ends up destroying mutuality. That is, erotic desire turns into madness when its object, the human woman, is transformed into divine perfection, into an object of absolute devotion, into an object to be worshipped, for this transformation of her into a goddess entails the destruction of her as a real human being, as much so as the man's desire to become a god destroys his own humanness.

> In the region of love, men are obsessed with the aims that have little to do with *giving* pleasure. (Does a goddess have needs?) They go through intercourse in the grip of the picture of sublime union, mad with desire for quasi-mystical experience in which there would be no separate pleasure of the woman to consider in any case, since at the climatic moment all sensations would be fused. This picture makes them forget, or actively deny, the fact that there is another separate sentient being there, whose pleasure is a separate thing and does count for something. (TD, 183)

Lucretius also points out that the illusion of the divinity of the other cannot be sustained. When the man realizes that his lover is actually an embodied human being, he will not be able to deal with it. He will not be able to accept the plain fact that she is a mortal who, as much as he, is subject to bodily necessity. Insofar as he discovers this, and to the extent that the illusion of her divinity becomes clear, he will be disgusted with her. Can a goddess be subject to flatulence, to the uncleanliness of menstruation? Unable to accept this, the man tries to keep the illusion going. He will insist that the lover conceal her true human self; he will insist on perfume, costume, and makeup; he will insist that the woman disguise herself, that she live dishonestly; disgusted with her real humanity, he will demand that she maintain herself as an aesthetic object.

Combine a desire for fusion that cannot be satisfied with the transformation of the object of love into a goddess and the result is disaster: the destruction of the human itself. The pain this generates is too much to bare; it must be avoided at all costs.

So, is there an alternative to the pain of obsession and disgust that a sick love inevitably leads to? Lucretius thinks there is. The first step in the therapy to cure the disease of erotic passion is to remove the false beliefs it carries. There are two such false beliefs: (1) the proper object of love is the divine, the goddess; and (2) the aim of love is a fusion with that divine object. Nussbaum summarizes Lucretius's cure for a diseased love as follows: "If the loved one is not turned into a goddess, there is no surprise and no disgust at her humanity. [In the cured state] . . . the lover could see the beloved clearly as a separate and fully human being. . . . Love's fantasies constrain and enclose both men and women, dooming the former to an exhausting alternation between worship and hatred, the other to a frantic effort of concealment and theater, accompanied by an equal hatred of everyday human beings" (TD, 182).

Nussbaum thinks that Lucretius is right to want to cure the madness of eroticism, its divine madness, we might call it, its mad desire to transcend our humanity. She thinks that he is right to propose that a lover learn how to embrace his or her own humanity and the humanity of the beloved. She is less sure that he is right when he recommends that lovers learn to re-embrace their mutual humanity by rekindling a kind of love that is a wiser form of eros. Lucretius thinks that it is possible for us to re-embrace the eros that early humans once knew, an eros without anxiety, without violence, without disgust and obsession, without madness, call this a more natural love, a more (pre?)-civilized love.

As Lucretius has it, only if we re-embrace this peaceful eros that we once knew, is a good marriage possible. Unlike his master, in fact, Lucretius thought that sexual, erotic love within marriage could be a good thing, if properly controlled. Indeed, he thought that marriage itself could be a institution that could contribute to the good life.

What would a good marriage look like for Lucretius? Well, it would be based on a love that recognized the humanity of both parties. There would be no pretending that the lover is a goddess. And there would be no passion for union. In a good marriage, the passion of eros would be controlled, and the passion to transcend the human would be kept in check by reason. There would be a recognition of mutuality and interdependency, an acknowledgment of the fact that both partners have needs; there would be an appreciation of the ordinary, the everyday. In a good marriage, eros would be transformed into *philia,* and hence marriage would be transformed into a cordial friendship.

Obedience to reason teaches the lovers that they must control their passions, and, as it were, achieve and maintain a sort of distance or detachment between the lover and the beloved. Keeping this distance will control and hence cure the misguided passion for fusion. This reasonable distance will require a kind of disengagement; it will entail an abandonment of anxious care for the other, a forswearing of jealously and obsession. It will replace disgust with our humanness with a rational embrace of it. In a good marriage, the mad erotic obsession to grasp and immobilize the other will be replaced with a loose and controlled cordial hug.

But we must ask, What are the side effects of this therapy of control that Lucretius prescribes? Is anything lost here? As Lucretius sees it, the only way to make a marriage happy is to remove from it the liabilities of erotic passion, its potential excesses. But, can we remove from eros its potential for madness without removing its potential for every intensity, the intensity of excitement, the intensity of joy? Is something missing when the lover and the beloved become just friends? This is not to say, of course, lovers should not be friends, or that friendship is not a form of love essential for human happiness, but rather to ask this: Is eros more than *philia?* or, at least, different? And, what is more important to ask, Is a life devoid of eros in fact a truly human life? Does eros bring a human joy that is not commensurate with the joy of friendship?

Nussbaum thinks that a human being who follows Lucretius's advice, a human being who refuses to embrace the joys of erotic passion, ends up living a life that is essentially other than a fully human life. I agree. It is one thing to desire these joys and to fail to find love, it is quite another to desire to transcend the desire altogether. What a price Lucretius's therapy seems to exact. As Professor Nussbaum says, "Lucretius cannot understand this joy [of erotic love]: for in the end, he is an Epicurean, and as an Epicurean, he cannot permit himself, beyond a certain point, to follow his own advice to 'yield to human life' " (TD, 191).

The irony of Lucretius's therapy to cure a diseased love that aims to transcend the human, the irony of his proposal that we re-embrace the human, is that it turns out to be just another technique for denying or refusing it. In the end he simply exchanges the madness of Dionysian abstract immediacy for a different sort of madness, call this the madness of Apollonian abstract distance—the madness of disengagement, reserve, numbness, aloofness, cordiality. The madness of controlled aloofness, the madness of disengagement and distance, as much so as the intoxication of the fantasy of union and fusion, have their consequences: both are techniques of transcendence; both are unable to embrace the human in all of its fragility and neediness; neither can embrace the anxiety over the potential excesses attendant to eros; and hence neither can embrace its joys.

In the end, it turns out that Lucretius's cure for the human urge to be a god is itself a form of the disease. For him, the happy person is the one who attains to a self-sufficient life, a life without neediness and vulnerability, a life of a god. Nussbaum rightly sees this, rightly calls his hand on this mistake. She asks, and implicitly answers in the affirmative, "Is this the attitude of a cured lover, or is it simply a new form of the disease that Lucretius's therapy was supposed to cure?" (TD, 191)

Where, according to Nussbaum, did Lucretius go wrong? First, she would point out that he did not go completely wrong. There is much we can learn from him: the importance of mutuality, the charge of dishonesty in the maintenance of the illusion of the goddess, the madness of the drive for union, the need to embrace our humanity, and so forth. But he did go wrong. She puts her objection to Lucretius in the form of the following question, "Is love really, in its nature, based . . . upon the idea of union? (TD, 188) She thinks it is not.

Indeed, Nussbaum thinks that if we are to be able to embrace eros, we must redefine its aim. She sees the proper aim as not being fusion, but what she calls "intimate responsiveness" (TD, 188). She agrees with Lucretius that the desire for fusion is madness; she thinks, however, that distance is not its cure. For her, the embrace of erotic passion need not eliminate, contra Lucretius, the desire for closeness; how could it? Eros is, by nature, a desire that drives two people to want to be close, as close as it is possible to be; in fact, even though distance may make the heart grow fonder, we cannot make sense of an erotic desire to be separated from the beloved; this would not be love. Closeness then captures the intimacy part of "intimate responsiveness." But eros also involves, for her, "responsiveness." That is, eros requires the two do not become one; there is simply no room for responsiveness when the two have been fused. Going on to explain what she means by intimate responsiveness, she says, "What the lover wants is to be extremely close to the person he or she loves, to be close enough to perceive and respond to every movement and every perceptible sign. In that closeness, the lover wants to achieve the other person's pleasure and his or her own—and, at the same time, to achieve a kind of knowledge of the other person, the sort of knowledge that consists in awareness and acknowledgment of every perceptible portion of that person's activity" (TD, 188).

Nussbaum says further that the aim of fusion is neither necessary nor sufficient for love as intimate responsiveness. She explains:

> Not necessary, because lovers can respond to one another as separate persons, without ever denying that they must always remain apart. . . . Not sufficient, because even if a lover could, *per impossible,* take his lover's body and mind into himself, making them parts of him, that would be, precisely, not to respond to them as hers, not to seek to please her as someone with a separate life. . . . It is, we might argue, this desire for closeness, attunement, and responsiveness that explains the way lovers hold, bite, and squeeze one another—not the impossible thought of union or fusion. We do not need to posit that error, even at the unconscious level. (TD, 189)

Can we accept Nussbaum's definition of love as intimate responsiveness? Perhaps to some extent. I certainly agree that her idea of love as intimate responsiveness is an advance over Lucretius's reduction of love to a controlled relation of friendly detachment. But can love as intimate responsiveness be the sufficient basis for a happy marriage? I do not deny that it is necessary; and I certainly don't deny that intimate responsiveness is a more human definition of eros than controlled detachment. Yet we must ask, Is Nussbaum's redefinition of eros rich enough to make for a happy marriage?

As I see it, if the embrace of marriage is to become a distinctively human form of the embrace of the human, and hence a central component in the human pursuit of happiness, then it must be based on a larger notion of love than is found in the idea of intimate responsiveness. It must be more, since I am convinced that intimate responsiveness alone is not sufficient to produce what Nussbaum wants, namely, a mutual acknowledgment of otherness, of separation, and hence of connection, all of which are the essential conditions for a happy marriage.

To my mind, what is missing from this definition of the love, when we try to make it the sufficient basis of a happy marriage, is something like a public dimension. Marriage, as a relation of love, is more than what goes on in the bedroom, or even the living room. Marriage, to be happy, must find a way to acknowledge itself as a worldly institution.

This is the way marriage begins, in a public space, in the midst of public declarations before others. In fact, this comes first; the intimacy comes only after this public legitimation (or it used to). Marriage is a legal as well as a moral institution, or what comes to the same thing, it is an institution. Accordingly, marriage carries in itself public responsibilities. The love in a happy marriage, therefore, cannot be a matter only of intimate responsiveness.

I do not claim that love as intimate responsiveness cannot sustain a certain kind of mutuality. I think it can. But the question I am raising is whether this kind of mutuality is sufficient to bring the otherness, the separateness of the other, fully into acknowledgment.

Marriage is a conversation of love, but it is not simply a conversation exclusively between the two lovers. It is also, and of moral necessity, a conversation that opens toward the world. Marriage, a happy marriage, must give the lovers a life beyond themselves. The conversation of love within a marriage must, at least on occasion, break out of the tight circle of intimacy. The lover and the beloved must find a way to be interested in something other than the welfare of each other. And I would add that I do not think that having children is sufficient to provide this interest.

Somehow the conversation of love, to make for a happy marriage, must find a way to open itself to a life with other human beings. Intimacy may bond the two to each other, but it does not provide sufficient resources for creating and sustaining an interest in being together with others; perhaps just the opposite. Yet without this interest in being with others, call this an ethical or political interest in the world, I boldly assert, the marriage will, like a plant deprived of water, wither and die, even if it does not end in divorce.

But entering into this conversation with each other and with others about our common life together is a risky business. It opens us to the dangers and excitement of disagreement, the agony and the ecstasy of struggle and conflict, the existential acknowledgment of difference and connection, and the seriousness of argument, something that may involve pain and hurt, even violence, yet also something that entails that the two take each other seriously as other. But herein is the real test of the acknowledgment of otherness, the real test of mutuality, the acid test of a good marriage. Entering this conversation forces us to ask and continually to re-ask, Can we keep the conversation of love going in the midst of conflict and disagreement? Or, does conflict and disagreement keep the love in a happy marriage alive? Can we continue to be together once we have fully acknowledged the other's right to his or her own voice? Or, more profoundly, can two people be together in a happy marriage if they do not mutually acknowledge the other's own voice?

While entering into this conversation is dangerous, it is also exciting. As Höldern once said, "Where the danger is, there also grows the saving power." The fact is, conversations at the dinner table cannot for long be sustained exclusively with exchanges of intimacy, however exciting this may be for a while, and every so often. Moreover, intimacy is not the only form of marital excitement, of marital passion, of marital joy. A marriage without political excitement, a sense of involvement and passionate interest in the world, will fall into just that everydayness that is deadly banality.

Marriage, a happy marriage, requires not only that the two fall into love with each other, it also requires that the two together fall in love with the world. Only then is the embrace of love and marriage truly an embrace of the human; only then does love become truly civilized.

Love and Rage

Love is a dangerous emotion: it can make raging monsters out of us, even the best of us. So why risk it? Maybe the best thing we human beings can do is to extirpate this dangerous passion of eros. This is what the Stoics recommended.

But at least one of the Stoics, perhaps the best of them, Seneca, was ambivalent about this therapy. This is the import of Nussbaum's essay on Seneca's *Medea*.[3] At play in Seneca's ambivalence is his attraction to a triad of incompatible sets of beliefs: (1) he believed, as the story of Medea shows clearly and incontrovertibly, that love will turn, perhaps inevitably and unavoidably, into murderous rage; he believed that this rage runs counter to moral purity and hence tranquillity and happiness; he believed love leads directly to tragedy; (2) like the Stoics he admired, he also believed that the best way to happiness is to extirpate this passion; but (3) like the human being that he was, he believed that eros is a beautiful human passion, that it is deeply connected to our humanness, that a life without it is deeply tragic.

It is Seneca's ambivalence about love that leads him to express his vision of it in tragic drama. For Seneca, human existence is tragic just because love, which lies at the core of our humanness, is itself essentially tragic. Love

---

3. "Serpents in the Soul: A Reading of Seneca's *Medea*" (TD, 439–83).

is tragic because a human life with it or without it will be a life of suffering. As Seneca seems to think, the only real question for human beings to ask is this, Which suffering is more tolerable? That is, which form of suffering is less disturbing to human tranquillity/happiness? Seneca's answer, the Stoic answer, is the latter: we must find a way to say "no" to the temptations of eros.

Clearly Seneca recognizes what the official position of Stoicism is: the extirpation of love is possible and it is necessary for the good life. He certainly wanted to agree that the loss of love is not the loss of anything valuable, indeed to the contrary; the fact is he wanted to think that the casting off of eros would be like the casting off a disease of the soul.

Seneca is drawn to agree with the Stoic that every love story is the same story, that is, the story of Medea. The common structure of the story of love is as follows. A life given over to love will, of necessity, be porous. This is true since love requires an openness to the other, a possibility of being penetrated by the other. Love is impossible if there is no way for the lovers to enter into the life of each other. For this to happen, each of the lovers must be willing to allow the boundary of his or her self to be crossed by something outside of his or her self; but not only this, they want this intrusion since they are convinced that a life alone is not happy. Willing to be and wanting to be open to the other makes for vulnerability and dependence. It makes for vulnerability since the self open to the other is a self subject to being affected by something outside of itself, something outside of its own control; it makes for dependence and neediness since the self's desire for the other shows the self to be less than sufficient unto itself; or what is the same thing, it shows that the self needs something outside of its control to complete its happiness.

But, according to the Stoic, this vulnerability and neediness of something outside of one's control is precisely what leads erotic passion to a bad end, to inevitable pain and suffering, to rage and violence. For the Stoic, there is no avoiding these painful consequences of opening ourselves to the other in the way that eros requires; the mutual interpenetration of the lovers will always turn to violation, to betrayal, to abuse, to departure. This in turn will transform eros into anger, into rage, into revenge, but finally into an effort to seal the self off from the other. The Stoic therapy can save us this pain: to avoid the hurt of being porous to the other, the Stoic recommends that we establish secure boundaries around ourselves; he advises us to secure and preserve our virginity; he tells us that we must seal ourselves off from external penetration, close off all the holes in the self that might allow outside forces into our lives, forces that are out of our control. This is what lovers may come to on the other side of the violence of betrayal and revenge, but, as the Stoic asks, why go through this hell only to come to see what good reason should have told us in the first place? If we followed good reason, we would see clearly that to be happy we must be self-sufficient, we must not need the other, we must not be vulnerable to anything outside ourselves.

Nussbaum summarizes the Stoic version of the story of love in this way:

> Love almost inevitably leads to wounds; so love will lead to anger and to a reactive attempt to root out the source of the disorder, restoring the boundaries of the self. But these attempts are almost always violent. They involve digging out what is other in oneself, assailing the source of the pain. And, furthermore, they may also be self-defeating. For love, reacting as anger, moves to seal off the wounds or holes that make love possible. So, in the end, what we get is the sealed self that the Stoic has had all along; only the road to this self must be through violence. Virginity once lost can be restored only by the sword. (TD, 456–57)

Having said all of this, having said that Seneca wanted to agree with the Stoic's version of the love story and with the Stoic therapy of desire, we must note, as Professor Nussbaum makes abundantly clear, that Seneca is deeply ambivalent about love. We simply cannot ignore Seneca's majestic and moving poetic expressions of love in the play. These expressions can only represent his own deep appreciation of love's power, its beauty, its importance. Perhaps we can say "no" to love, and perhaps we ought to, but for Seneca, the Stoic therapy was not all that easy to swallow.

As Seneca presents it, the story of Medea is the hard case for the Stoic. The reason for this is that she is a virtuous person, a person whose love was once beautiful and happy. If love can go wrong here, how much more easily is it liable to fail among the less virtuous? Medea shows us how even the most beautiful love can turn into ugliness; she shows us how the passion of love can turn even the most virtuous person into a monster.

But even the ugliness in Medea's murderous rage is, in Seneca's expression of it, deeply ambiguous. As we might say, there is a beauty in this ugliness, something virtuous in her monstrous rage. Even though she takes murderous revenge on her husband Jason for his betrayal, a revenge that includes the killing of her own children, born and unborn, she seems somehow morally justified. After all she has been true, loyal, and faithful to her marriage; she is the one who has been betrayed. Indeed, there would be something wrong with her if she were not enraged by Jason's affair, by his abandonment of her. Her rage is an appropriate human response to injustice. As we might say, the intensity of her rage is a measure of just how much her love and marriage mattered to her, of just how beautiful and how valuable it was.

And yet despite her moral entitlement to rage, we cannot help but feel the horror, the foulness, of her revenge, the inhumanness of her deeds. How can killing one's own children ever be justified, ever virtuous? Surely Medea has turned from a virtuous person into a poisonous snake; surely she is no longer to be admired; surely now she must be pitied, if not condemned.

Seneca expresses his own ambivalence over the value of eros by putting the conflict into Medea's soul. In the course of the play when she thinks about killing her children she is pulled in two opposite directions: as a mother she is horrified at what she is about to do her own children, as a betrayed lover she remembers that the children are Jason's. She oscillates, "Why, soul, do you totter back and forth? A double tide tosses me; I am uncertain of my course. . . . Anger puts love to flight, mother-love anger. Grief, yield to mother-love. [But then]. . . . Again grief grows and hate boils, and the Fury of old takes my hand. Anger, where you lead I follow" (TD, 450).

And Seneca also oscillates. As Nussbaum convincingly puts it, this oscillation can be framed within the debate between the Aristotelian and the Stoic Schools on the value of eros. Aristotle's position on love in general, and on Medea in particular, Nussbaum puts as follows: "The Aristotelian holds that we can have passionate love in our lives and still be people of virtue and appropriate action; that the virtuous person can be relied upon to love the right sort of person in the right way at the right time, in the right relation to other acts and obligations. Medea's problem is not a problem of love per se, it is a problem of inappropriate, immoderate love. The virtuous person can avoid this problem" (TD, 441).

In contrast, the Stoic thinks that the problem is with love per se. He thinks this is precisely what Medea shows, since she is, after all, a virtuous person. For the Stoic then, love can and inevitably will turn even the best human being into a monster; therefore, the happy life is a life without it. Aristotle is wrong, love cannot be controlled; rather it must be extirpated. Furthermore, Aristotle is wrong to think that a life without love would be less than happy.

Let us consider how this debate might proceed. The Aristotelian might well say to the Stoic that Medea's story is obviously not the story of all love. Rather is it an exceptional story, a story of excess, and hence not the story of the inevitable course of a life that allows love into it. Most lovers never resort to murder, much less to the murder of their own children. Medea's story is therefore of little help in evaluating the place of love in the good life.

While the Aristotelian does not deny that cruelty sometimes accompanies eros in fact, she does attribute this infrequent cruelty to bad luck, to *tuche*. But, we must remember, for the Aristotelian, being subject to fortune, to uncontrolled external happenings, is precisely the necessary condition for moral virtue to arise. This explains why Aristotle thinks that the gods, who are not subject to luck, are without the moral virtues (TD, 470). The morally virtuous person cannot avoid, and must not even want to avoid luck, since virtue requires a context of uncontrolled happenings. However, the Aristotelian does insist on this: the virtuous person "will be able to stop short of the really bad forms of cruelty" (TD, 474).

The Stoic reply to this is startling. What the Stoic says is that you will always and inevitably hurt the one you love, if not in fact, at least in fantasy. Moreover, you can't control the rage that love will infect you with.

To reply to the specific charge that Medea is not representative, but the story of excess, the Stoic says this: cruelty may accompany erotic passion far more frequently than the Aristotelian is willing to acknowledge. As Nussbaum comments, the facts seem to be on the side of Seneca: "Consider the many acts of physical abuse, especially of women and children; consider the acts of betrayal; consider the ingenious vindictive reprisals of the betrayed toward former lover and toward rival, the manipulation of children's lives and emotions, the financial warfare, the excessive litigation—consider these things and you will discover that the risks and uncertainties associated with erotic passion do indeed produce a great deal of bad and destructive action" (TD, 472).

But even if cruelty were factually enacted only infrequently, there can be little doubt of the frequency of cruelty in fantasy. This cruelty, the Stoic thinks, is an unavoidable companion of erotic passion. There is some question as to whether we can ever be safe, even the best of us, from crimes of thought and wish. Even the happiest of loves can turn, even if just in passing, to unhappiness, to murderous wishes of harm to the other. Along these lines, Nussbaum interprets Seneca as follows: "[E]ven if you should stop short of evil external action in unhappy love, you will never be safe from thinking violent and angry thoughts, forming fantasies of murder and evil, against your former lover and/or your rival. You will still, almost in spite of yourself, be likely to find yourself weaving murderous spells, wishing horrors. [And against the Aristotelian], [t]hese thoughts are not under the control of right reason and good character" (TD, 476).

Quickly the Aristotelian responds by saying that an inner wish is not nearly as bad as the wish carried out; a wish to do harm to the other is not as bad as actually doing harm. But surely the Aristotelian must concede that a heart that wishes murderous deeds, even if they are not carried out, is not the heart of a virtuous person.

Undaunted by the Stoic's argument, the Aristotelian is now ready to play his strongest hand. If love is of the right sort it will be for the other for the other's own sake. Loving the other this way acknowledges the separateness of the other and hence is not possessive and manipulative. If the other should leave, or betray his beloved, then she should be willing, out of her love and concern for his own happiness, to let him go, as perhaps good parents who really love their children in the right way should be willing to let them go away to live separate lives. If the virtuous person really loves someone for his own sake, she should be willing, tenderly and understandingly and without rage or anger, to let him go.

The Stoic's reply is convincing. She asks, "What kind of love is it that does not want to be together with the beloved? that would not be hurt by abandonment or betrayal? Wouldn't this loss, even the threat of it, be a cause of a deep disturbance in the soul? And isn't this always a possibility in erotic, passionate attachment?" The Stoic's argument is more convincing to my mind than Aristotle's. Somehow Aristotle's picture of the virtuous person, of moral purity, where there are no excesses, does not ring true to our human experience. Certainly we all know all too well that the volatility of erotic passion does carry in itself the ever-present threat of excess, of harm, of rage. And we know too, that even the best of us cannot subdue it.

Even if we can accept the Stoic's diagnosis of the nature of eros, do we have to accept his proposed therapy for its ills? I would like to think not. Let us be clear about what the Stoic therapy requires. The Stoic prescription is for radical surgery: the good life is possible only if we cut our hearts out. As the Stoic doctor sees it, health is possible only if, and to the extent that, a person finds a way to extirpate the passion of love, erotic love especially, but perhaps all love.

This therapy is again a prescription for transcending our humanness. The good human life is possible only if we transcend our human desires and live as gods, without needs, self-sufficient and secure from the harm others will cause us if we let them into our lives, if we become dependent on them, if we need them, if we love them. The hard conclusion of the Stoic, contra Aristotle, is simply this: "[T]here is no safe way of combining deep personal love (especially, but probably not only, erotic love) with spotless moral purity" (TD, 480).

This conclusion is especially hard for Seneca to accept. For him, the Stoic therapy of desire must be embraced, but not without its tragic consequences. As Medea shows, love can never be what the Aristotelian imagines it can be, a passion that can be happily and harmoniously integrated into the virtuous life; but as the Aristotelian knows, it is equally true that a life without it can never be *eudaimon.* "So either way we live, we will be, it seems, imperfect" (TD, 480).

Is there an alternative to these alternatives? This is an especially urgent question for someone like me and, if I read her correctly, Nussbaum, since both I and she think that a life without love would be unhappy. Both of us agree that a life without love would be essentially incomplete, perhaps essentially less than fully human. Is there then a way of embracing love without denying, or subduing, or eliminating, or otherwise transcending, its excesses, its cruelties?

Does Nussbaum see a way to do this? She agrees with the Stoics against Aristotle that we cannot domesticate eros, and she agrees with Aristotle against the Stoics that we cannot live happily without it. But she sees something common to these two sides, something that she calls into question in her attempt to formulate an alternative. Both the Aristotelian and the Stoic take their stands within the medical analogy, both are doctors of the soul, both are obsessed with finding a way to secure health against the threat of disease. Nussbaum suggests that the only way to forge an alternative to the dilemma that the two sides of this debate pose is to move beyond the opposition of disease and health. As she says, "What this play suggests, in the end, is a conception of the ethical stance that turns its back—at least some rare times and in some ways—on one aspect of the medical analogy, its tireless insistence on perfect health" (TD, 481).

Does this mean that Nussbaum thinks that we human beings must be content never to achieve perfect health, perfect virtue? Does she think that we must be content with the fact that, as long as we love, there will always be a sickness in us? Does she mean that as human beings we must settle for an inevitable moral imperfection? These are tricky questions.

If her advice is to abandon the pursuit for perfect happiness, perfect moral virtue, perfect moral health, then what is her ideal of perfection? Certainly it could not be the ideal of a god, since the gods lack moral virtue, although they do posses perfection in some sense. More critically, it could not be a godlike perfection, since this would run counter to the great burden of Nussbaum's argument, namely, the attempt to say that the desire to transcend our humanity is the deepest human sickness. For her, the desire to transcend the human always hides a deep contempt for the human. More constructively, Nussbaum's general burden is to find a viable way to embrace our humanness; and with regard to the present issue, her burden is to try to find a way of embracing love without having to deny its excesses.

If we are not simply to settle for the imperfections of our humanness, what are we to do? Are we to think of human perfection differently? Perhaps this is what Nussbaum means by saying that we must take our ethical stance outside of the opposition between health and sickness. But what could this mean? This is an even more difficult question when we realize that Nussbaum seems to be suggesting that we can accept love into our lives only when we recognize it as a "transmoral" value. Does she mean to say that morality must be rooted in a transmoral ground? Or what all of this comes to: Is Nussbaum suggesting that we human beings who accept love into our lives must simply accept it as a mystery, a mystery that cannot be put into the language of moral discourse?

Perhaps the answer to this question can be found in Nussbaum's own version of the ending to Seneca's play. In it she presents Medea's final ascension in a chariot pulled by serpents. Pulled along by her passions, Medea "goes off from our world, into the sun, from the place of moral judgment to the place where there are no gods" (TD, 483). And she goes on to say that in this ascension, we are witnessing "the triumph of love" (TD, 483).

I would not for a moment deny the mystery of love, but I do have a problem with Nussbaum's idea that the triumph of love comes only when it is moved beyond the place of moral judgment. As I see it, this is simply, and quite to the contrary of what Nussbaum wants, just another attempt to transcend the human. Is there an alternative to Nussbaum's alternative? Is there a way of truly embracing human love as it is, liabilities and all?

Nussbaum herself comes close to offering such a suggestion. We do not need to go outside of morality in order to find the resources we need for the existential embrace of love as an indispensable human good. We need simply to expand our moral categories. Nussbaum begins this, but she does not go far enough. She suggests that happy love must incorporate into itself mercy, patience, and understanding. As she says, "Here we have sympathetic understanding without detachment; here we have a source of gentleness to both self and other that can modify one's passions even where there is wrongdoing and even where there is both anger and ill-wishing" (TD, 482).

Not that Nussbaum might object to this, but it is odd in this context that she does not make mention of *forgiveness*. As I see it, this is the virtue without which love cannot survive. It is a virtue that does not deny love's excesses, love's fragility, rather it presupposes these; it is a virtue that does not deny that love, and especially marriage, is a matter of promise and trust; rather, forgiveness makes trust and promise possible.

No one that I know of was more keenly aware of the importance of for-giveness in human affairs than Arendt. Like Nussbaum, Arendt, also an Aristotelian, makes much of the fragility of human life. In Arendt's language, human existence in the world is essentially fragile because human action is subject to what she calls an intrinsic unpredictability and irreversibility. This is very close to Nussbaum's focus on the human context of exposure to *tuche*. Arendt thinks that we can meet the contingencies of human life in the world only if we embrace both the power of promise, what we might call, the power unique to human beings of establishing ties that bind us together, and the virtue of forgiveness, the virtue that alone can stop the consequences of our action, short of murderous and violent revenge. She says:

> The possible redemption from the predicament of irreversibility—of being unable to undo what one has done though one did not, and could not, have known what he was doing—is the faculty of forgiving. The remedy for unpredictability, for the chaotic uncertainty of the future, is contained in the faculty to make and keep promises. The two faculties belong together in so far as one of them, forgiving, serves to undo the deeds of the past, whose "sins" hang like Damocles' sword over every new generation, and the other, binding oneself through promises, serves to set up in the ocean of uncertainty, which the future is by definition, islands of security without which not even continuity, let alone durability of any kind, would be possible in the relationships between men. (HC, 221–13)

I think Arendt is right. In fact, I think Nussbaum might well agree.

Perhaps I can put the point like this. In reaction to actual betrayal or abandonment, or to the threat of it, or even to the fear of it, I may well feel, and may in fact be, morally entitled to rage and revenge toward my lover. But the spiral of rage can, and will most likely lead me into inhuman wishes and thoughts, if not actual cruelty and harm. As Arendt says, the consequences of our actions go far beyond what we are aware of and we are hardly ever in control of them once the flames of rage ignite. The human urge is to punish, and most often when this urge is followed we are led toward the inhuman, to-ward violence and brutality. Can we stop this urge? Can we annul the ever-present possibility that love will make monsters out us, even the best of us? And can we stop it without sealing ourselves off from the intensity of the pas-sion, from its intoxicating joys and unsurpassable blessings? Sometimes we can't. But equally, sometimes we can. And if we do, it will be, I suggest, because we have found a way to forgive. There is no other way; but then again perhaps this is quite enough.

Love and Death

Paradoxically, there is no bond more porous or more solid than that established in marriage. This is so because the marriage bond is grounded in mutual freedom. So long as both continue to choose to be together, there is nothing more solid; indeed, the gates of hell cannot prevail against it. Yet, the relation is not in the control of either partner alone. It is certainly within the power of each to choose otherwise, to choose not to be together; no bond is more fragile.

The traditional marriage ceremony makes it clear that the bond, which is being established, is grounded in the mutual freedom of each of the separate individuals that the concluding pronouncement will unite. The ceremony begins with the consent, the mutually exchanged series of "I wills": "I will have; I will love, comfort, honor, keep, etc." And in some ceremonies, the witnesses are asked if they will help these two uphold their mutual agreements (an acknowledgment that it will be difficult), to which they are to respond, "We will." This is followed by vows of taking and receiving, of mutual having and holding, and by a mutual giving and receiving of rings.

The marriage is, like any promise, only as good as it is; only as good as the two make it; only as good as the two are to their words of promise. Much can go wrong, things beyond the control of either, sickness or health, riches or poverty, temptations and betrayal. Sometimes the promises cannot be upheld. Divorce is always a possibility. And as I have argued earlier, the two can only be together freely, if they are free to leave. This is Stanley Cavell's point in saying that every legitimate marriage is a remarriage, that is, a marriage that has come face-to-face with the realization that divorce is a real existential possibility. We could call this the truth of departure: the realization that I am free to stay only if I am free to leave.

Divorce, however, is not the only kind of departure a marriage must reckon with. As the ceremony acknowledges explicitly, marriage establishes a bond that holds "until death do us part." Every marriage does in fact end in such a departure, in such a loss. Marriage, like human life itself, is mortal. Does the mortality of marriage, the inevitability of loss it entails, contribute to the Epicurean/Stoic argument that the happiest life is one that seals itself off from such hurt?

Specifically, let us turn again to Lucretius, to Nussbaum's interpretation of his attempt to confront human mortality. Let me be clear that in what follows I will be extrapolating from Nussbaum's interpretation of Lucretius. Indirectly, the question I want to raise here is this: Is love, especially as it is found in marriage, worthwhile, given its inevitable end? This question is similar to the broader question that is the focus of Lucretius's inquiry: is human life worthwhile, given that it is mortal? Moreover, the answers that he proposes are relevant for our question.

There is, however, a difference between Lucretius's broader question and mine in one essential respect. The death of a person cannot represent a loss for that person in the way that the death of a lover or spouse can and will represent a loss for the other. As Wittgenstein once put it, "Death is not an experience that one lives through." But in the context of marriage, I think we must add, "The death of the beloved is an experience that the other must live through." Or to vary what Kierkegaard once said about time, we could say, "There is no grief in the grave, but there is grief beside the grave." It is this grief beside the grave that the Epicurean/Stoic thinks is both possible and necessary to eliminate if the good life is to be lived.

I think it will be obvious that what Lucretius says about the relation of the sweetness of life to the fact of death can be transposed into a discussion of the relation of the sweetness of love and marriage to the fact of its vulnerability to loss. As the Epicurean might reason, the natural tendency among human beings is to relish the sweetness of love, to bathe in the deeply satisfying joy of being together in marriage. This natural human embrace of love and marriage, however, leads human beings to a disturbance deep in the soul, call this the fear of losing the sweetness of love, the anxiety of losing the beloved. And this disturbance is not merely anticipatory. When the loss actually comes, this naive embrace of the sweetness of love may end in bitterness, sadness, grief, and misery. "The love of life, Lucretius claims, is natural in all sentient creatures, and so all creatures go to death with reluctance" (TD, 193).

The problem with this natural attitude, as Lucretius sees it, is that it has not reflected adequately on human finitude. In fact, in a kind of reflex reaction to the natural fear of death, most human beings search for immortality. Or to put this in terms of love, most human beings who know its sweetness, seek ways of preserving it forever. They turn from the reality of death to the fantasy of a love that never dies. As one line of a contemporary love song has it, "If love don't last forever, what's forever for?"

Lucretius thinks that the pursuit of immortality, whether of love or life, is a profound sickness. It is sure to lead to misery and unhappiness. As an

Epicurean doctor of the soul, he proposes a cure. We will be cured of the pursuit of immortality if we surgically remove from the human soul its source: the irrational fear of death.

Although I am more interested here in the cure that Lucretius proposes than in his diagnosis of the illness, let me present very briefly the two basic elements of that diagnosis: first, the symptoms produced by the fear of death are shown to be the symptoms of a debilitating disease; and secondly, an argument is given to show that this fear of death is in fact irrational. These two elements of the diagnosis combine to show that fear of death will inevitably impede human flourishing and hence must be checked; and also that with proper reflection and right reasoning this fear can be checked.

As Lucretius recognizes, most people do not admit to a fear of death. This denial presents the Epicurean doctor of the soul with a challenge. The doctor must lead the patient to an acknowledgment that she does in fact fear death, but he must do this indirectly. He proceeds as follows: he describes to the patient certain patterns of behavior he has observed in human beings, all the while hoping that the patient will see herself in these images, and that the penny will drop. What these patterns of behavior are designed to disclose is this: even though people often *say* that they are have no fear of death, their lives often *show* something quite different.

First, human beings often find themselves blindly obedient to religious authority. Rather than doing what is rational, many simply follow the commands of what they take to be the voice of the gods, a voice usually mediated by some shaman, or prophet, or priest. Blindly heeding these divine commands, instead of good reason, people are led to harm others and even themselves. Obedience to religious authority causes pain and not happiness; it may even cause a father to be willing to sacrifice his daughter (Agamemnon) or his son (Abraham).

But why are human beings so willing to sacrifice their own reason? Why are human beings so willing to be dependent on religious authorities? Quite simply, because they think that the priests have something to offer in return for their loyalty and dependence. And what is this, other than the promise of the immortality of the soul?

Secondly, whenever we are plagued by the fear of death, acknowledged or not, we often fail to enjoy the pleasures of this life. Strangely this inability to enjoy life may be generated by a love of life. When we love life, when we love others, our friends, our family, our lovers or spouses, and when we realize that we can lose them, when we realize that these loves cannot last forever, we may find them unsatisfying. Such a person cannot enjoy the moment simply because the moment does not last. In such a person the fear of death is again at play: if we cannot have our joys forever, then they are not worth having.

This failure to enjoy life leads to a third symptom, to "a kind of aimless and restless frenetic activity that has no point at all, other than the avoidance of one's own self and one's own finite condition" (TD, 197). This is a complex pattern of behavior, but all too common. When someone finds no pleasure and enjoyment in life (because he loves these pleasures and joys so much that he cannot bear the fact that time is forever erasing them and will finally erase them for good), he seeks to avoid his deep discontentment and misery in a frenetic pursuit of enjoyment and pleasure as distractions from his unhappiness. Lucretius could well be describing the despair of the Kierkegaardian aesthete when he says of such a person that he "flees himself": "Here's a man who often goes outside, leaving his house, because he's tired of being home. Just as suddenly he turns back, since he feels no better outdoors. He rushes off to his country house . . . he turns back as soon as he reaches the threshold; or, heavy, he seeks forgetfulness in sleep. But in spite of all his efforts he clings to that self, which we know he never can succeed in escaping, and hates it" (TD, 198).

If this path of self-avoidance is so self-destructive, then why do so many people follow it? As Lucretius sees it, the cause of this illness is usually an unacknowledged despair over finitude, that is, an unacknowledged fear of death. People are simply not aware that they are running from death. The logic is simple: the fear of death keeps the person from the enjoyment of life; this causes the person to flee from life; avoidance of life in turn leads to misery and pain, and ultimately unhappiness.

Finally, there is the drive to accumulate wealth, power, and fame. But hardly ever are any of these goals achieved honorably and without harm to others and to oneself. The pursuit of fame and fortune, fueled by envy and greed, often entails criminal acts, often betrayals of lovers, friends, family, truth, and duty. As Lucretius hopes to disclose to his patient, these pursuits are clearly not pursuits of happiness, but just the opposite.

So again, why do so many seek these prizes? Reflection yields the answer: these goals represent a kind of pursuit of immortality. If achieved, they assure remembrance; they mark one's significance; they show that one's life counted for something. But this pursuit is predicated on a fear that death will wipe out one's significance. Again, even if the people who pursue these goals do not realize it, and most often they do not, it is the fear of death that is motivating them.

In the end, however, everyone who pursues the path of fame and fortune will find at the end of life a deep disappointing realization: the pursuit of immortality causes the person to miss life completely. But sometimes along the way, some can be brought to this realization before it is too late. At this point, the Epicurean doctor of the soul is ready to apply the second step of his therapy. Now he must show the patient that her fear of death is irrational.

As Nussbaum interprets him, Lucretius presents four arguments that the fear of death is irrational. The first argument has to do only with the broad question of whether life is worthwhile because it ends in death. The argument turns on the claim that death cannot be a bad thing for that person since that person will not experience his or her own death. Hence the fear of one's own death is irrational. As Nussbaum notes, much can be, and has been, made of this argument.

This argument, and others, like the symmetry argument,[4] that he gives bearing only on the issue of whether one's own death is a bad thing for that person, are not at the center of my interests here. My interest is in whether, in the case of love and marriage, the death of the other is something that it is rational to fear. In this case, death is something a spouse can and most likely will experience. It is therefore still an issue as to whether the death of the beloved is a bad thing and hence rational to fear.

Lucretius does offer arguments that are relevant to this issue, what Nussbaum calls the banquet argument and the population argument. The second of these is the oft-heard argument to the effect that if we did not die there would not be room for us. This is kind of a twist on the Adam and Eve story in this sense: as the biblical story has it, the discovery of mortality carries with it a discovery of eros; to keep the species going, given that we die, we must repopulate the earth with our children. As Lucretius reasons, given that we keep re-populating the earth, we must die, otherwise there wouldn't be enough room.

The banquet argument is more interesting. Nussbaum puts Lucretius's argument as follows: "[L]ife is like a banquet: it has a structure of time that reaches a natural and appropriate termination; its value cannot be prolonged far beyond that, without spoiling the value that preceded" (TD, 203). This is the argument that is most relevant for our purposes because it raises the issue

---

4. This is Nussbaum's name for the following argument of Lucretius as to why it is irrational to fear death: the time before we were born is of no concern to us since before we were born we did not exist. Not existing, we could neither be harmed, nor suffer pain; and moreover, neither does this state represent a loss for us. Death, however, is a perfectly symmetrical form of nonexistence. As such, death should not be of concern to us, and for the same reasons (TD, 203).

of time. This is relevant because love and marriage are relationships that begin, develop, and end in time and because the death of one lover puts an end to that relationship and brings grief to the other who must go on living in time. In this light, we may wonder, is it rational to fear the death of the beloved? And if so, does this make it irrational to marry or to love?

Let us consider then what Nussbaum calls "the sweet and deadly music of time." As she argues, love, especially marriage,

> has a structure that evolves and deepens over time; and it will centrally involve sharing future-oriented projects. This orientation to the future seems to be inseparable from the value we attach to these relationships; we cannot imagine them taking place in an instant without imagining them stripped of much of the human value they actually have. In fact, what can take place in an instant could hardly be called love at all. For love is not, or not only, a feeling that can be had in a moment; it is a pattern of concern and interaction, a way of living with someone. (TD, 208–9)

If love and marriage do have this temporal structure, then it seems rational to fear the death of the other which will bring the relation to an end.

Lucretius seems to agree that love and marriage, and life in general, has this temporal structure. This, after all, seems to be one of the points of the banquet argument. However, he thinks that it is irrational to fear the death of oneself, or, by implication, the death of the other. The argument he gives is what Nussbaum calls the additive argument. If the argument holds, then Lucretius will be able to say that granting the temporal structure of life (and love) does not make it rational to fear death, one's own or the other's.

Extrapolating, we might say that Lucretius wants to argue that the sweetness of love (and life) is spoiled by the bitters of the fear of death, and that the sweetness can only be enjoyed if that fear is seen to be irrational and is removed from the soul. The additive argument aims to show this.

The argument goes something like this. The sweetness of the moment is so sweet that we would like to hold on to it forever. Yet we know that the moment is always fleeting. We therefore pursue the fantasy of making the moment last forever. But the moment, Lucretius argues, would be spoiled by adding eternity to it, that is, by making the historical moment into something without an end, and thus essentially ahistorical: depriving the moment of its end would spoil its sweetness. This is, he thinks, and I agree, to miss the moment, to transcend the historical. To wish for immortality is to wish that life would have no end, and this would rob it of its sweetness. For this reason, he argues, the wish for immortality, or the fear of death, is irrational. The only way to dispel the wish for immortality, a wish that would spoil the sweetness of the moment, is to dispel the fear of death that generates the wish. We can know the sweetness of the time only by getting rid of the fear of its loss.

This is the heart of Lucretius's additive argument: eternity cannot add to the sweetness of the pleasurable moments of life. Nussbaum puts the argument thusly: "True pleasure . . . is not additive: having more, or having a longer episode of it, does not make it better or more valuable; nor does the sheer number of episodes of it add to its worth. . . . Perfect Epicurean pleasures . . . do not have a temporally extended or limited structure. They are, like Aristotle's *energeiai,* complete in a moment, complete once we do or act at all" (TD, 211, 213).

At this point, Lucretius's argument falls apart in contradiction. The sweetness of life and love would be lost if they were made eternal. Yet, according to the additive argument, the moment of sweetness has no temporally extended structure. But what is a moment without temporal extension? What is a moment invulnerable to being lost or unaffected by the passage of time? Such a moment can only be a kind of eternal now. But herein Lucretius is hoisted on his own petard! He wants to say that the sweetness of the moment is spoiled by the fear of its loss and by the pursuit of making it last forever; at the same time, he wants to say that the sweetness of the moment is eternal, and therefore, it is irrational to fear its loss. He can't have it both ways.

As it turns out then, Lucretius ends up denying the temporal structure of the pleasures of life, and by implication, the temporal structure of love. Lucretius's argument for the irrationality of the fear of death and his proposed cure for this ill depend essentially on this denial.

This contradiction is more apparent when we realize that Lucretius's diagnosis of the ills of the religious pursuit of immortality is followed by a proposed cure that we should live as immortal gods, immune to time and hence to the fear of death. Nussbaum puts the aim of Lucretius's therapy as follows: "to rise above mortality altogether and to make ourselves into gods. But isn't this the religious view of life once again, in a slightly different form, furnished with a new conception of the divine . . . but still feeding on the same old longing for transcendence?" (TD, 217)

What is the moral of this story? What can we learn from Lucretius about love and death? One thing surely: the longing for immortality, or the fantasy of immortal love is just one more instance of the persistent human wish to transcend its own humanness. And something more: Lucretius teaches us that even the most intense desire to embrace the human, and Lucretius certainly has this desire, may end up as just another form of transcendence. As Nussbaum notes, in the end Lucretius simply trades one form of transcendence for another. He exchanges the otherworldly longing for immortality for an invulnerability to time, for a *this-worldly* inward detachment (TD, 217), a detachment that amounts to a transformation of time into an eternal and invulnerable moment.

What Lucretius did, and yet did not quite see, is that the sweetness of life and love are inextricably bound to time, and hence to loss, and ultimately, death. As we might put this connection—a connection that he did not see adequately—the sweetness of life and love are not spoiled by the fact of death but have the sweetness they have *because* of the fact of death. I say he did not adequately see this connection because he did not realize that the human fear of death is the human expression and acknowledgment of the sweetness of life and love. As I would say, the human fear of death, far from being irrational, is an existential testimony to the value of love and life. In the fear and trembling of our consciousness of our mortality, the sweetness of life and love find their deepest intensity. If our desire is to embrace life and love, then we must be willing to embrace the natural human fear of death, of separation; it would be a wish to transcend our humanness to want to extirpate that fear from our souls. To embrace the human is to embrace our mortality and the mortality of the ones we love.

Lucretius thought that the fear of death robbed life and love of its sweetness, but the fact is, it is the denial of the fear of death that does this. The pursuit of immortality does this, but so does Lucretius's therapy of inward detachment. What Lucretius's therapy does is put a distance between me and the one I love. It teaches me how to steal myself from external happenings; it teaches me self-sufficiency; it teaches me to be unaffected by what happens to the other. What it does not see is the price of this detachment. That price is the sweetness of love.

But if the human embrace of love entails that we embrace the bitters and the sweets, is it worth it? Certainly we have the power to say "no"; it is not irrational to live without love. But we also have the power to say "yes"; it is not irrational to love. What is outside of our power to have, what is irrational to wish for, is the one without the other, the "yes" without the possibility of the "no."

So is the embrace of love worth it? As it turns out, this is just a specific form of the broader question, Is the embrace of our humanness worth it? I, of course, cannot answer this question for anyone except myself. What I hope to have made clear however is that the most fundamental either/or for human beings is just this existential choice: either a refusal of our humanness or a faithful embrace of it.

And what is my choice? I like to think of myself as standing in the world in fear and trembling, yet in faith, extending my arms open to others, to the world. As it happens, I think, sometimes I actually do this. In these moments, I am sure the embrace of the human is worth it. May it be at least as well with you.

INDEX